THE EVERYTHING
STIR-FRY COOKBOOK
2ND EDITION

Dear Reader,

Coming from a large Vietnamese family, cooking and food were always integral components to my upbringing. Our kitchen would be filled with the sounds and smells of the most amazing foods made by my mom and aunties. As they would create dishes from our heritage, they would recount old stories and interweave them with life tips. And of course, there would always be a lot of laughter with the kitchen chaos. Through their teachings, I learned that food is not only meant to nourish our bodies but to also bring happiness to those whom we cook for.

The only challenge about learning how to cook from my mom and aunties is that they never used recipes. For them, it was about knowing a basic technique and trusting in your palette to adjust as needed. They were all about having their mise en place ready so that when it was time to do the actual cooking, they could quickly bring together mouthwatering dishes to feed an army. At the heart of it, stir-frying carries this spirit. But don't be fooled; just because something is stir-fried doesn't automatically mean it's an Asian dish.

Through this book I hope to show you some great recipes that can be prepared as is or modified according to your flavor preference. I've included some commonly found stir-fries such as Mongolian Beef and some delicious unconventional stir-fries such as Balsamic-Glazed Lamb and Chimichurri Skirt Steak. I hope you enjoy it and are able to share some of these dishes with your loved ones.

Nam Nguyen

Welcome to the EVERYTHING® Series!

These handy, accessible books give you all you need to tackle a difficult project, gain a new hobby, comprehend a fascinating topic, prepare for an exam, or even brush up on something you learned back in school but have since forgotten.

You can choose to read an Everything® book from cover to cover or just pick out the information you want from our four useful boxes: e-questions, e-facts, e-alerts, and e-ssentials.

We give you everything you need to know on the subject, but throw in a lot of fun stuff along the way, too.

We now have more than 400 Everything® books in print, spanning such wide-ranging categories as weddings, pregnancy, cooking, music instruction, foreign language, crafts, pets, New Age, and so much more. When you're done reading them all, you can finally say you know Everything®!

QUESTION

Answers to
common questions

FACT

Important snippets
of information

ALERT

Urgent
warnings

ESSENTIAL

Quick
handy tips

PUBLISHER Karen Cooper

MANAGING EDITOR, EVERYTHING® SERIES Lisa Laing

COPY CHIEF Casey Ebert

ASSOCIATE PRODUCTION EDITOR Mary Beth Dolan

ACQUISITIONS EDITOR Lisa Laing

SENIOR DEVELOPMENT EDITOR Brett Palana-Shanahan

EVERYTHING® SERIES COVER DESIGNER Erin Alexander

Visit the entire Everything® series at *www.everything.com*

THE
EVERYTHING®
STIR-FRY
COOKBOOK

2ND EDITION

Nam Nguyen

Avon, Massachusetts

This book is dedicated to Mom, Dad, my siblings,
and to all the amazing foodies in my family.

An Everything® Series Book.
Everything® and everything.com® are registered trademarks of F+W Media, Inc.

Published by Adams Media, a division of F+W Media, Inc.
57 Littlefield Street, Avon, MA 02322. U.S.A.
www.adamsmedia.com

ISBN 10: 1-4405-6157-5
ISBN 13: 978-1-4405-6157-3
eISBN 10: 1-4405-6158-3
eISBN 13: 978-1-4405-6158-3

Printed in the United States of America.

10 9 8 7 6 5 4 3 2 1

Always follow safety and common-sense cooking protocol while using kitchen utensils, operating ovens and stoves, and handling uncooked food. If children are assisting in the preparation of any recipe, they should always be supervised by an adult.

Photographs by Nam Nguyen.
Nutritional statistics by Nicole Cormier, RD.

This book is available at quantity discounts for bulk purchases.
For information, please call 1-800-289-0963.

Contents

Acknowledgments

I would like to thank my incredible family and friends who have supported me through all of my Foodventures. Without your encouragement and willingness to be my guinea pigs, this book and *The Culinary Chronicles* would have never existed. I apologize for all of the times (and the times to come) I've made you wait until I have taken a hundred photos of a dish before we can eat. And finally deep gratitude and admiration to our mother who started all of this in the first place. We love and miss you, Mom.

Introduction

STIR-FRYING DATES BACK OVER two millennia to China where hot fires were created in brick stoves. Typically the stovetops had an opening directly over the flames where an inverted domed pan, called a wok, could snuggly fit. Classic woks are roundbottomed and direct the heat toward the central area of the pan. The rounded shape also lends well to the curved spatula often used when stir-frying to assist in the handling of the food. Modern-day woks are now available with flat bottoms in order for them to sit flush on electric and gas ranges.

The key to success with stir-frying is to have all of your items prepared and organized (your mise en place) before you begin the actual cooking. You will want all of your produce and aromatics chopped up in small pieces so that they can be quickly and evenly cooked. Your wok or pan should be heated so that it is nice and hot before you add ingredients to it. Typically when you stir-fry, you will want to use your wrist to create a shaking motion to toss the ingredients around; however, some recipes will ask for you to allow the ingredients to sear in the wok/pan before moving it around. As for deep-frying in woks/pans, you will also want to gently move the ingredients around in the oil, flipping the food often to create an even fry.

There are an overwhelming number of benefits to stir-frying. Not only is the cooking process usually quick once you have your mise en place together, but it is also quite forgiving. Recipes are simply loose guidelines. If you do not have one product, you can substitute with another ingredient for an equally delicious result. Measurements are also only suggested amounts. For example, if a recipe lists 1 tablespoon soy sauce, taste it first and adjust according to your salt-level preference.

Sautéing is also quite similar to stir-frying. Both methods require a little preparation before the cooking process begins and use a high level of heat to cook the ingredients. Whereas stir-frying traditionally uses woks, sautéing typically employs a large skillet. However, the sides of both pans allow for the tossing and flipping of the ingredients while they cook. The other difference is that traditional sautéing employs a combination of oil and butter for the cooking fat. The belief is that butter offers a richer flavor to a dish, and the combination of oil helps increase the smoking point so that the butter does not burn. With that said, do not limit your stir-fries to only Asian dishes as the method can be applied to dishes from all over the world.

When it comes to stir-frying, your only limit is your imagination!

CHAPTER 1

Stir-Fry Essentials

As our society becomes more interested in healthy eating and the quality of the foods we are putting into our bodies, cooking at home is more popular and exciting than ever. Food movements such as farm to table and the desire to eat sustainable foods have inspired us to take more responsibility for how and what we eat. Stir-frying lends well to this shift because the quick cooking allows diners to focus on the true flavor of the ingredients while saving valuable time in the kitchen. The average time for stir-frying a dish is only five to seven minutes. Better still, stir-frying is one of the simplest cooking techniques to learn. All it takes are a few cooking tips and the right ingredients and you're ready to start stir-frying!

The Art of Stir-Frying

Basically, stir-frying involves cooking food at high heat in a small amount of oil. With a few exceptions (such as allowing beef to sear briefly when it is first added to the pan), it's important to keep the ingredients moving constantly during stir-frying. The constant stirring motion ensures that all the food comes into contact with the bottom surface of the pan, where the heat is most intense. It also keeps the food from sticking to the pan.

Getting Ready to Stir-Fry

While the technique of stir-frying is quite straightforward, there are a few basic principles that make the process of stir-frying go more smoothly. It's important to organize your mise en place, that is, prepare all the ingredients ahead of time and have those items close to your wok or pan. Once you start stir-frying, you won't have time to chop an onion or measure out the ingredients for a sauce to add at the end. Organization is essential for a smooth stir-fry process.

Most stir-fry recipes call for meat, poultry, or seafood to be marinated prior to stir-frying. A marinade helps tenderize meat, and it's a great way to add extra flavor to a stir-fry. In most cases you will want to start marinating the meat before doing anything else as it will require the longest inactive time. While meat is marinating, take the opportunity to focus on the remaining prep work, such as chopping vegetables, preparing a sauce, and cooking rice.

Whenever possible, try to cut the stir-fry ingredients into uniform-sized pieces so that they will take approximately the same amount of time to cook. Make sure vegetables are thoroughly dry before adding them to a stir-fry; wet vegetables won't cook properly and can cause the hot oil to spatter. Canned vegetables should be rinsed and drained to remove excess sodium and flush any flavors the canning process may have imparted. If using frozen vegetables such as spinach, thaw and drain them well before adding them into the wok. Frozen vegetables that retain less water such as edamame beans or peas can be added directly into the wok without thawing.

The Basics of Stir-Frying

The process of stir-frying will unfold smoothly if you follow these basic guidelines:

- Make sure that all the ingredients for the stir-fry are near the stove, so that you can reach for them quickly.
- Add the oil to a preheated pan, tilting the pan so that the oil drizzles along the sides. Since the ingredients will be moving around the wok, it is important the sides are well oiled.
- Before adding the main ingredients, add the aromatics such as ginger and garlic to flavor the oil.
- If the stir-fry includes meat or poultry, add that first. Let it sear briefly, then stir-fry until it changes color and is nearly cooked through. (The beef should have no trace of pink, and the chicken should have turned white.)
- When adding vegetables, add the thicker, denser vegetables first, as they will take more time to cook. Feel free to add a small amount of water or soy sauce if the vegetables begin to dry out during stir-frying.

Keep these instructions in mind as you try the recipes in the following chapters.

Wok Versus Frying Pan

Selecting the wrong equipment can turn stir-frying from a quick and easy task into an exercise in frustration. The right equipment, on the other hand, will help ensure a successful result. When it comes to cooking equipment, the most important decision you'll need to make is what type of pan to use. Asian cuisine cooks traditionally use a wok for many types of cooking, from steaming to stir-frying. With its high, sloping sides and rounded or flat bottom, the wok's unusual design is perfect for stir-frying. Unlike with a standard frying pan, in a wok you can stir and toss food with ease without worrying about it winding up on the floor. The wok bottom also rests directly on the heat source, allowing food to cook more quickly. Many popular cookware stores now carry woks and other international cookware. However, you can also purchase them through online vendors.

While most people prefer a wok for stir-frying, the frying pan has its fans as well. Many cookware shops carry stir-frying pans that are specifically designed both for stir-frying and other types of pan-frying. Here are a few basic features you should look for when choosing a frying pan for stir-frying:

- **Heavy material.** A frying pan made of cast iron or heavy-gauge aluminum (such as Calphalon's hard anodized pans) can handle heat without scorching. If you try stir-frying with a pan made of lighter material, such as Teflon, you may ruin the pan.
- **Deep sides.** While it won't have a wok's deep, sloping sides, a frying pan with deeper sides will make stirring easier.
- **Tight-fitting lid.** Even stir-fry recipes sometimes call for the food to be covered and briefly steamed or simmered in addition to stir-frying.

In the end, whether you use a wok or frying pan for stir-frying is really a matter of personal preference. You may want to start out stir-frying with a frying pan and wait to purchase a wok until you are sure you'd like to continue stir-frying.

A Stir-Fry Cook's Best Friend—the Wok

When purchasing a wok, factors to consider include the wok's size, design, and the type of material it is made from. Most important is whether the wok is made of a type of material that can handle high heat. While the original woks were made of cast iron, today the majority of Chinese chefs favor carbon steel. Carbon steel is lightweight, durable, and a good conductor of heat, so food cooks evenly. Better still, carbon steel woks are inexpensive— a good wok can often be purchased for under $25.

How to Choose a Wok

Cast iron still has its fans, particularly since its conduction of heat is superior to carbon steel. However, the heaviness of cast iron makes it more difficult to drain food or quickly clean out the wok before stir-frying the next batch of ingredients.

Originally, woks were roundbottomed, designed to sink into the pit of a Chinese woodstove. While roundbottomed woks are still commonly used in commercial restaurants and on gas stoves, their shape makes them a difficult choice for flat electric stoves. Not only does the food cook unevenly, but the rounded wok can reflect heat back on the stovetop element, causing permanent damage. When stir-frying first took hold in the West, designers attempted to solve the problem by creating a collar for the wok to rest on that would be placed on the stovetop element. A more recent innovation is the flatbottomed wok, which can sit directly on the stovetop element. However, some people still prefer to use a roundbottomed wok with a collar.

ALERT

In theory, an electric wok seems like a great way to ensure even heating during stir-frying while freeing up a stovetop element. In practice, however, electric woks may fail to generate enough heat for stir-frying (although they are good for keeping cooked food warm). Generally, higher-end electric woks tend to perform better than less-expensive models.

While some restaurants can use woks up to three feet wide, twelve to fourteen inches is a good size for home use, as larger woks won't fit comfortably on noncommercial stoves. However, college students or anyone living alone may prefer a smaller wok, between nine and twelve inches in diameter, particularly if space is an issue.

How to Season and Clean a Wok

A carbon steel wok must be seasoned in order to perform properly. Seasoning a wok replaces the sticky protective coating put on by the manufacturer with an oil coating that protects the surface, and it also helps keep food from sticking to the pan. Over time, the wok will develop its own nonstick coating and will require less oil for stir-frying.

The first step in seasoning a wok is to wash it in hot water and scrub it with a scouring pad to remove the manufacturer's coating. (Unless you need to reseason it at some point, this is the only time you should use a harsh cleanser on the wok.) Rinse the cleaned wok and dry it on a stovetop element over high heat. Once the wok is dry, remove it from the element, and use a paper towel to rub a small amount of oil around the inside. Heat the wok over medium-low heat for ten minutes, and use a clean paper towel to wipe off the oil. You will probably find black residue on the paper towel. Keep repeating the process—rubbing oil over the wok, heating, and wiping—until the paper towel contains no black residue.

When cleaning a wok, the two most important things to remember are to avoid using a scouring pad or abrasive cleanser and to dry the wok thoroughly. Scouring pads and harsh cleansers can remove the protective coating, and wet woks can rust.

Cooking Utensils

In addition to your standard cooking utensils, you may also want to consider stocking up on a few less-common items, some of which are specifically designed for stir-frying.

- **Wok spatula.** A wok spatula has a wider base than a regular spatula, making it easier to lift and stir food during stir-frying.
- **Wok lid.** In addition to covering the food during simmering or steaming, the interior of the wok lid comes in handy for transferring food from the preparation area to the wok.
- **Mandoline.** A mandoline is a cutting tool that is handy for cutting vegetables into thin matchsticks (also called cutting the vegetables "julienne style").
- **Colander.** Investing in a good colander will keep you from going through an endless supply of paper towels to drain meat after stir-frying.
- **Cooking chopsticks.** Longer than regular chopsticks, cooking chopsticks are used for everything from stirring food and lightly beating eggs to separating long noodles in a pot of boiling water.
- **Slotted spoon.** Even stir-fries sometimes call for the meat to be immersed and cooked in hot oil, or for vegetables to be blanched before combining them with the other ingredients in the stir-fry. A slotted spoon makes it easier to remove the food from the hot oil or boiling water.

Essential Ingredients for Stir-Frying

There are a few basic ingredients that you'll want to keep on hand so that you can whip up a stir-fry on short notice. While some of these, such as rice vinegar or hoisin sauce, may be new to you, most are readily available in the ethnic or international section of local supermarkets.

Sauces and Seasonings

There are a number of sauces and seasonings that lend flavor to stir-fry dishes. Soy sauce is an indispensable ingredient in Asian cuisine, from Japanese shoyu to Indonesian kecap manis, which is a thick version of soy sauce sweetened with palm sugar. Since stir-frying is most closely associated with Chinese cuisine (and to a lesser extent, Thai cuisine), most of the recipes in this book are made with Chinese soy sauce. The two main types of soy sauce used in Chinese cooking are light and dark soy sauce. Both are made from fermented soy beans. However, while light soy sauce (usually referred to in recipes simply as "soy sauce") is quite salty, the addition of molasses gives dark soy sauce a darker color and a richer texture and flavor.

FACT

If you can't find Chinese light soy sauce in the supermarket, Kikkoman brand soy sauce can be used as a substitute. Persons on a low-sodium diet may prefer to use Kikkoman, because Chinese light soy sauce brands are typically quite high in sodium. If you're not watching your sodium intake, be prepared to add a bit of salt (or a seasoning substitute) when using Kikkoman instead of Chinese light soy sauce in recipes.

Every protein marinade needs an acidic liquid to help tenderize it, and rice wine plays that role in Asian stir-fry cooking. Rice wine can often be found at your local supermarket or Asian grocery store. However, if you are in a bind, dry sherry makes an acceptable substitute.

Like rice wine, rice wine vinegar is made with fermented glutinous rice, but it goes through a more extensive fermentation process. Rice wine vinegar is frequently used in sauces and vinaigrettes. Like rice wine, rice wine vinegar can often be found in the ethnic section of local supermarkets.

If it is unavailable, try substituting a mellow-flavored vinegar such as cider vinegar instead of regular white vinegar.

Chili paste is a spicy condiment made with chilies, vinegar, and other seasonings. If you're not a fan of handling hot chili peppers, chili paste makes a convenient substitute.

Made from toasted sesame seeds, sesame oil has a wonderful nutty flavor. You'll recognize sesame oil by its rich dark color and aromatic scent. Sesame oil is used in marinades and added to stir-fries at the end of cooking for extra flavor. A little goes a long way though, so be sure to use it sparingly.

Hoisin sauce is made by combining soybean paste with chilies, garlic, and other seasonings. It has a sweet and spicy flavor. In stir-frying, the thick brown paste is frequently added to sauces and sometimes to marinades as well. Hoisin sauce is sometimes called duck sauce because it is spread on the pancakes that are traditionally served with Peking duck.

ESSENTIAL

While it is the most well known, hoisin sauce is not the only soybean-based sauce used in stir-fries (and Chinese cooking). Black bean sauce is made with soybeans that are fermented with garlic and other seasonings. Several popular stir-fries use black bean sauce or the fermented black beans themselves. Depending on where you live, finding black bean sauce may require a trip to the Asian grocery store or shopping online.

Essential Fresh Ingredients

Sometimes called the "holy trinity" of Chinese cuisine, garlic, ginger, and green onion have a particularly important role to play in stir-frying. Both garlic and ginger are added to the heating oil to help prevent an oily flavor from being imparted to the other ingredients. Scallions (also called green onion) lend a mild onion flavor to stir-fries. They may be added to the oil with the garlic and ginger, stirred in with the other ingredients during stir-frying, or sprinkled on the dish at the end as a garnish. All three are sometimes added to marinades to give meat or seafood extra flavor.

Unless a recipe specifically calls for powdered ginger, always use fresh ginger in stir-fry dishes. You can peel the ginger or leave the peel on as desired. When using green onion in stir-fries, cut off the ends and cut the green onion on the diagonal into the size called for in the recipe. Normally, all of the green onion is used. However, you can also use only the green or white parts to enhance the appearance of the dish.

Canned Asian Vegetables

For many people, their first introduction to Asian vegetables came when they ordered a stir-fry dish made with bamboo shoots and water chestnuts. The popularity of these two vegetables stems partly from their easy availability—bamboo shoots and water chestnuts (along with baby corn and straw mushrooms) are readily available on local supermarket shelves. Always rinse canned Chinese vegetables after opening or blanch briefly in boiling water to remove any taste from the can. Like all canned vegetables, Chinese vegetables are heated to kill any bacteria before canning, so they need to be stir-fried only long enough to heat them through.

While canned vegetables are convenient, nothing beats fresh Chinese vegetables for flavor. Fresh water chestnuts have a sweet flavor that canned water chestnuts lack. Both water chestnuts and bamboo shoots are available year-round in the produce section of Asian markets. Feel free to use them in place of canned vegetables in any of the recipes.

Rice, Noodles, and Cornstarch

Stir-fries are frequently meant to be accompanied by rice. Rice is a staple grain in southern China, where it is frequently consumed at every meal. While long-grain white rice is the rice of choice throughout much of China, the type of rice you use is really a matter of personal preference. Feel free to use other types of rice, such as medium grain or healthy brown rice.

FACT

The main difference between white and brown rice is the level of processing that takes place. All rice is hulled, but in white rice the brown or reddish layers of bran underneath the hull are removed as well. Besides giving brown rice its darker color, these layers of bran are a rich source of B vitamins, making brown rice more nutritious than white varieties.

A number of popular stir-fries, including pad Thai, are made with noodles. While Asian noodles may not come in the variety of shapes that characterize Italian pasta, there is more variety in the basic ingredients used to make the noodles. In addition to standard wheat-based flour, Asian noodles are made from rice flour and mung bean starch. The unusual ingredients give these noodles specific properties: both are superabsorbent, soaking up the seasonings and sauce they are cooked with. They also puff up nicely when deep-fried.

Cornstarch, made from the starchy substance contained inside corn kernels, plays a major role in stir-fry cooking. It is used in marinades to seal in the other ingredients and protect foods from the hot oil, and it is added to sauces as a thickener.

While cornstarch is a popular thickener in North America, starches made from tapioca, arrowroot, and even water chestnut are used throughout Asia. When a recipe calls for a cornstarch and water mixture to thicken the sauce, feel free to experiment with replacing the cornstarch with one of these other starches. Just remember that each has slightly different properties: for example, tapioca starch thickens more quickly than cornstarch, and arrowroot starch will actually thin out again if overcooked.

Dried Ingredients

While they are more commonly found in long-simmering dishes such as soups and stews, dried ingredients are regularly used in stir-fries. Depending on where you live, it may require a trip to the Asian market or going online (see Appendix B) to buy them. But you will find it is well worth the effort to have these items in your culinary repertoire.

Dried Chinese mushrooms are ubiquitous in Chinese cuisine, lending a rich flavor that fresh mushrooms lack. Like other dried ingredients, dried mushrooms need to be reconstituted through soaking in hot water. The strained soaking liquid from these mushrooms is frequently added to the sauce. Some noodles are quite delicate and should be soaked in warm water instead of boiled. For instance rice noodles or bean thread noodles should be softened in water before adding into a stir fry.

Common Cooking Problems

No cooking technique is completely foolproof. Here are solutions to the most common problems that can arise during stir-frying.

Food Sticking to the Wok

Food sticking is one of the most common problems in stir-frying. The usual culprit is a wok that hasn't been preheated. Never add hot oil to a cold wok—always heat the wok for at least thirty seconds before adding the oil. The wok should be nearly smoking, and you should be able to feel the heat when you place your hand two to three inches above the wok's bottom.

Burning the Aromatics

Flavoring oil with aromatics (such as garlic and ginger) is a well-known cooking technique, designed to prevent an oily flavor from being imparted to the food. When you're stir-frying, however, there is a danger that the garlic will burn, adding a bitter flavor to the dish. Following the basic steps for stir-frying and stir-frying quickly will take care of much of the problem. If you're still having difficulties, instead of stir-frying the garlic and ginger for ten seconds, try pressing down on the garlic and ginger with a spatula after adding them to the wok, forcing them to quickly release their flavor into the hot oil.

A Lumpy Cornstarch Mixture

Thickening a sauce with cornstarch is one of those techniques that seems like it should be simple but can go wrong very quickly if you don't follow the correct steps. Never add the cornstarch directly to a sauce heating in the wok or skillet. The cornstarch will not combine properly with the hot liquid, and the sauce will be lumpy. Instead, prepare a cornstarch slurry by dissolving the cornstarch in a small amount of cold water. Pour the slurry into the heated sauce and stir until the sauce thickens. You can also add the cornstarch to the sauce before it is heated, whisking in the cornstarch to combine it with the other ingredients.

Keep in mind that no matter how thoroughly you stirred it, it takes only a few minutes for grains of cornstarch to separate out of the slurry and settle on the bottom of the bowl. Always remember to stir the cornstarch and water mixture before adding it to the sauce.

CHAPTER 2

Condiments, Marinades, and Sauces

Simple Stir-Fry Sauce

*Add this simple sauce in the final stages of stir-frying. If you like, thicken the sauce by adding
1 teaspoon of cornstarch dissolved in 4 teaspoons of water. Add the cornstarch and water mixture
directly into the sauce in the wok or skillet, stirring quickly to thicken.*

INGREDIENTS | YIELDS ½ CUP

3 tablespoons soy sauce

3 tablespoons water

1 tablespoon oyster sauce

2 teaspoons red wine vinegar

2 teaspoons granulated sugar

1 teaspoon garlic salt

¼ teaspoon black pepper

Combine all the ingredients in a small bowl. Use as called for in a recipe, or store in a sealed container in the refrigerator until ready to use. (Use the sauce within 3 or 4 days.)

PER RECIPE | Calories: 70 | Fat: 0g | Protein: 3.3g | Sodium: 5,547 mg | Fiber: 0.5g | Carbohydrates: 14g | Sugar: 9g

Quick Chicken Marinade

*Use this simple but flavorful marinade with 1 pound of chicken breasts cut into 1" cubes.
Be sure to add the cornstarch last so that it seals in the other flavors.*

INGREDIENTS | YIELDS ¼ CUP

2 tablespoons dry sherry, Chinese rice wine, or white cooking sherry

2 tablespoons light soy sauce

½ teaspoon black pepper

½ teaspoon sesame oil

2 garlic cloves, minced

1 tablespoon cornstarch

1. In a small bowl, whisk the marinade ingredients together.

2. Place the chicken cubes in a bowl and marinate the chicken in the refrigerator for 30 minutes. Use as called for in a stir-fry recipe.

PER RECIPE | Calories: 126 | Fat: 2.3g | Protein: 2.6g | Sodium: 1,800mg | Fiber: 0.7g | Carbohydrates: 16g | Sugar: 3g

Orange Sauce

*If you want a thicker sauce, leave the water out of the sauce and combine the water with
1½ teaspoons cornstarch in a separate small bowl. Add the sauce as called for in the recipe,
bring to a boil, and then add in the cornstarch and water mixture, stirring to thicken.*

INGREDIENTS | YIELDS ⅔ CUP

6 tablespoons orange juice
1 tablespoon fresh orange zest
2 tablespoons water
1 tablespoon rice vinegar
1 tablespoon dark soy sauce
2 teaspoons light soy sauce
2 teaspoons brown sugar
¼ teaspoon red pepper flakes

Combine the orange juice, zest, water, rice vinegar, dark soy sauce, light soy sauce, brown sugar, and red pepper flakes in a bowl. Either use immediately in a stir-fry recipe or store in a sealed container in the refrigerator until ready to use. (Use the sauce within 3 or 4 days.)

PER RECIPE | Calories: 101 | Fat: 0.2g | Protein: 2g | Sodium: 1,502mg | Fiber: 0.8g | Carbohydrates: 23g | Sugar: 18g

Orange Marinade

*The orange flavor in this marinade goes very nicely with pork,
as in Spicy Orange Pork Chops (see Chapter 6).*

INGREDIENTS | YIELDS ¼ CUP

2 tablespoons orange juice
1 tablespoon fresh orange zest
1 tablespoon water
1 tablespoon soy sauce
1 teaspoon brown sugar
1 garlic clove, finely minced
¼ teaspoon red pepper flakes
½ scallion, finely chopped
2 teaspoons cornstarch

In a small bowl, whisk together all items of the marinade. Use to marinate ¾–1 pound lean pork for at least 20 minutes.

PER RECIPE | Calories: 104 | Fat: 0.2g | Protein: 2.4g | Sodium: 1,503mg | Fiber: .8g | Carbohydrates: 23g | Sugar: 18g

Basic Chinese Brown Sauce

*Either store-bought beef broth or beef bouillon cubes dissolved
in boiling water can be used in this recipe.*

INGREDIENTS | YIELDS ⅔ CUP

½ cup beef broth

1 tablespoon soy sauce

1 tablespoon oyster sauce

1 tablespoon Chinese rice wine or dry
sherry

1 teaspoon granulated sugar

1 teaspoon sesame oil

¼ teaspoon black pepper

2 teaspoons cornstarch

1. In a bowl, whisk together the beef broth, soy sauce, oyster sauce, rice wine, sugar, sesame oil, and pepper until combined.

2. Whisk in the cornstarch. Either use the sauce immediately or store in a sealed container in the refrigerator until ready to use. (Use the sauce within 3 or 4 days.) Stir the sauce before adding it to the stir-fry to bring up any cornstarch that has settled on the bottom.

PER RECIPE | Calories: 107 | Fat: 5g | Protein: 3g |
Sodium: 1,783mg | Fiber: 4g | Carbohydrates: 13g | Sugar: 4.5g

Sweet-and-Sour Sauce

*To turn this into a dipping sauce, simply bring the ingredients to a boil in a medium
saucepan over low heat, stirring constantly. Use the dipping sauce immediately
or store in a sealed container in the refrigerator until ready to serve.*

INGREDIENTS | YIELDS 1 CUP

¼ cup granulated sugar

¼ cup vinegar

2 tablespoons ketchup

¾ cup water

1 tablespoon cornstarch

1. Combine the sugar, vinegar, ketchup, and water in a medium bowl.

2. Whisk in the cornstarch. Use as called for in the stir-fry recipe. Stir the sauce before adding to the stir-fry to bring up any cornstarch that has settled on the bottom. If not using immediately, store the sauce in a sealed container in the refrigerator. (Use the sauce within 3 or 4 days.)

PER RECIPE | Calories: 265 | Fat: .09g | Protein: 0.5g |
Sodium: 341mg | Fiber: 1g | Carbohydrates: 65g | Sugar: 57g

Pineapple Sweet-and-Sour Sauce

A 14-ounce can of pineapple chunks will give you the right amount of juice needed for this sauce. Reserve the pineapple chunks to add directly to the stir-fry, if called for in the recipe. The brown sugar complements the sweetness of the pineapple, while the vinegar and salt give the sauce a multifaceted flavor.

INGREDIENTS | YIELDS 1 CUP

¾ cup pineapple juice
½ teaspoon salt
3 tablespoons vinegar
¼ cup brown sugar
1 tablespoon cornstarch

1. In a small bowl, combine the pineapple juice, salt, vinegar, and brown sugar.

2. Whisk in the cornstarch. Use the sauce as called for in a recipe. If not using immediately, store the sauce in a sealed container in the refrigerator. (Use within 3 or 4 days.) Stir the sauce before adding it to the stir-fry to bring up any cornstarch that has settled on the bottom.

PER RECIPE | Calories: 346 | Fat: .2g | Protein: .7g | Sodium: 1,199mg | Fiber: 0.4g | Carbohydrates: 85g | Sugar: 72g

Pineapple Sweet-and-Sour Dipping Sauce

This sauce can be used as a dipping sauce with Pork Egg Rolls (see Chapter 3) or any kind of spring roll.

INGREDIENTS | YIELDS 1¼ CUPS

2 tablespoons cornstarch
2 tablespoons water
5 tablespoons brown sugar
¾ cup pineapple juice
½ teaspoon salt
¼ cup vinegar
½ green bell pepper, seeded and diced
½ red bell pepper, seeded and diced
2 tablespoons pineapple chunks

1. In a small bowl, dissolve the cornstarch in 2 tablespoons water. Set aside.

2. In a saucepan, bring the brown sugar, pineapple juice, and salt to a boil over medium heat. Stir in the vinegar. Add the cornstarch and water mixture, stirring to thicken.

3. Add the bell peppers and pineapple chunks. Stir briefly to heat through. If not using immediately, store the sauce in a sealed container in the refrigerator. (Use within 3 or 4 days.)

PER RECIPE | Calories: 472 | Fat: .5g | Protein: 2g | Sodium: 1,209mg | Fiber: 3g | Carbohydrates: 115g | Sugar: 91g

Hot and Sour Sauce

This tangy sauce uses ketchup as the main base. You may also substitute with tomato paste, however, use only ¾ of the measurement listed for the ketchup.

INGREDIENTS | YIELDS 1¼ CUP

2 tablespoons low sodium soy sauce

¼ cup rice wine vinegar

½ cup ketchup

¼ cup water

½ tablespoon sambal chili paste

½ tablespoon granulated sugar

½ teaspoon red pepper flakes

½ teaspoon minced garlic

½ teaspoon minced ginger

1 tablespoon cornstarch

1 tablespoon minced chives

1. In a medium sized bowl, whisk together all the ingredients except the cornstarch and chives.

2. Once the sugar has dissolved, whisk in the cornstarch and then the chives.

3. Store the sauce in a sealed container in the refrigerator. (Use the sauce within 3 or 4 days.).

PER RECIPE | Calories: 210 | Fat: 0.6g | Protein: 45g | Sodium: 2,326mg | Fiber: 1g | Carbohydrates: 48g | Sugar: 34g

Sesame Sauce

Sesame sauce makes a great dipping sauce for spring rolls, or it can be added to a stir-fry dish at the end of cooking, as in Sesame Pork with Noodles (see Chapter 9). If chili paste is already included in the recipe, do not add it to the sauce.

INGREDIENTS | YIELDS ½ CUP

4 tablespoons chicken broth

2 tablespoons red wine vinegar or Chinese red rice vinegar

2 tablespoons soy sauce

2 tablespoons sesame oil

½ tablespoon granulated sugar

¼ teaspoon chili paste

2 garlic cloves, finely minced

2 teaspoons cornstarch

1. Combine the chicken broth, vinegar, soy sauce, sesame oil, sugar, chili paste, and garlic in a bowl.

2. Whisk in the cornstarch. Either use the sauce immediately or store in a sealed container in the refrigerator until needed. (Use the sauce within 3 or 4 days.) Stir the sauce before adding to the stir-fry to bring up any cornstarch that has settled on the bottom.

PER RECIPE | Calories: 341 | Fat: 28g | Protein: 3.6g | Sodium: 2,093mg | Fiber: 0.4g | Carbohydrates: 18g | Sugar: 7g

Peking Sauce

This versatile sauce is both sweet and slightly spicy from the chili paste.
It can be used in any stir-fry dish and also as a barbecue sauce.

INGREDIENTS | YIELDS ¼ CUP

1 tablespoon water
1 tablespoon hoisin sauce
1 tablespoon plum sauce
½ tablespoon ketchup
½ teaspoon sambal chili paste
1 tablespoon sesame oil
1 garlic clove, minced finely
1 scallion, diced

In a bowl, whisk together all the ingredients until incorporated. If using in a stir-fry recipe, store in a sealed container in the refrigerator until ready to use. (Use the sauce within 3 or 4 days.)

PER RECIPE | Calories: 237 | Fat: 14g | Protein: 1g | Sodium: 383mg | Fiber: .9g | Carbohydrates: 28g | Sugar: 24g

Oyster-Flavored Marinade for Beef

Flavored with oyster sauce, this marinade is a great way to add flavor to a simple beef and vegetable stir-fry that doesn't include a finishing sauce, as in the recipe for Beef Stir-Fry with Vegetables (see Chapter 4).

INGREDIENTS | YIELDS ¼ CUP

3 tablespoons oyster sauce
2 tablespoons dark soy sauce
1 teaspoon sugar
2 teaspoons sesame oil
½ teaspoon salt
½ teaspoon black pepper
½ teaspoon garlic powder
1 tablespoon cornstarch

In a medium bowl, whisk all the marinade ingredients together until combined. Place the beef in the bowl and toss to cover well. Allow the beef to marinate for approximately 20 minutes before use.

PER RECIPE | Calories: 178 | Fat: 9g | Protein: 3g | Sodium: 4,453mg | Fiber: .8g | Carbohydrates: 21g | Sugar: 4.7g

Curry Sauce

For best results, use Madras curry powder in this recipe.

INGREDIENTS | YIELDS ¾ CUP

½ cup chicken broth

3 tablespoons curry powder

¼ teaspoon cumin powder

2 teaspoons brown sugar

1 tablespoon dark soy sauce

½ teaspoon chili paste (optional)

Curry

While many people believe that curry is a single dry spice, curry powder is a compilation of spices that may or may not include curry leaves. Furthermore, the word *curry* actually comes from the Tamil word *kahri*, meaning "sauce."

In a small bowl, combine the chicken broth, curry powder, cumin powder, brown sugar, dark soy sauce, and chili paste if using. Either use immediately in a stir-fry recipe or keep covered in a sealed container in the refrigerator until ready to use. (Use the sauce within 3 or 4 days.)

PER RECIPE | Calories: 155 | Fat: 4.6g | Protein: 6g | Sodium: 1,435mg | Fiber: 6.4g | Carbohydrates: 4.6g | Sugar: 9.6g

Teriyaki Sauce

This quick sauce can be thickened with the addition of ½ teaspoon cornstarch dissolved in 2 tablespoons of water.

INGREDIENTS | YIELDS ¾ CUP

¾ cup low-sodium soy sauce

½ cup water

1 tablespoon mirin

1 tablespoon sake

3 tablespoons light brown sugar

½ tablespoon minced garlic

1 tablespoon minced ginger

1. In a small saucepan over medium heat, whisk together all the ingredients and let the liquids come a low boil.

2. Reduce the heat to low and simmer the sauce until thickened, about 8–10 minutes. Use immediately or store covered in the refrigerator for 1 week.

PER RECIPE | Calories: 302 | Fat: 0.4g | Protein: 12.8g | Sodium: 1,079mg | Fiber: 2g | Carbohydrates: 60g | Sugar: 43g

Ponzu Sauce

Traditional ponzu utilizes the yuzu citrus fruit that is indigenous to eastern Asia. Yuzu is very fragrant and tart. If you can't find yuzu, substitute lemon juice mixed with a few squeezes of orange and grapefruit juice.

INGREDIENTS | YIELDS 2 CUPS

1 cup yuzu juice
¼ cup rice vinegar
1 cup low-sodium soy sauce
1 tablespoon mirin
2 tablespoons bonito flakes
1 (4") piece dried konbu (Japanese kelp)
1 teaspoon sesame oil
2 scallions, finely minced

1. In a small saucepan over medium heat, combine the yuzu juice, rice vinegar, soy sauce, mirin, bonito flakes, and dried konbu, and simmer for 5 minutes. Remove from heat and allow the sauce to sit for 4–6 hours.

2. Strain the sauce and stir in the sesame oil and scallions. Use immediately or store in covered in the refrigerator for up to 1 week.

PER RECIPE | Calories: 245 | Fat: 5.4g | Protein: 17g | Sodium: 1,443mg | Fiber: 3.4g | Carbohydrates: 37g | Sugar: 11.6g

Chili Ponzu Marinade

If you're short on time, try using bottled ponzu sauce that can be found in local Asian groceries.

INGREDIENTS | YIELDS 1 CUP

1 cup ponzu sauce
½ tablespoon sambal chili paste
1 tablespoon orange zest
1 garlic clove, finely minced
¼ teaspoon black pepper
½ teaspoon toasted sesame seeds
¼ cup vegetable oil

1. In a medium bowl, stir the ponzu sauce, chili paste, zest, garlic, pepper, and sesame seeds together.

2. Stream in the oil, whisking constantly. Refrigerate in a sealed container until needed. (Use the marinade within 1 week.)

PER RECIPE | Calories: 510 | Fat: 55g | Protein: .8g | Sodium: 115mg | Fiber: 1.1g | Carbohydrates: 4.6g | Sugar: 2g

Ginger Miso Dressing

This dressing can be used with both cold and warm salads.

INGREDIENTS | YIELDS ½ CUP

1 tablespoon low-sodium soy sauce

1 tablespoon miso paste

¼ cup rice wine vinegar

½ tablespoon sugar

1 teaspoon sesame oil

1 tablespoon toasted sesame seeds

1 tablespoon minced ginger

1 teaspoon minced garlic

¼ teaspoon black pepper

¼ cup vegetable or canola oil

1. In a blender, combine all the items with the exception of the vegetable oil. Pulse several times until the ingredients have broken down.

2. On the lowest setting, slowly stream in the vegetable oil and blend until dressing is fully emulsified. Dressing can be stored in the refrigerator for up to 2 days.

PER RECIPE | Calories: 195 | Fat: 10g | Protein: 0.05 | Sodium: 1,545mg | Fiber: 0.1g | Carbohydrates: 19g | Sugar: 8g

Miso-Soy Marinade

This marinade is perfect for seafood, especially a firm white fish like sea bass.

INGREDIENTS | YIELDS 1 CUP

⅓ cup mirin

½ cup sake

2 tablespoons low-sodium soy sauce

3 tablespoons light miso paste

1 tablespoon honey

1 tablespoon brown sugar

½ teaspoon white pepper

1 scallion, finely diced

1 tablespoon vegetable oil

Whisk all the ingredients together. Refrigerate in a sealed container until needed. (Use the marinade within 2 days.)

PER RECIPE | Calories: 519 | Fat: 16.8g | Protein: 8.9g | Sodium: 3,727mg | Fiber: 3.6g | Carbohydrates: 54g | Sugar: 35g

Tonkatsu Sauce

A traditional accompaniment to Tonkatsu (see Chapter 6), tonkatsu sauce is both sweet and tangy.

INGREDIENTS | YIELDS ½ CUP

4 tablespoons barbecue sauce

4 tablespoons ketchup

1 tablespoon soy sauce

2 teaspoons Worcestershire sauce

2 teaspoons rice wine vinegar

½ teaspoon mustard powder

1 teaspoon garlic powder

½ teaspoon black pepper

In a small bowl, whisk all the ingredients together. Refrigerated sauce can be kept in a sealed container for 7 days.

PER RECIPE | Calories: 185 | Fat: .5g | Protein: 2.7g | Sodium: 2,410mg | Fiber: 1.3g | Carbohydrates: 44g | Sugar: 31.5g

Tsuyu

This Japanese sauce can be used with Agedashi Tofu (see Chapter 3) or with cold soba noodles.

INGREDIENTS | YIELDS 2½ CUPS

2 cups water

1 tablespoon dried dashi soup stock

¼ cup low-sodium soy sauce

¼ cup mirin

Dashi

Dashi is Japanese stock, typically consisting of dried kelp, bonito flakes, dried mushrooms, and additional seasonings. If you don't have the time to make your own dashi, the soup stock is sold in dried powder form in Asian grocery and specialty food stores.

1. In a small saucepan, bring the water to a slow boil over medium-high heat. Add dashi soup stock, reduce the heat to medium low, and simmer for 4–5 minutes.

2. Add the soy sauce and mirin and simmer for an additional 2–3 minutes. Remove from heat and cool. Tsuyu can be stored in the refrigerator for 3–5 days.

PER RECIPE | Calories: 33 | Fat:0.02g | Protein: 4g | Sodium: 3,607mg | Fiber: 0.5g | Carbohydrates: 4.8g | Sugar: 1g

Korean-Inspired Marinade

Marinade's role as flavor enhancer is particularly important in stir-frying, which is all about quick cooking as opposed to slow simmering. Use this flavorful marinade to marinate between 1 and 1½ pounds of beef before stir-frying.

INGREDIENTS | YIELDS ½ CUP

2 tablespoons orange juice

2 tablespoons soy sauce

1 tablespoon honey

1 tablespoon brown sugar

1 tablespoon rice wine or sherry

1 tablespoon sesame oil

¼ teaspoon black pepper

½ Asian pear, finely grated

1 scallion, sliced

1 teaspoon toasted sesame seeds

1. Prepare the beef for stir-frying, cutting according to the recipe directions.

2. In a large bowl, whisk together the marinade ingredients. Place the beef in the bowl, ensuring that it has been evenly coated. Cover the bowl and allow the beef to marinate in the refrigerator for at least 1 hour.

PER RECIPE | Calories: 358 | Fat: 15g | Protein: 3.3g | Sodium: 180mg | Fiber: 3.6g | Carbohydrates: 52g | Sugar: 42g

Peanut Sauce

This easy sauce is used as a condiment for beef or chicken satay (see Chicken "Satay" with Peanut Sauce in Chapter 3).

INGREDIENTS | YIELDS 1½ CUPS

1 cup creamy peanut butter

1 tablespoon grated ginger

2 teaspoons sesame oil

1 tablespoon soy sauce

2 garlic cloves, minced

1 teaspoon red pepper flakes

2 tablespoons rice vinegar

¼ teaspoon kosher salt

¼ cup peanut oil

1. In a blender, add the peanut butter, ginger, sesame oil, soy sauce, garlic, red pepper flakes, rice vinegar, and salt. Blend until combined.

2. On the lowest setting, stream in the peanut oil until completely emulsified, approximately 2–3 minutes. Sauce should be used within the same day.

PER RECIPE | Calories: 2,122 | Fat: 193g | Protein: 66.8g | Sodium: 2,676mg | Fiber: 16.8g | Carbohydrates: 58g | Sugar: 24g

Tamarind Chili Sauce

The tartness from the tamarind juice coupled with the heat from chilies makes this the perfect dipping sauce for dishes such as Crispy Fried Shrimp Balls (see Chapter 3) or egg rolls.

INGREDIENTS | YIELDS ¼ CUP

3 tablespoons tamarind juice concentrate

1½ tablespoons fish sauce

1 tablespoon warm water

½ tablespoon lime juice

1 tablespoon palm sugar

1 teaspoon minced garlic

1 red chili, minced finely

In a medium bowl, whisk together all the ingredients and refrigerate for 15 minutes. Sauce can be stored in the refrigerator for up to 1 week.

PER RECIPE | Calories: 130 | Fat: 0.3g | Protein: 1.7g | Sodium: 15.2mg | Fiber: 2g | Carbohydrates: 33g | Sugar: 28g

Nuoc Cham Sauce

This Vietnamese dipping sauce pairs well with egg rolls or spring rolls.

INGREDIENTS | YIELDS 1½ CUPS

½ cup fish sauce

½ cup granulated sugar

½ cup fresh lime juice

¼ cup warm water

1 Thai chili, finely diced, or ½ teaspoon sambal chili paste

1. Combine fish sauce, sugar, lime juice, and water. Stir until sugar is dissolved.

2. Stir in chilies. Use immediately refrigerate in a covered container for up to 2 weeks.

PER RECIPE | Calories: 423 | Fat: 0.2g | Protein: 0.7g | Sodium: 5mg | Fiber: 3g | Carbohydrates: 112g | Sugar: 102g

Nuoc Cham

Nuoc cham is a common Vietnamese dipping sauce that is primarily made of fish sauce, sugar, and lime juice. Depending on the type of dish it is paired with, nuoc cham can contain shredded carrots, minced ginger, or garlic.

Citrusy Mediterranean Marinade

Be sure to use extra-virgin olive oil in this recipe. While pure olive oil has the high smoke point needed for stir-frying, extra-virgin olive oil is the best choice for marinades and salad dressings.

INGREDIENTS | YIELDS 1 CUP

5 tablespoons orange juice

3 tablespoons lemon juice

¼ cup red wine vinegar

2 cloves garlic, chopped

½ teaspoon dried oregano

2 tablespoons freshly chopped basil

⅛ teaspoon black pepper

¼ cup olive oil

1. Combine the orange juice, lemon juice, vinegar, garlic, oregano, basil, and black pepper in a medium bowl.

2. Whisk in the olive oil. Refrigerate in a sealed container until needed. (Use the marinade within 1 week.)

PER RECIPE | Calories: 548 | Fat: 54g | Protein: 1.3g | Sodium: 18mg | Fiber: 0.9g | Carbohydrates: 14g | Sugar: 7.6g

Fajita Marinade

Both sea salt and kosher salt contain fewer additives and have a richer flavor than ordinary table salt. Use one of these in this marinade to bring out the other flavors in the recipe.

INGREDIENTS | YIELDS ¼ CUP

2 tablespoons lime juice

½ tablespoon lime zest

1 teaspoon chili powder

1 teaspoon kosher salt

¼ teaspoon ground cumin

¾ teaspoon freshly ground black pepper

⅛ teaspoon garlic salt

1 tablespoon extra-virgin olive oil

1. In a small bowl, combine the lime juice, zest, chili powder, salt, cumin, black pepper, and garlic salt.

2. Whisk in the olive oil. Either use the marinade immediately or store in a sealed container in the refrigerator. Use within 1 week, stirring the marinade before adding to the meat, poultry, or tofu.

PER RECIPE | Calories: 143 | Fat: 14g | Protein: 0.8g | Sodium: 2,680mg | Fiber: 2.3g | Carbohydrates: 6.3g | Sugar: 0.7g

Tequila Lime Marinade

This quick marinade is ideal for chicken or beef. Due to the alcohol and amount of citrus in this recipe, avoid marinating for longer than 15 minutes to maintain the texture of the meat.

INGREDIENTS | YIELDS ½ CUP

2 tablespoons tequila

2 tablespoons lime juice

½ tablespoon honey

½ tablespoon grated lime zest

¼ teaspoon cumin powder

¼ teaspoon red pepper flakes

¼ teaspoon kosher salt

¼ teaspoon black pepper

3 tablespoons vegetable oil

1 teaspoon finely diced jalapeño pepper

1 tablespoon finely chopped cilantro

1. In a medium bowl, combine the tequila, lime juice, honey, lime zest, cumin powder, red pepper flakes, kosher salt, and black pepper.

2. Whisk in the oil and then stir in the jalapeños and cilantro. Either use the marinade immediately or store in a sealed container in the refrigerator for up to 1 week. Stir the marinade before using.

PER RECIPE | Calories: 473 | Fat: 41g | Protein: 0.5g | Sodium: 592mg | Fiber: 1.3g | Carbohydrates: 13g | Sugar: 9.4g

Roasted Tomato Salsa

Also known as salsa roja, this salsa's heat level can be adjusted by the number of serrano chilies that are added. You can also vary the types of chilies by using either poblanos or Anaheim chilies.

INGREDIENTS | YIELDS 2 CUPS

2 pounds Roma tomatoes, quartered

1 medium yellow onion, peeled and quartered

4 serrano chilies, sliced in half and seeded

2 jalapeño peppers, sliced in half and seeded

10 garlic cloves, peeled

3 tablespoons olive oil

1 cup chopped cilantro leaves

½ tablespoon kosher salt

¼ teaspoon black pepper

1. Preheat oven to 450°F. Place the tomatoes, onions, serrano chilies, jalapeños, and garlic on a baking sheet. Drizzle with olive oil and toss to coat.

2. Transfer the baking sheet to the oven and roast for 15–20 minutes, flipping the items halfway through the roasting process. Allow to cool on the baking sheet.

3. Pour roasted vegetables into a food processor with the cilantro, salt, and pepper. Pulse until smooth.

4. Salsa can be stored in the refrigerator for 3 days.

PER RECIPE | Calories: 621 | Fat: 42g | Protein: 11g | Sodium: 3,599mg | Fiber: 14g | Carbohydrates: 57g | Sugar: 29g

Tomatillo Salsa

Tomatillos are a close cousin to the gooseberry. They are wrapped in a thin husk, which must be removed before eating.

INGREDIENTS | YIELDS 2½ CUPS

3 pounds fresh tomatillos, chopped

¼ cup chopped cilantro

1 large jalapeño pepper, seeded and chopped

1 serrano chili, seeded and chopped

1 (4-ounce) can roasted green chilies, chopped

¼ cup diced yellow onion

1 tablespoon minced garlic

½ tablespoon lime juice

⅛ teaspoon cumin powder

½ teaspoon kosher salt

¼ teaspoon black pepper

1. Place the tomatillos, cilantro, jalapeño, serrano, green chilies, onion, and garlic in a food processor. Pulse until smooth.

2. Transfer mixture to a saucepan and add the lime juice, cumin, salt, and pepper. Simmer over low heat for 8–10 minutes and then remove from heat. Cool to room temperature and refrigerate for at least 4 hours.

3. Salsa can be stored in the refrigerator for up to 1 week.

PER RECIPE | Calories: 508 | Fat: 14g | Protein: 16g | Sodium: 1,205mg | Fiber: 28g | Carbohydrates: 96g | Sugar: 60g

Fresh Pico de Gallo

This bright and herbaceous condiment is the perfect accompaniment for dishes like fish tacos or Beef Tostadas (see Chapter 4). Try adding in ½ cup corn kernels or ½ cup rinsed black beans for added flavor and crunch.

INGREDIENTS | YIELDS 2½ CUPS

2 cups fresh tomatoes, seeded and diced

½ cup finely diced white onion

¼ cup chopped fresh cilantro

½ tablespoon finely diced and seeded serrano chili

1 teaspoon grated lime zest

1 tablespoon fresh lime juice

¼ teaspoon ground cumin

1 teaspoon kosher salt

¼ teaspoon ground pepper

Combine all the ingredients in a large bowl and mix well. Cover with plastic wrap and refrigerate for at least 1 hour.

PER RECIPE | Calories: 108 | Fat: 0.9g | Protein: 4.5g | Sodium: 2,382mg | Fiber: 6.5g | Carbohydrates: 24g | Sugar: 13g

Spicy Avocado Crema

Drizzle this bright crema over tacos or tostadas.

INGREDIENTS | YIELDS 1½ CUPS

1 ripe avocado, peeled, seeded, and diced (about 1½ cups)

½ cup Mexican crema or crème fraîche

¼ cup chopped fresh cilantro

1 teaspoon finely diced and seeded serrano pepper

1 tablespoon fresh lime juice

¼ teaspoon cumin powder

1 teaspoon kosher salt

¼ teaspoon ground pepper

Combine all the ingredients in a food processor or blender. Pulse until thoroughly combined. Place in a bowl, cover with plastic wrap, and refrigerate for at least 1 hour.

PER RECIPE | Calories: 331 | Fat: 29g | Protein: 4.4g | Sodium: 2,375mg | Fiber: 14g | Carbohydrates: 19.6g | Sugar: 1.7g

Chimichurri Sauce

Chimichurri is a beloved sauce from Argentina and goes well over almost all types of protein.

INGREDIENTS | YIELDS 1 CUP

1 cup roughly chopped fresh cilantro

1 cup roughly chopped Italian parsley

4 sprigs fresh oregano

2 teaspoons minced garlic

1 serrano chili pepper, seeded and diced

½ tablespoon grated lime zest

2 tablespoons lime juice

¼ teaspoon red pepper flakes

1 tablespoon honey

½ cup olive oil

½ tablespoon kosher salt

¼ tablespoon black pepper

1. In a food processor or blender, add the cilantro, parsley, oregano, garlic, serrano chili, lime zest and juice, red pepper flakes, and honey. Pulse several times to break down the herbs.

2. Stream in the olive oil and blend until the items have fully incorporated. Season with salt and pepper. Sauce can be stored in a sealed container in the refrigerator for up to 1 week.

PER RECIPE | Calories: 1,065 | Fat: 108g | Protein: 2.6g | Sodium: 3,575mg | Fiber: 3.6g | Carbohydrates: 28g | Sugar: 18g

Garlic Aioli

If you prefer a less pronounced garlic flavor in this aioli, use roasted garlic in lieu of fresh.

INGREDIENTS | YIELDS 1 CUP

1 cup quality mayonnaise

2 tablespoons minced garlic

1 tablespoon lemon juice

2 tablespoons chopped Italian parsley

¼ teaspoon kosher salt

2 tablespoons vegetable oil

In a medium bowl, whisk all the ingredients together and refrigerate, covered for at least 30 minutes. Garlic aioli can be stored in a sealed container for 2 days in the refrigerator.

PER RECIPE | Calories: 1,855 | Fat: 202mg | Protein: 3.7g | Sodium: 1,853mg | Fiber: 0.6g | Carbohydrates: 13g | Sugar: 1.6g

Wasabi Aioli

Wasabi root can be difficult to find at your local grocery store. Feel free to substitute with either wasabi powder or wasabi paste.

INGREDIENTS | YIELDS 1 CUP

1 cup quality mayonnaise

½ tablespoon wasabi paste or 1½ teaspoons fresh grated wasabi

1 teaspoon lime juice

¼ teaspoon kosher salt

2 tablespoons vegetable oil

In a bowl, whisk all the ingredients together. Refrigerate, covered, for at least 30 minutes. Wasabi aioli can be stored in a sealed container for 2 days in the refrigerator.

PER RECIPE | Calories: 1,829 | Fat: 202g | Protein: 2.6g | Sodium: 1,844mg | Fiber: 0.4g | Carbohydrates: 7.4g | Sugar: 1.1g

Basil Pesto

Although most modern cooks employ the use of a food processor or blender to make pesto, traditionalist believe that grinding the ingredients together with a mortar and pestle brings out a greater flavor to the end product.

INGREDIENTS | YIELDS 2 CUPS

2 garlic cloves, roughly chopped
½ cup toasted pine nuts
½ cup grated Parmesan cheese
Juice of ½ lemon
2½ packed cups fresh basil leaves
½ teaspoon kosher salt
¼ teaspoon black pepper
¾ cup extra-virgin olive oil

1. In a food processor or blender, pulse together the garlic and pine nuts.

2. Add the cheese, lemon juice, basil leaves, salt, and pepper. Pulse several more times.

3. With the food processor/blender on, slowly stream in the olive oil until the pesto is fully incorporated and smooth. You may need to scrape down the sides in between.

4. Either use the pesto immediately or store in a sealed container in the refrigerator until ready to use. (Use the pesto within 1 week or place in a container with a layer of olive oil on top and freeze.)

PER RECIPE | Calories: 1,690 | Fat: 177g | Protein: 23g | Sodium: 1,952mg | Fiber: 2.7g | Carbohydrates: 10g | Sugar: 1.5g

Marinara Sauce

This sauce is quite versatile and can be used as a base for pasta dishes, sauced over proteins, or as a dipping sauce for appetizers such as Meatballs with Marinara Sauce (see Chapter 3).

INGREDIENTS | YIELDS 4 CUPS

2 tablespoons olive oil

1 tablespoon minced garlic

1 small white onion, finely diced

½ teaspoon red pepper flakes

½ teaspoon dried oregano

1 (32-ounce) can San Marzano tomatoes, crushed

1 teaspoon kosher salt

¼ teaspoon black pepper

2 tablespoons roughly torn basil leaves

1. In a large saucepan, heat the olive oil over medium heat. Add the garlic and onions and cook until softened and translucent, about 3–4 minutes.

2. Add in the pepper flakes and oregano and cook for 1 additional minute.

3. Pour in tomatoes with juice and allow to come to a soft boil. Lower the heat to medium low and simmer, partially covered, for 15–20 minutes. Stir the sauce every few minutes, and once the sauce has thickened, remove from heat.

4. Season with salt, pepper, and basil. With an immersion blender, pulse the sauce several times so that it is smoother but still has a chunky texture.

PER RECIPE | Calories: 438 | Fat: 28g | Protein: 8.6g | Sodium: 3,655mg | Fiber: 11g | Carbohydrates: 46g | Sugar: 24.5g

Bloody Mary Dipping Sauce

This quick sauce is a fun riff on the popular brunch cocktail.
Serve with Steak Bites (see Chapter 3) or shrimp cocktail

INGREDIENTS | YIELDS 1½ CUPS

1 (14½-ounce) can diced tomatoes, drained

2 tablespoons tomato paste or ketchup

2 tablespoons vodka

1 tablespoon Worcestershire sauce

1½ teaspoons prepared horseradish

1 teaspoon Tabasco sauce

½ teaspoon celery salt

¼ teaspoon ground pepper

Place all the ingredients into a large bowl. Using an immersion blender, pulse until the ingredients have incorporated and the texture of the sauce is somewhat smooth. This can also be done in a blender. Refrigerate for 30 minutes before serving. Sauce can be stored in the refrigerator for up to 2 days.

PER RECIPE | Calories: 175 | Fat: 0.7g | Protein: 4.7g | Sodium: 2,216mg | Fiber: 5.5g | Carbohydrates: 26g | Sugar: 15g

Cilantro-Mint Chutney

Try using this herbaceous chutney alongside Lamb Samosas
(see Chapter 3) or Vegetarian Samosas (see Chapter 3).

INGREDIENTS | YIELDS 1 CUP

1½ cups chopped cilantro

1½ cups chopped mint leaves

1 small white onion, quartered

1 serrano chili, seeded and chopped

1½ tablespoons tamarind juice concentrate

½ tablespoon salt

¼ cup water

Place all the ingredients in a food processor. Pulse until the ingredients have broken down into a thick sauce. Use within the same day.

PER RECIPE | Calories: 187 | Fat: 2.6g | Protein: 10g | Sodium: 3,690mg | Fiber: 14.5g | Carbohydrates: 38.6g | Sugar: 12g

Mango Chutney

Chutneys are a common South Asian condiment that have a similar consistency to a relish. Fruit chutneys can be made in a variety of flavors such as apples, pears, or apricots.

INGREDIENTS | YIELDS 2 CUPS

2 tablespoons vegetable oil

1 small red onion, diced

¼ teaspoon red pepper flakes

¼ teaspoon whole mustard seeds

1 tablespoon minced ginger

3 cups cubed ripe mango

¼ teaspoon apple cider vinegar

½ cup water

1 teaspoon curry powder

¼ teaspoon kosher salt

¼ teaspoon white pepper

1. In a saucepan over medium heat, heat the oil. Add the onion, pepper flakes, mustard seeds, and ginger. Stir and cook until the onion has become translucent, about 5–7 minutes.

2. Add the mangoes and cook for an additional 2 minutes.

3. In a small bowl, whisk together the vinegar, water, and curry powder. Stir into the mango mixture and reduce the heat to low. Allow mixture to simmer for 30 minutes until the chutney has thickened and become syrupy.

4. Stir in salt and pepper. Transfer the chutney into a bowl and place in a water bath to cool. Chutney can be jarred and kept in the refrigerator for up to 2 weeks.

PER RECIPE | Calories: 622 | Fat: 29g | Protein: 4.3g | Sodium: 608mg | Fiber: 11.8g | Carbohydrates: 96g | Sugar: 76g

Cuban Mojo Marinade

Use this flavorful marinade to liven up chicken or pork stir-fries.

INGREDIENTS | YIELDS 2 CUPS

¼ cup lime juice

¼ cup lemon juice

1 cup orange juice

1½ tablespoons minced garlic

1 tablespoon minced jalapeño pepper

¼ cup chopped oregano

¼ cup chopped cilantro leaves

¼ cup vegetable oil

Whisk all the ingredients together in a bowl. Marinade can be kept in the refrigerator for 2 days.

PER RECIPE | Calories: 686 | Fat: 55.7g | Protein: 4.3g | Sodium: 25mg | Fiber: 8g | Carbohydrates: 51.5g | Sugar: 23g

Cucumber-Mint Raita

Raita is a delicious condiment served with spicy dishes to help cool the palate.

INGREDIENTS | YIELDS 1½ CUPS

1 cup plain low-fat yogurt

½ cup diced English cucumber

1 tablespoon chopped mint leaves

¼ teaspoon coarsely ground toasted cumin seeds

¼ teaspoon garam masala

½ teaspoon kosher salt

¼ teaspoon black pepper

¼ teaspoon cayenne powder

In a bowl, combine all the ingredients and stir well. Refrigerate for 20 minutes before serving.

PER RECIPE | Calories: 172 | Fat: 4g | Protein: 13.7g | Sodium: 1,358mg | Fiber: 1.3g | Carbohydrates: 21.2g | Sugar: 18g

CHAPTER 3

Appetizers and Small Bites

Ahi on Wonton Chips

Ahi is a type of yellowfin tuna that has a beautiful reddish color.
When unavailable, hamachi also works well with this dish.

INGREDIENTS | SERVES 6

½ cups Chili Ponzu Marinade (see Chapter 2)

4 ounces fresh ahi tuna, diced

1 cup vegetable oil

12 wonton skins, cut into triangles

½ teaspoon kosher salt

½ cup Wasabi Aioli (see Chapter 2)

3 tablespoons minced chives

BFFs with the Fishmonger

When preparing seafood, particularly when served rare, it is important to use the freshest product possible. Purchase your seafood from trusted sources and get to know your fishmonger, who can suggest the best products of the day.

1. In a large bowl, combine the marinade with the tuna. Allow the fish to marinate in the refrigerator for 5 minutes.

2. In a wok, heat the oil over medium-high heat. In batches, fry the wonton skins to golden brown and transfer to plates lined with paper towels. Season immediately with salt. Continue until all wontons have been fried.

3. Carefully discard all but 1 tablespoon of the oil remaining in the wok. Heat to medium high and flash-fry the tuna for 30 seconds before removing to a plate.

4. Top each wonton chip with a mound of tuna, a drizzle of Wasabi Aioli, and a sprinkle of chives. Serve immediately.

PER SERVING | Calories: 643 | Fat: 60g | Protein: 11g | Sodium: 543mg | Fiber: 0.6g | Carbohydrates: 15g | Sugar: 5g

Fried Green Tomatoes

Picked from the vine before they have fully ripened, firm green tomatoes are a great addition to stir-fries.

INGREDIENTS | SERVES 4

3 large green tomatoes, sliced into
   ½" slices

¼ teaspoon black pepper

1 teaspoon kosher salt, divided

½ cup all-purpose flour

1 large egg

½ cup buttermilk

¼ cup cornmeal

½ cup panko bread crumbs

1 cup vegetable oil

¼ teaspoon cayenne pepper

1 cup Garlic Aioli (see Chapter 2)

Overcrowding a Pan

When cooking, it's important to not overcrowd the pan or wok. Having too many items in a pan at once lowers the temperature and does not allow food to cook properly.

1. Season the tomatoes with pepper and ½ teaspoon salt. Put the flour in a shallow dish. In another dish, whisk together the egg and buttermilk. In a third shallow dish, combine the cornmeal and bread crumbs.

2. Heat a wok or skillet over medium heat until it is nearly smoking. Add the oil.

3. One at a time, place a slice of tomato into the flour and shake off excess. Dip into the egg wash and finally into the bread crumb mixture. Be sure to evenly coat and shake off excess breading. Gently transfer the breaded tomato slices into the wok.

4. Once browned, flip the tomatoes on the other side to continue frying. This will take approximately 2 minutes on each side. Remove the fried tomatoes and drain on plates lined with paper towels. Sprinkle the hot slices with cayenne pepper and remaining salt.

5. Repeat until all the tomatoes have been fried; serve immediately with Garlic Aioli.

PER SERVING | Calories: 1,095 | Fat: 106g | Protein: 7.3g | Sodium: 1,120mg | Fiber: 2.5g | Carbohydrates: 30g | Sugar: 7.6g

Pork Egg Rolls

Ground turkey can easily be substituted in this recipe. Serve with fresh lettuce leaves and dipping sauces such as Sweet-and-Sour Sauce (see Chapter 3) or Nuoc Cham Sauce (see Chapter 2).

INGREDIENTS | YIELDS 25 ROLLS

1 pound lean ground pork

1 tablespoon dark soy sauce

2 tablespoons oyster sauce

1 teaspoon minced garlic, divided

1 teaspoon minced ginger, divided

1 cup shredded carrots

2 scallions, finely chopped

1 teaspoon sesame oil

1 teaspoon black pepper

25 (6" x 6") egg roll wrappers

2 eggs, beaten

2 cups peanut or vegetable oil

1. In a large bowl, mix together the ground pork, soy sauce, oyster sauce, garlic, ginger, carrots, scallions, and sesame oil. Add the black pepper.

2. One at a time, place an eggroll wrapper on a flat surface with one of the points facing toward you. Spoon about 2 tablespoons of the filling in a line toward the bottom half of the wrapper. Brush the top corner and sides with the beaten egg. Fold in the sides of the wrapper and tightly roll the egg roll up until it is closed. Press to seal, set aside, and continue with the remaining ingredients.

3. Heat the oil in a wok over high heat to 375°F. In batches, fry the egg rolls until golden brown, about 5–6 minutes. Remove the fried egg rolls to plates lined with paper towels to drain. Serve hot.

PER SERVING | Calories: 147 | Fat: 10.2g | Protein: 7.4g | Sodium: 142mg | Fiber: 1.3g | Carbohydrates: 7.3g | Sugar: 0.7g

Prawn and Scallion Egg Rolls

For a variation of this quick dish, add a small slice of bacon or drizzle of pesto on top of the prawns before rolling them up.

INGREDIENTS | SERVES 12

24 large prawns, shelled and deveined

¼ teaspoon black pepper

2 teaspoons fish sauce

12 (6" x 6") egg roll wrappers, cut into diagonals

6 scallions, cut into quarters

1 large egg, beaten

2 cups peanut or vegetable oil

1½ cups Nuoc Cham Sauce (see Chapter 2)

Curled Prawns

To help keep your prawns or shrimp from curling during the cooking process, cut small slits along the under belly and "snap" them into a straight line.

1. In a large bowl, combine prawns, pepper, and fish sauce. Allow the prawns to marinate in the refrigerator for 5 minutes.

2. One at a time, place an egg roll wrapper half on a flat surface with the longest side of the triangle toward you. Place 1 prawn at the bottom of the triangle and lay 1 scallion on top of it. Brush the top corner and sides with the beaten egg. Fold in the sides of the wrapper and continue rolling the egg roll up until it is closed. Press to seal, set aside, and continue with the remaining ingredients.

3. Heat the oil in a wok to 375°F. In batches, fry the egg rolls until golden brown, about 3 minutes. Remove the fried egg rolls to plates lined with paper towels to drain. Serve egg rolls hot with Nuoc Cham Sauce.

PER SERVING | Calories: 217 | Fat: 12.8g | Protein: 10.5g | Sodium: 78.5mg | Fiber: 2.3g | Carbohydrates: 17g | Sugar: 10g

Salmon Firecracker Rolls

Salmon holds up well in this dish, though you can substitute with a firm white fish such as tilapia.

INGREDIENTS | SERVES 4

1 (4-ounce) salmon fillet

1 cup Miso-Soy Marinade (see Chapter 2)

1 teaspoon toasted sesame seeds

½ teaspoon red pepper flakes

8 (6" x 6") egg roll wrappers

8 (4" x 4") pieces toasted seaweed

1 large egg, beaten

½ cup Tamarind Chili Sauce (see Chapter 2)

Healthy Salmon

Salmon are found in the North Atlantic and Pacific and are considered an oily fish. They are known to have a vast number of health benefits including high omega-3 fatty acids that help lower the amount of lipids circulating in the bloodstream.

1. Slice the salmon into 8 even strips.

2. In a medium bowl, whisk the marinade, sesame seeds, and pepper flakes together. Add in the salmon and gently mix so that the fish is evenly coated. Refrigerate for 30 minutes.

3. One at a time, place an egg roll wrapper on a flat surface with one of the points facing toward you. Lay a seaweed sheet on top of the wrapper, then place 1 strip of salmon, horizontally toward the bottom. Brush the top corner and sides with the beaten egg. Fold in the sides of the wrapper and tightly roll the egg roll up until it is closed. Press to seal, set aside, and continue with the remaining ingredients.

4. Heat the oil in a wok to 375°F. In batches, fry the egg rolls until golden brown, about 2–3 minutes so that the center of the salmon will remain rare. Remove the fried egg rolls to plates lined with paper towels to drain. Slice the egg rolls in half on a diagonal. Serve hot with Tamarind Chili Sauce.

PER SERVING | Calories: 291 | Fat: 7g | Protein: 11g | Sodium: 1,132mg | Fiber: 2.2g | Carbohydrates: 39g | Sugar: 23g

Tex-Mex Egg Rolls

These scrumptious and fulfilling eggrolls can be served with Fresh Pico de Gallo (see Chapter 2) and Spicy Avocado Crema (see Chapter 2).

INGREDIENTS | SERVES 24

1 cup cooked cubed chicken breast

1 cup shredded pepper jack cheese

½ cup black beans, drained and rinsed

½ cup corn kernels

½ cup diced tomatoes

¼ cup sour cream

2 tablespoons minced jalapeño peppers

¼ cup chopped cilantro leaves

2 scallions, sliced

1 teaspoon kosher salt

¼ teaspoon cumin powder

¼ teaspoon paprika

¼ teaspoon black pepper

24 (6" x 6") egg roll wrappers

1 large egg, beaten

2 cups vegetable oil

1. In a large bowl, combine the chicken, cheese, beans, corn, tomatoes, sour cream, jalapeños, cilantro, scallions, salt, cumin, paprika, and black pepper. Mix well.

2. One at a time, place an egg roll wrapper on a flat surface with one of the points facing toward you. Spoon about 2–3 tablespoons of the filling in a line toward the bottom half of the wrapper. Brush the top corner and sides with the beaten egg. Fold in the sides of the wrapper and tightly roll the egg roll up until it is closed. Press to seal, set aside, and continue with the remaining ingredients.

3. Heat the oil in a wok to 375°F. In batches, fry the egg rolls until golden brown, about 4–5 minutes. Remove the fried egg rolls to plates lined with paper towels to drain. Slice the egg rolls in half on the diagonal. Serve hot.

PER SERVING | Calories: 227 | Fat: 20g | Protein: 4.5g | Sodium: 194mg | Fiber: 0.6g | Carbohydrates: 6.6g | Sugar: 0.5g

Banana-Nutella Egg Rolls

To accompany these egg rolls, try serving them with
coconut ice cream or a drizzle of warm caramel sauce.

INGREDIENTS | SERVES 8

2 large ripe bananas, peeled
8 (6" x 6") egg roll wrappers
½ cup Nutella spread
2 tablespoons water
2 cups peanut or canola oil
2 tablespoons confectioners' sugar

1. Slice each banana lengthwise, then cut each of those pieces in half.

2. One at a time, place an egg roll wrapper on a flat surface with one of the diagonal points facing toward you. Spread about 1 tablespoon of Nutella on the bottom portion of the wrapper, leaving ¼" border along the edge.

3. Place one of the slices of banana at the bottom. Brush the top corner and sides with water. Fold in the sides of the wrapper and continue rolling the egg roll up until it is closed. Press to seal, set aside, and continue with the remaining ingredients.

4. Heat the oil in a wok to 375°F. In batches, fry the egg rolls until golden brown, about 3 minutes. Remove the fried egg rolls to plates lined with paper towels to drain.

5. Place each banana egg roll on a plate and sift confectioners' sugar over the top. Serve warm.

PER SERVING | Calories: 272 | Fat: 18.2g | Protein: 10.5g | Sodium: 52mg | Fiber: 4g | Carbohydrates: 21g | Sugar: 8g

Calamari Fritti

Depending on your preference, serve this crispy calamari with Marinara Sauce
(see Chapter 2) or Basil Pesto (see Chapter 2) as a dipping sauce.

INGREDIENTS | SERVES 4

¼ cup buttermilk

1 teaspoon garlic salt

1 teaspoon onion powder

¼ teaspoon cayenne powder

1 pound calamari, cleaned and cut into
    1" rings, tentacles left whole

2 cups vegetable oil

1 cup all-purpose flour

¼ cup yellow cornmeal

1 teaspoon kosher salt

½ teaspoon black pepper

Lemon wedges

1. In a large bowl, mix the buttermilk, garlic salt, onion powder, and cayenne together. Add the cleaned calamari, ensuring it's well covered in the liquid. Cover the bowl with plastic wrap and place in the refrigerator for at least 45 minutes.

2. Place a large colander in the sink and pour the calamari with buttermilk mixture into it. Gently shake the colander to drain off the marinade. Use paper towels to blot off excess liquids.

3. Preheat oil in a wok to 375°F.

4. In a large zip-top bag, add the flour, cornmeal, salt, and pepper. Add the calamari and zip the bag closed. Shake well to evenly coat the calamari. Pour the contents of the bag into a large colander (or you can do this in batches) and sift the calamari to get rid of any extra flour.

5. In batches, carefully add the calamari into the hot oil and cook for about 3–4 minutes or until lightly golden and crispy.

6. Transfer the fried calamari to a paper-towel-lined plate. Repeat until all the calamari has been fried. Serve immediately with lemon wedges.

PER SERVING | Calories: 1,221 | Fat: 111g | Protein: 21g | Sodium: 1,246mg | Fiber: 1.3g | Carbohydrates: 35g | Sugar: 1g

Tequila-Lime Calamari

This quick dish has but a few ingredients and focuses on bright flavors.
Serve as an appetizer or on top of arugula for a delicious salad.

INGREDIENTS | SERVES 4

½ cup Tequila Lime Marinade (see Chapter 2)

1 pound calamari tubes, cut into 1" pieces

2 tablespoons vegetable oil

1 tablespoon lime juice

2 tablespoons extra-virgin olive oil

2 tablespoons chopped Italian parsley

½ teaspoon kosher salt

Milk to the Rescue

Want to help your calamari stay tender? Soak them in milk overnight.

1. Combine the marinade with the calamari in a large bowl. Refrigerate for 5 minutes.

2. Heat a wok to medium-high heat and add the vegetable oil. Swirl the oil around the wok and add the calamari. Toss and stir-fry the calamari for 2–3 minutes.

3. Remove the calamari to a plate and drizzle with lime juice, olive oil, and parsley. Season with salt and serve immediately.

PER SERVING | Calories: 339 | Fat: 25g | Protein: 17.5g | Sodium: 493mg | Fiber: 0.1g | Carbohydrates: 6g | Sugar: 2.2g

Chicken "Satay" with Peanut Sauce

This quick and delicious appetizer is a deconstructed version of the popular satay dish. If you prefer to grill the chicken, soak wooden skewers in water for a couple hours before threading the chicken on them.

INGREDIENTS | SERVES 8

2 garlic cloves, minced

1 teaspoon minced ginger

2 tablespoons soy sauce

1 teaspoon sesame oil

¼ teaspoon red pepper flakes

4 tablespoons vegetable oil, divided

1 pound boneless, skinless chicken breast, cut into 1" cubes

2 scallions, sliced

2 tablespoons crushed roasted peanuts

1 cup Peanut Sauce (see Chapter 2)

1. In a large bowl, whisk together garlic, ginger, soy sauce, sesame oil, pepper flakes, and 2 tablespoons oil. Add chicken and toss to coat well. Refrigerate 30 minutes.

2. Heat the remaining oil in the wok over medium-high heat. Add in the chicken with the marinade liquid. Stir-fry for 3–4 minutes until the chicken is cooked through.

3. Place the chicken on a plate and drizzle the liquids over the top. Top the chicken with scallions and peanuts. Serve with Peanut Sauce.

PER SERVING | Calories: 310 | Fat: 25g | Protein: 17g | Sodium: 513mg | Fiber: 1.5g | Carbohydrates: 5.7g | Sugar: 2.2g

Crispy Anchovies

Can't find fresh anchovies? Try substituting with fresh white smelt.

INGREDIENTS | SERVES 6

1 cup all-purpose flour

1 teaspoon kosher salt

½ teaspoon black pepper

1 teaspoon garlic powder

1 cup milk

1 cup yellow cornmeal

2 cups canola oil

1 pound fresh anchovies, heads off and gutted

1 tablespoon minced garlic

2 red chilies, finely diced

¼ cup chopped Italian parsley

Lemon wedges

1 cup Wasabi Aioli (see Chapter 2)

The Misunderstood Anchovy

In the past, anchovies have had a tough rap. However, fresh anchovies are absolutely delicious and have little in common with canned anchovies.

1. Place the flour, salt, pepper, and garlic powder in a shallow dish and whisk together.

2. Pour the milk into another shallow dish. Place the cornmeal in a third dish.

3. Heat the oil in a wok to 375°F.

4. Working in batches, dredge the anchovies in the seasoned flour, then the milk, and toss into the cornmeal. Shake off excess coating and slide anchovies into the wok. Fry the anchovies on both sides for a total of about 2–3 minutes. Drain on wire rack. Repeat with remaining batches.

5. Carefully discard all but 1 tablespoon of oil in the wok. Add the garlic and chilies and cook for 30 seconds. Add in the parsley and fried anchovies and toss a few times. Serve immediately with lemon wedges and aioli.

PER SERVING | Calories: 1,299 | Fat: 114g | Protein: 27g | Sodium: 3,461mg | Fiber: 2g | Carbohydrates: 39g | Sugar: 3.5g

Crispy Artichokes with Garlic Aioli

Once peeled, artichokes can oxidize and quickly turn brown. To prevent this, add them to a cold water bath with ice cubes and lemon juice.

INGREDIENTS | SERVES 4

4 large artichoke hearts, quartered

2 lemons cut into wedges

1 cup all-purpose flour

½ teaspoon garlic salt

½ teaspoon black pepper

2 cups canola oil

½ tablespoon kosher salt

¼ teaspoon cayenne pepper

1 cup Garlic Aioli (see Chapter 2)

1. Place the artichoke hearts and half the lemon wedges in a large bowl. Fill the bowl with ice cubes and cold water.

2. In another large bowl, combine the flour, garlic salt, and pepper.

3. Heat the oil in a wok to 375°F.

4. Remove artichokes from water and carefully dry with paper towels. Toss the artichokes in the flour mixture and gently shake off excess.

5. When oil is ready, working in batches, fry the artichokes until golden, about 3–4 minutes. Transfer to a plate lined with paper towels.

6. Season with salt and cayenne and serve hot with aioli and remaining lemon wedges.

PER SERVING | Calories: 1,550 | Fat: 160g | Protein: 4.5g | Sodium: 1,643mg | Fiber: 1.9g | Carbohydrates: 30g | Sugar: 1.2g

Meatballs with Marinara Sauce

These meatballs are fun appetizers to serve using decorative toothpicks. You can also make a meatball submarine sandwich using a sandwich roll and topping it with mozzarella cheese.

INGREDIENTS | SERVES 8

¼ pound ground beef

¼ pound ground pork

¼ cup grated Parmesan cheese

1 tablespoon Italian seasoning

1 teaspoon black pepper

¼ teaspoon red pepper flakes

½ tablespoon minced garlic

¼ cup Italian bread crumbs

1 large egg, beaten

2 tablespoons cold water

2 tablespoons vegetable oil

2 cups Marinara Sauce (see Chapter 2)

1. In a large bowl, mix together the ground beef, ground pork, Parmesan cheese, Italian seasoning, black pepper, red pepper flakes, garlic, bread crumbs, egg, and cold water. Roll about 2 tablespoons of the mixture into a ball. Repeat with the remaining meat mixture.

2. Heat a wok over medium heat. Add the oil and swirl it around the wok. In batches, evenly brown the meatballs, which will take approximately 3 minutes.

3. Once all the meatballs have browned, add them all back to the wok. Pour the marinara sauce into the wok. Spoon the sauce over the tops of the meatballs to glaze them. Cover the wok and lower the heat. Simmer for 5–7 minutes until the sauce has thickened.

4. Remove the meatballs from the sauce and place on a platter. Insert a toothpick or small skewer into each meatball. Pour the Marinara Sauce into a small bowl and place alongside the meatballs for dipping.

PER SERVING | Calories: 157 | Fat: 11.2g | Protein: 8.2g | Sodium: 326mg | Fiber: 1g | Carbohydrates: 6g | Sugar: 1.8g

Crab Rangoon

*Using fresh crab gives a deep flavor to these fried wontons;
however, imitation crab meat can also be used when needed.*

INGREDIENTS | SERVES 6

8 ounces softened cream cheese

4 ounces cooked lump crab meat

1 tablespoon minced chives

¼ teaspoon cayenne powder

¼ teaspoon garlic powder

¼ teaspoon black pepper

½ teaspoon kosher salt

24 wonton skins

2 cups peanut or vegetable oil

1 cup Sweet-and-Sour Sauce (see Chapter 2)

Faux Crab

Imitation crab meat is usually found in "stick" form. Typically it is made of a fish paste from white fish like pollock.

1. In a medium bowl, mix the cream cheese, crab meat, chives, and seasonings together.

2. Take one wonton skin and brush the edge of each side with water. Place about 1 tablespoon of the mixture in the center of the skin. Fold 2 ends of the wrapper together, pinching to seal. Fold the other ends together to make a little parcel. Use your fingers and pinch together all the seams to thoroughly seal. Repeat with the remaining wonton skins.

3. Heat the oil in a wok to 375°F. In batches, fry the wontons for 2–3 minutes until golden brown. Remove to a plate lined with paper towels to drain. Repeat until all parcels have been fried.

4. Serve with immediately with Sweet-and-Sour Sauce.

PER SERVING | Calories: 541 | Fat: 37g | Protein: 18g | Sodium: 565mg | Fiber: 4.8g | Carbohydrates: 38g | Sugar: 12g

Korean Beef Lettuce Wraps

In lieu of lettuce, feel free to use squares of toasted seaweed.

INGREDIENTS | SERVES 4

½ cup Korean-Inspired Marinade (see Chapter 2)

½ pound rib eye steak, thinly sliced

2 tablespoons gojuchang paste

2 tablespoons soy sauce

1 teaspoon sesame oil

½ tablespoon honey

½ tablespoon rice wine vinegar

2 tablespoons vegetable oil

8 Bibb lettuce leaves

1 cup julienned cucumbers

1 cup julienned carrots

Gojuchang

Gojuchang is a common Korean condiment that is made of ground red chili, fermented soybeans, rice flour, and spices.

1. In a large bowl, combine the marinade with the steak. Refrigerate for 1 hour.

2. In another bowl, whisk together the gojuchang paste, soy sauce, sesame oil, honey, and rice wine vinegar. Refrigerate until you're ready to serve.

3. Heat a wok over medium-high heat and add the vegetable oil. Once the oil has come to temperature, add in the beef and stir-fry for 3–4 minutes until browned. Transfer the beef to a plate.

4. To assemble the wraps, take 1 lettuce leaf and place a few pieces of the beef on it. Top with some cucumber and carrots and drizzle on some of the prepared gojuchang sauce.

PER SERVING | Calories: 293 | Fat: 16g | Protein: 13g | Sodium: 1,083mg | Fiber: 3g | Carbohydrates: 22g | Sugar: 15g

Pork Larb-Gai Lettuce Wraps

Larb-gai packs a lot of flavor, from the tang of the lime juice to the bright, herbaceous notes of the mint.

INGREDIENTS | SERVES 4

2 tablespoons vegetable oil
½ tablespoon minced garlic
2 red chilies, minced
½ pound ground pork
1 tablespoon fish sauce
2 tablespoons lime juice
¼ cup sliced red onions
¼ cup chopped mint leaves
2 scallions, sliced
8 Bibb lettuce leaves

1. Heat the wok over medium heat and add the oil. Add the garlic and cook until fragrant—about 30 seconds.

2. Add chilies and cook for 1 additional minute, then add the pork.

3. Using a wooden spoon, stir the pork around the wok while breaking it apart to a crumbled consistency. Cook the pork until it is no longer pink, approximately 3–4 minutes.

4. Remove the wok from the heat. Stir in the fish sauce, lime juice, onions, mint, and scallions.

5. To assemble the wraps, divide the mixture into eighths. Take 1 lettuce leaf and place 1 portion of the larb-gai in the center.

PER SERVING | Calories: 235 | Fat: 18g | Protein: 11g | Sodium: 53mg | Fiber: 1.7g | Carbohydrates: 5.7g | Sugar: 2.2g

Chicken Lettuce Wraps

Blanched cabbage leaves can also serve as an alternative to lettuce.

INGREDIENTS | SERVES 4

2 tablespoons oyster sauce

1 tablespoon soy sauce

1 tablespoon rice wine vinegar

1 teaspoon sesame oil

1 teaspoon sugar

½ teaspoon black pepper

½ pound boneless, skinless chicken breast, sliced into thin strips

4 tablespoons vegetable oil, divided

½ tablespoon minced garlic

2 shallots, thinly sliced

1 cup sliced oyster mushrooms

½ cup shiitake mushrooms

¼ cup chicken broth

2 scallions, cut into 1" pieces

8 Bibb lettuce leaves

½ cup Peking Sauce (see Chapter 2)

1. In a medium bowl, whisk together the oyster sauce, soy sauce, rice wine vinegar, sesame oil, sugar, and black pepper. Add the chicken and toss to coat. Refrigerate for 30 minutes.

2. Heat a wok over medium heat, then add 2 tablespoons oil. Add the garlic and shallots and cook for 30 seconds, then add the mushrooms. Toss the items in the wok several times and then pour in the chicken broth. Cook the mushrooms until tender, about 4–5 minutes. Remove to a plate.

3. Add the remaining oil to the wok; once it is heated, add in the chicken. Stir-fry for 2–3 minutes.

4. Add the mushroom mixture back into the wok along with the scallions. Cook together for another 2 minutes.

5. To assemble the wraps, divide the mixture into eighths. Take 1 lettuce leaf and place 1 portion of the chicken mixture in the center. Serve with Peking Sauce as a dipping condiment.

PER SERVING | Calories: 324 | Fat: 23g | Protein: 14g | Sodium: 821mg | Fiber: 1.8g | Carbohydrates: 14g | Sugar: 7.3g

Tofu Lettuce Wraps

Tofu is high in protein and serves as a wonderful substitute for meat.

INGREDIENTS | SERVES 4

1 (12⅓-ounce) block firm tofu

2 tablespoons low-sodium soy sauce

1 tablespoon gojuchang paste

1 tablespoon honey

1 teaspoon sesame oil

2 scallions, sliced

2 tablespoons vegetable oil

1 shallot, thinly sliced

½ tablespoon minced garlic

1 small red bell pepper, seeded and diced

1 cup edamame beans

¼ teaspoon black pepper

½ teaspoon toasted sesame seeds

8 Bibb lettuce leaves

Demystifying Tofu

Tofu is a result of adding coagulants to soymilk and then pressing the "curds" into blocks. Although stocked full of health benefits, the flavor of tofu is rather benign. However, tofu will take on marinade flavors beautifully.

1. Using paper towels, pat the tofu dry. Cut the tofu into cubes.

2. In a medium bowl, whisk together the soy sauce, gojuchang paste, honey, sesame oil, and scallions. Add in the tofu cubes and mix until well coated. Refrigerate for 1 hour.

3. Heat the vegetable oil in a wok over medium heat. Add the shallots and garlic and cook for 30 seconds.

4. Toss in the bell pepper and edamame and stir-fry for 2 minutes.

5. Add in the tofu with the marinade. Stir-fry for an additional 2 minutes and sprinkle in the black pepper and sesame seeds.

6. To assemble the wraps, divide the mixture into eighths. Take 1 lettuce leaf and place 1 portion of the tofu mixture in the center. Serve hot.

PER SERVING | Calories: 264 | Fat: 15g | Protein: 16g | Sodium: 562mg | Fiber: 4.5g | Carbohydrates: 18g | Sugar: 8g

Potstickers

Dumpling skins tend to be thicker than wonton skins and typically do not contain eggs in the dough. However, when dumpling skins aren't available, feel free to substitute with wonton skins. For a dipping sauce, mix 1 part rice wine vinegar with 2 parts soy sauce.

INGREDIENTS | SERVES 6

½ pound ground pork

1 cup finely shredded cabbage

2 scallions, sliced

2 teaspoons minced ginger

2 tablespoons soy sauce

1 teaspoon sesame oil

½ teaspoon pepper

24 dumpling skins

2 tablespoons vegetable oil

¼ cup water

¼ cup chopped scallions

Stock Your Freezer

Potstickers can be made ahead and frozen. Prepare the dumplings through step 2, then lay out the potstickers on a baking sheet and place in the freezer. Once frozen, transfer the potstickers to a container or resealable bag. They can be stored in the freezer for up to 1 month. Continue with step 3, but add a few additional minutes to the cooking time.

1. In a large bowl, combine the pork, cabbage, scallions, ginger, soy sauce, sesame oil, and pepper. Refrigerate for 30 minutes.

2. Take 1 dumpling skin and use your finger to brush water along the edge of the circle. Place about 1 tablespoon of the mixture in the center of the skin. Fold the dumpling skin over and firmly press the sides to seal completely. While you are forming the potstickers, create a flattened bottom. You can also pleat the edges if you like.

3. Heat the oil in a wok over medium heat. Place the potstickers, flattened side down, in one layer and fry for 1–2 minutes.

4. Carefully pour the water into the wok and cover. Allow the pot stickers to steam for an additional 2–3 minutes. Remove the lid and continue cooking until the water has evaporated.

5. Place the potstickers on a plate and sprinkle the tops with scallions. Serve hot.

PER SERVING | Calories: 248 | Fat: 13g | Protein: 10g | Sodium: 507mg | Fiber: 1g | Carbohydrates: 20g | Sugar: 0.8g

Sweet-and-Spicy Chicken Wings

*To tell if these chicken wings are cooked, pierce one with a knife—
the juice from the wing should run clear when the meat is cooked through.*

INGREDIENTS | SERVES 4

12 chicken wings

½ teaspoon black pepper

¼ teaspoon cayenne powder

½ tablespoon garlic salt

½ cup rice flour

½ cup vegetable or peanut oil

1 clove garlic, minced

2 slices ginger, minced

4 tablespoons chopped scallions, divided

1 red jalapeño pepper, thinly sliced

½ cup Sweet-and-Sour Sauce (see Chapter 2)

1. In a large bowl, season the wings with black pepper, cayenne, and garlic salt.

2. Toss the seasoned wings with the rice flour and set aside.

3. Add the oil to a wok over medium-high heat. Once the oil reaches temperature, gently shake off excess flour from the wings and carefully add them to the wok. Fry until golden brown and cooked through—about 7–8 minutes. Remove the chicken wings and drain on a platter lined with paper towels.

4. Carefully drain all but 1 tablespoon of the oil from the wok. Over medium heat, add in the garlic, ginger, 2 tablespoons scallions, and jalapeño. Stir-fry for 15 seconds.

5. Add in the Sweet-and-Sour Sauce. Allow the sauce to come to a boil and return the chicken wings to the wok. Toss the wings to coat well. Transfer to a platter and sprinkle the tops with remaining scallions. Serve immediately.

PER SERVING | Calories: 444 | Fat: 23g | Protein: 28g | Sodium: 1,035mg | Fiber: 0.8g | Carbohydrates: 27g | Sugar: 7.6g

Thai-Spiced Hot-and-Sour Wings

*Arrowroot powder is frequently used as a thickener in Thai recipes.
You can substitute cornstarch if arrowroot powder is unavailable.*

INGREDIENTS | SERVES 4

12 chicken wings

1 teaspoon salt

1 teaspoon black pepper

2 tablespoons fish sauce

1 tablespoon soy sauce

3 tablespoons tamarind juice
   concentrate

6 tablespoons water, divided

2 tablespoons vegetable or peanut oil

2 tablespoons minced ginger

6 Thai red chilies, cut in half, seeded,
   and finely chopped

1 tablespoon arrowroot powder

Tangy Tamarind

Tamarind is the sticky pulp contained in the pods of the tamarind tree. Juice from the pulp is used to give a distinctive sweet-and-sour flavor to many Southeast Asian dishes.

1. Place the chicken wings in a bowl. Rub the salt and pepper over the wings and let stand for 10 minutes.

2. In a small bowl, combine the fish sauce, soy sauce, tamarind juice, and 4 tablespoons water. Set aside.

3. Heat a wok or skillet over medium-high heat until it is almost smoking. Add the oil. When the oil is hot, add the ginger and the chilies. Stir-fry for 30 seconds.

4. Add the chicken wings. Let sit for 1 minute, then stir-fry, moving the wings around the pan. Continue stir-frying for 5 minutes, or until the wings are browned.

5. Pour the prepared sauce over the chicken wings. Reduce the heat, cover, and simmer for 10 minutes or until the wings are cooked. Remove the wings from the pan.

6. In a small bowl, stir the arrowroot powder with the remaining 2 tablespoons water. Add the arrowroot powder/water mixture to the sauce in the wok, turning up the heat so that the sauce comes to a boil and stirring quickly to thicken. When the sauce has thickened, approximately 2–3 minutes, pour it over the chicken wings. Serve hot.

PER SERVING | Calories: 386 | Fat: 34g | Protein: 29g | Sodium: 931mg | Fiber: 2g | Carbohydrates: 13g | Sugar: 7g

Steak Bites

These juicy steak bites will be a hit at your next party.
Bloody Mary Dipping Sauce (see Chapter 2) is the perfect accompaniment.

INGREDIENTS | SERVES 8

1 pound rib eye or sirloin steak, cut into 1½" cubes

2 tablespoons Montreal steak seasoning

4 tablespoons vegetable oil, divided

2 tablespoons unsalted butter

1½ cups Bloody Mary Dipping Sauce (see Chapter 2)

1. In a large bowl, toss the beef cubes with the seasoning and 2 tablespoons oil.

2. Heat a wok over medium-high heat. Add the remaining oil and butter. Once the butter has melted, add the beef cubes in a single layer. Do not disturb the cubes for 30–45 seconds to allow the beef to develop a nice golden brown color. Then toss and stir to allow the steak bites to cook for an additional minute. You want the beef to have a nice sear but not cook all the way through.

3. Place the steak bites on a platter and insert a small skewer or decorative toothpick in each cube. Serve alongside a bowl of the dipping sauce.

PER SERVING | Calories: 183 | Fat: 12.5g | Protein: 12.5g | Sodium: 309mg | Fiber: 0.6g | Carbohydrates: 3.2g | Sugar: 2g

Shrimp Spring Rolls

Although shrimp is used in this recipe, almost any type of protein would be just as delicious.

INGREDIENTS | SERVES 4

½ pound shrimp, peeled and deveined

2 garlic cloves, minced

2 tablespoons fish sauce

¼ teaspoon black pepper

2 tablespoons vegetable oil

8 rice paper spring roll wrappers

8 lettuce leaves

2 cups cooked vermicelli noodles

1 cup cucumbers, thinly sliced

1 cup shredded carrots

1 cup fresh mint leaves

1 cup cilantro leaves

1½ cups Nuoc Cham Sauce (see Chapter 2)

Spring Roll Versus Egg Roll

"Egg rolls" refer to delicious rolls that are fried and crispy. "Spring rolls" are fresh rolls and utilize rice paper sheets. Egg rolls should be served hot whereas spring rolls can be served cold or at room temperature.

1. In a medium bowl, mix the shrimp, garlic, fish sauce, and black pepper together. Refrigerate for 10 minutes.

2. Heat a wok with the oil over medium-high heat. Add the shrimp and stir-fry for 2–3 minutes, until they turn pink. Remove to a plate.

3. Take 1 piece of rice paper and dip into a shallow dish of water to soften. Lay the softened rice paper on a plate. Place 1 piece of lettuce in the center and top with ¼ cup of the noodles in a line. Top with a few cooked shrimp, slices of cucumber, carrots, mint leaves, and cilantro. Fold in the sides and tightly roll up until it is closed. Repeat with the remaining ingredients.

4. Serve with Nuoc Cham Sauce.

PER SERVING | Calories: 304 | Fat: .4g | Protein: 15g | Sodium: 218mg | Fiber: 3.7g | Carbohydrates: 43.5g | Sugar: 28g

Tofu Spring Rolls

The filling in these spring rolls would also be a delicious vegetarian option in egg rolls if you substitute light soy sauce for the oyster sauce. Serve them with either Nuoc Cham Sauce (see Chapter 2) or Peanut Sauce (see Chapter 2).

INGREDIENTS | SERVES 4

2 tablespoons vegetable oil

2 shallots, thinly sliced

½ tablespoon minced garlic

1 cup sliced shiitake mushrooms

2 cups baby spinach

½ cup shredded carrots

2 scallions, sliced

3 cups fried tofu cut into thin strips

2 tablespoons oyster sauce

1 tablespoon rice wine

1 teaspoon sesame oil

¼ teaspoon black pepper

8 rice paper spring roll wrappers

1. Heat a wok with the oil over medium heat. Add the shallots and garlic and cook for 30 seconds.

2. Add the mushrooms and stir-fry for 1–2 minutes. Add the spinach, carrots, and scallions. Continue cooking the items until the vegetables have softened, approximately 2 more minutes.

3. Toss in the tofu and stir in the oyster sauce, rice wine, sesame oil, and pepper. Cook for an additional 2 minutes. Remove from heat and let cool to room temperature.

4. Take 1 piece of rice paper and dip into a shallow dish of water to soften. Lay the softened rice paper on a plate. Place a few spoonfuls of the mixture in a line toward the middle of the rice paper. Fold in the sides and tightly roll up until it is closed. Repeat with the remaining ingredients.

PER SERVING | Calories: 198 | Fat: 15g | Protein: 2.3g | Sodium: 359mg | Fiber: 1.1g | Carbohydrates: 13g | Sugar: 1g

Bacon-Wrapped Shrimp

If you prefer to use your oven broiler, place all the wrapped shrimp on a baking sheet.
Place directly underneath the broiler to brown, flipping halfway through the cooking process.

INGREDIENTS | SERVES 6

24 extra-large shrimp, deveined and
   shelled, with tails on
½ teaspoon black pepper
6 slices bacon, quartered
1 tablespoon vegetable oil
2 cups Basil Pesto (see Chapter 2)

1. Season shrimp with pepper. One at a time, wrap a piece of bacon around each shrimp. Use a toothpick to secure.

2. Heat oil in a wok over medium heat. Add the wrapped shrimp in a single layer. Cook for 2 minutes on each side or until the bacon is crispy and the shrimp turn pink. Drain the shrimp on plates lined with paper towels. Repeat until all the shrimp have been cooked.

3. Serve warm with pesto as a dipping sauce.

PER SERVING | Calories: 406 | Fat: 42g | Protein: 6.5g | Sodium: 514mg | Fiber: 0.5g | Carbohydrates: 2g | Sugar: 0.2g

Miso-Glazed Scallops

Be sure not to overcook your scallops as they will take on a rubbery texture.

INGREDIENTS | SERVES 6

12 diver scallops
1 cup Miso-Soy Marinade (see
   Chapter 2)
1 tablespoon vegetable oil
¼ cup chives cut into 2" pieces

1. Rinse the scallops and pat dry. In a shallow dish, add the scallops and marinade. Refrigerate for 20 minutes.

2. Heat a wok or skillet over medium-high heat until it is nearly smoking. Add the oil. When the oil is hot, add in the scallops in a single layer. Allow the scallops to sear for 1 minute without moving them around. Flip them and cook for an additional 1–2 minutes.

3. Place the scallops on a plate and lay 2 pieces of the chives, crisscrossed, on the tops. Serve hot.

PER SERVING | Calories: 107 | Fat: 5g | Protein: 1.5g | Sodium: 621mg | Fiber: 0.6g | Carbohydrates: 9g | Sugar: 5.8g

Mushroom Medley Crostini

Feel free to use whichever mushrooms you prefer in this dish.

INGREDIENTS | SERVES 6

2 tablespoons olive oil
1 tablespoon unsalted butter
½ tablespoon minced garlic
2 tablespoons minced shallots
½ cup sliced crimini mushrooms
½ cup sliced shiitake mushrooms
½ cup sliced button mushrooms
½ cup sliced oyster mushrooms
¼ teaspoon red pepper flakes
¼ cup dry white wine
1 teaspoon fresh thyme leaves
1 tablespoon Worcestershire sauce
¼ teaspoon black pepper
½ cup crumbled goat cheese
12 slices toasted baguette
2 tablespoons chopped chives

1. Heat a wok over medium heat. Add the olive oil and butter.

2. Cook the garlic and shallots for 30 seconds. Add the mushrooms and red pepper flakes. Stir and toss a few times before adding in the wine. Allow the mushrooms to cook until tender, approximately 4–5 minutes.

3. Mix in the thyme leaves, Worcestershire sauce, and black pepper.

4. Remove from heat and stir in the goat cheese.

5. Top the baguette slices with a few spoonfuls of the mushroom mixture. Sprinkle the tops with chives and repeat with the remaining ingredients. Serve warm.

PER SERVING | Calories: 258 | Fat: 7.6g | Protein: 7.9g | Sodium: 446mg | Fiber: 1.8g | Carbohydrates: 38g | Sugar: 2g

Crispy Fried Shrimp Balls

These shrimp balls are not only delicious but are quite eye catching. Serve with Tamarind Chili Sauce (see Chapter 2) or Sweet-and-Sour Sauce (see Chapter 2).

INGREDIENTS | SERVES 6

½ pound shrimp, peeled and deveined

1 tablespoon fish sauce

1 egg white

1 teaspoon black pepper

1 tablespoon cornstarch

1 tablespoon plus 2 cups vegetable oil, divided

1 package wonton skins

½ cup Tamarind Chili Sauce (see Chapter 2)

1. In a food processor, pulse the shrimp, fish sauce, egg white, black pepper, cornstarch, and 1 tablespoon oil several times until the mixture turns into a paste but still has some small pieces of shrimp.

2. Slice the wonton skins into thin strips. Lay the strips in a layer on a cutting board.

3. Form the shrimp paste into balls approximately 1½ tablespoons in size. You may need to wet your hands in between to keep them from sticking.

4. Roll each ball into the wonton strips so that they cover the entire ball. Repeat until all balls have been wrapped.

5. Heat the remaining 2 cups oil in a wok to 375°F. In batches, fry the shrimp balls until they turn golden brown, approximately 3–4 minutes. Drain the fried balls on plates lined with paper towels. Serve hot with Tamarind Chili Sauce.

PER SERVING | Calories: 733 | Fat: 73g | Protein: 8.7g | Sodium: 70mg | Fiber: 0.7g | Carbohydrates: 12.6g | Sugar: 9.5g

Salt and Pepper Chicken

This same method can be used with chicken wings.

INGREDIENTS | SERVES 6

1 pound boneless, skinless chicken breasts

2 egg whites

1 tablespoon soy sauce

1 tablespoon rice wine

2 tablespoons five-spice powder

1 teaspoon garlic powder

½ teaspoon red pepper flakes

1 tablespoon plus 2 cups vegetable oil, divided

1 cup rice flour

1 tablespoon kosher salt

¼ cup sliced scallions

1. Cut the chicken into 1" pieces.

2. In a large bowl, mix the egg whites, soy sauce, rice wine, five-spice powder, garlic powder, pepper flakes, and 1 tablespoon oil. Add the chicken, tossing to coat evenly. Refrigerate for 1 hour.

3. Heat the remaining 2 cups oil in a wok to 375°F. In a shallow dish, whisk together the rice flour and salt.

4. Working in batches, toss the chicken into the flour mixture to coat evenly. Shake off excess flour and add the chicken to the wok. Fry until the chicken has turned golden brown and is cooked through, approximately 3–4 minutes. Drain on plates lined with paper towels and repeat with the remaining chicken.

5. Place the chicken on a plate and sprinkle scallions over the top. Serve hot.

PER SERVING | Calories: 856 | Fat: 77g | Protein: 19g | Sodium: 255.5mg | Fiber: 0.8g | Carbohydrates: 22g | Sugar: 0.3g

Agedashi Tofu

The ideal texture for agedashi tofu is crispy on the outside and creamy on the inside.

INGREDIENTS | SERVES 6

2 cups peanut oil or vegetable oil

1 (12-ounce) block soft tofu, cut into 1½" cubes

1 cup potato starch or cornstarch

1¼ cup Tsuyu (see Chapter 2)

¼ cup sliced scallions

¼ cup dried bonito flakes

Dried Bonito Flakes

Bonito flakes, or hanakatsuo, are a staple in Japanese cuisine. They are made from the bonito fish that has been dried and fermented.

1. Heat the oil in a wok to 375°F.

2. Blot the tofu dry with paper towels. Pour the potato starch or cornstarch into a shallow dish.

3. In batches, toss the tofu into the starch and coat evenly. Gently shake off the excess starch and add to the wok. Fry the tofu until golden brown, approximately 2–3 minutes. Drain on plates lined with paper towels. Repeat with the remaining tofu.

4. Pour 1 heaping tablespoon of Tsuyu into a bowl. Place 1 or 2 fried tofu cubes in the bowl and top with scallions and bonito flakes. Serve immediately.

PER SERVING | Calories: 732 | Fat: 72g | Protein: 2.3g | Sodium: 322mg | Fiber: 1.6g | Carbohydrates: 23g | Sugar: 1.3g

Lamb Samosas

If you prefer, use ground beef in the filling. Serve these delicious little pies with Cilantro-Mint Chutney (see Chapter 2).

INGREDIENTS | SERVES 6

2 tablespoons plus 2 cups peanut or vegetable oil

1 cup diced onions

2 scallions, sliced

2 garlic cloves, minced

½ teaspoon garam masala

½ teaspoon ground coriander

¼ teaspoon red pepper flakes

6 ounces ground lamb

¼ teaspoon black pepper

½ cup frozen peas

½ teaspoon turmeric powder

1 cup diced boiled potatoes

1 teaspoon kosher salt

1 (1-pound) package thawed puff pastry dough

Samosa Dough

Samosas are traditionally made with a pastry dough consisting of flour, salt, water, and ghee.

1. Heat 2 tablespoons of oil in a wok to medium heat. Add the onions, scallions, and garlic and cook until translucent, about 5 minutes.

2. Stir in the garam masala, coriander, and red pepper flakes.

3. Add the lamb and cook while breaking the meat up into crumbles. Once browned, approximately 3–4 minutes, add in the black pepper, frozen peas, and turmeric. Stir the mixture around for an additional minute.

4. Add the potatoes and salt. Mix well so that all items in the wok have incorporated together. Remove from heat and cool.

5. Cut the puff pastry dough into 18 squares. Taking 1 square of dough at a time, place a heaping spoonful of filling in the center. Fold over to create a triangle. Pinch and crimp the edges of the triangle to thoroughly seal. Continue with the remaining ingredients.

6. Heat the remaining oil in a wok to 350°F. In batches, fry the samosas for 1–2 minutes on each side until golden brown. Drain on plates lined with paper towels and serve warm.

PER SERVING | Calories: 414 | Fat: 32g | Protein: 19.5g | Sodium: 422mg | Fiber: 6.3g | Carbohydrates: 17g | Sugar: 4.4g

Vegetarian Samosas

*Serve these savory samosas with Mango Chutney (see Chapter 2)
or Cilantro-Mint Chutney (see Chapter 2).*

INGREDIENTS | SERVES 6

2 tablespoons plus 2 cups peanut oil or vegetable oil

1 cup diced onions

2 scallions, sliced

½ teaspoon garam masala

¼ teaspoon red pepper flakes

½ cup frozen peas

½ teaspoon turmeric powder

2 cups diced boiled potatoes

1 teaspoon kosher salt

1 (1-pound) package thawed puff pastry dough

1. Heat 2 tablespoons oil in a wok to medium heat. Add the onions and scallions and cook for 2 minutes or until translucent. Stir in the garam masala and red pepper flakes. Cook for 2 minutes.

2. Add in the frozen peas and turmeric. Stir the mixture around for an additional minute.

3. Add in the potatoes and salt. Mix well so that all items have incorporated together. Remove from heat and cool.

4. Cut the puff pastry dough into 18 squares. Taking 1 square of dough at a time, place a heaping spoonful of filling in the center. Fold over to create a triangle. Pinch and crimp the edges of the triangle to thoroughly seal. Continue with the remaining ingredients.

5. Heat the remaining oil in a wok to 350°F. In batches, fry the samosas for 1–2 minutes on each side until golden brown. Drain on plates lined with paper towels and serve warm.

PER SERVING | Calories: 734 | Fat: 76g | Protein: 1.8g | Sodium: 398mg | Fiber: 2.4g | Carbohydrates: 12.5g | Sugar: 2.6g

CHAPTER 4

Beef and Lamb

Beef Stir-Fry with Vegetables

Canned vegetables such as bamboo shoots need to be only quickly reheated because they are already cooked, which makes for a shorter stir-fry time.

INGREDIENTS | SERVES 4

¾ pound boneless sirloin

Oyster-Flavored Marinade for Beef (see Chapter 2)

3 tablespoons vegetable or peanut oil, divided

2 thin slices ginger

1 teaspoon salt

½ cup canned sliced bamboo shoots, rinsed

1 tablespoon Chinese rice wine, dry sherry, or water

1 medium zucchini, cut on the diagonal into ½" slices

1 medium red bell pepper, seeded and cut into strips lengthwise

½ teaspoon black pepper

1. Cut the beef across the grain into thin strips approximately 2" long. Place the beef in a bowl and add the marinade. Marinate the beef for 15 minutes.

2. Heat a wok or skillet on medium-high heat until it is nearly smoking. Add 2 tablespoons oil, swirling the wok or skillet so that it covers the sides. When the oil is hot, add the ginger and let brown for 2–3 minutes. Remove the pieces of ginger.

3. Add the beef, laying it flat in the pan. Let sear for about 30 seconds, then stir-fry the beef, moving it around quickly with a spatula until the beef is no longer pink and is nearly cooked through. Remove and drain in a colander or on paper towels.

4. Clean out the wok and add 1 tablespoon oil. When the oil is hot, add salt and the bamboo shoots. Stir-fry briefly for about 1 minute, splashing the bamboo shoots with the rice wine or sherry.

5. Add the zucchini and bell pepper. Continue stir-frying for about 2 minutes or until the zucchini turns a darker color and is tender but still firm.

6. Add the beef back into the skillet and season with black pepper. Stir-fry for another minute to mix all the ingredients together. Serve immediately.

PER SERVING | Calories: 185 | Fat: 6.8g | Protein: 19.8g | Sodium: 1,758mg | Fiber: 1.6g | Carbohydrates: 9.5g | Sugar: 4g

Stir-Fried Beef with Snow Peas

Snow peas are a wonderful addition to stir-fries, and they pair nicely with beef. They have a crunchy texture and sweet flavor that makes them perfect for stir-frying.

INGREDIENTS | SERVES 4

¾ pound sirloin steak

2 tablespoons soy sauce, divided

1½ tablespoons cooking wine or dry white sherry

½ teaspoon sesame oil

2 teaspoons cornstarch

2 tablespoons vegetable or peanut oil, divided

2 cloves garlic, chopped

8 ounces snow peas, trimmed

How to Cut Beef Across the Grain

Pick up a cut of flank or shoulder steak and you'll notice lines or "grains" running across it. These are the muscle fibers. To cut the steak across the grain, cut perpendicular to these fibers. If you cut the meat along the fibers, it will turn out very tough.

1. Cut the beef across the grain into thin slices approximately 1½" long. Place the beef in a bowl and add 1 tablespoon soy sauce, cooking wine or sherry, sesame oil, and cornstarch. Marinate the beef for 15 minutes.

2. Heat a wok or skillet over medium-high heat until it is nearly smoking. Add 1 tablespoon oil. When the oil is hot, add the garlic. Stir-fry for 10 seconds.

3. Add the beef. Let it sear for 1 minute, then begin stir-frying, stirring and tossing the meat. Remove the beef from the wok after 2 minutes or when it is no longer pink and is nearly cooked through. Drain the meat in a colander or on paper towels.

4. Heat 1 tablespoon oil in the wok or skillet over medium-high heat. When the oil is just starting to smoke, add the snow peas. Stir-fry the snow peas, moving them around the pan until they turn dark green (about 2 minutes).

5. Add the beef back into the pan. Stir-fry, combining the beef with the snow peas and remaining soy sauce. Serve hot.

PER SERVING | Calories: 158 | Fat: 4.8g | Protein: 20g | Sodium: 500mg | Fiber: 1.5g | Carbohydrates: 6.6g | Sugar: 2.4g

Beef with Asparagus

This simple stir-fry is a great way to celebrate the arrival of asparagus season each spring. You may substitute broccoli, mushrooms, or bamboo shoots throughout the remainder of the year, when asparagus is no longer in season.

INGREDIENTS | SERVES 4

¾ pound flank or sirloin steak

1 tablespoon light soy sauce

1 tablespoon Chinese rice wine or dry sherry

1 teaspoon granulated sugar

½ teaspoon black pepper

½ teaspoon salt

2 teaspoons plus 4 tablespoons vegetable or peanut oil, divided

1½ teaspoons cornstarch

3 tablespoons chicken broth

2 tablespoons oyster sauce

1 tablespoon dark soy sauce

½ teaspoon minced ginger, divided

½ teaspoon minced garlic, divided

1 pound asparagus, cut on the diagonal into thin slices

1. Cut the steak across the grain into thin strips 1½"–2" long. Place the beef strips in a bowl and add the light soy sauce, rice wine or sherry, sugar, black pepper, salt, 2 teaspoons oil, and cornstarch. Marinate the beef for 15 minutes.

2. In a small bowl, combine the chicken broth, oyster sauce, and dark soy sauce. Set aside.

3. Heat a wok or skillet over medium-high heat until it is nearly smoking, and add 2 tablespoons oil. When the oil is hot, add half the ginger and garlic. Stir-fry for 10 seconds.

4. Add the beef. Sear for 1 minute, then stir-fry the beef, stirring and moving the beef around the pan for an additional minute or until it is no longer pink. Remove the beef with a slotted spoon and drain in a colander or on paper towels.

5. Heat 2 tablespoons oil in the wok or skillet. When the oil is hot, add the remainder of the garlic and ginger. Stir-fry for 10 seconds.

6. Add the asparagus. Stir-fry for 1 minute, then add the chicken broth mixture and bring to a boil. Cover and cook until the asparagus turns a bright green and is tender but still crisp (about 2 more minutes).

7. Uncover and add the beef back into the pan. Stir-fry for 2 more minutes to mix everything together. Serve hot.

PER SERVING | Calories: 180 | Fat: 6.3g | Protein: 21g | Sodium: 1,087mg | Fiber: 2.5g | Carbohydrates: 9g | Sugar: 3.3g

Broccoli Beef

This no-fuss version of the popular restaurant dish is perfect for busy weeknights. Serve over rice for a complete meal.

INGREDIENTS | SERVES 4

¾ pound flank steak

3 tablespoons vegetable or peanut oil, divided

2 cloves garlic, chopped

2 cups chopped broccoli

1 teaspoon salt

½ teaspoon black pepper

⅓ cup Basic Chinese Brown Sauce (see Chapter 2)

1. Cut the flank steak across the grain into thin strips 1½"–2" long.

2. Heat a wok or skillet over medium-high heat until it is nearly smoking. Add 2 tablespoons oil. When the oil is hot, add the garlic. Press the garlic down with a spatula so that it releases its juices into the oil.

3. Add the beef, laying it flat in the pan. Let sear (brown) briefly, then stir-fry the meat, stirring and tossing for 2 minutes or until it is no longer pink. Remove the beef from the pan and drain in a colander or on paper towels.

4. Add 1 tablespoon oil. When the oil is hot, add the broccoli and sprinkle with salt and pepper. Stir-fry for 3–4 minutes, until the broccoli turns a darker green and is tender but still crisp.

5. Push the broccoli to the sides of the wok or skillet. Add the sauce in the middle and bring to a boil, stirring quickly to thicken. When the sauce has thickened, add the meat back into the pan. Cook for 1 minute, stirring to mix everything together. Serve hot.

PER SERVING | Calories: 164 | Fat: 6.8g | Protein: 19.5g | Sodium: 873mg | Fiber: 1.3g | Carbohydrates: 5.3g | Sugar: 1.3g

Spicy Hunan Beef

Hunan cuisine is known for its wide use of chilies, garlic, and ginger.

INGREDIENTS | SERVES 4

1 pound flank steak

1 tablespoon soy sauce

2 tablespoons rice wine or dry sherry, divided

2 teaspoons cornstarch

1 tablespoon dark soy sauce

1 tablespoon white rice vinegar

1 tablespoon water

1½ teaspoons sesame oil

⅛ teaspoon white pepper

3½ tablespoons vegetable or peanut oil, divided

2 teaspoons minced ginger

1 tablespoon minced garlic

2 tablespoons minced chili pepper

1 teaspoon chili paste

1 teaspoon granulated sugar

1. Cut the steak across the grain into thin strips 1½"–2" long. Place the beef in a bowl and add the soy sauce, 1 tablespoon rice wine or dry sherry, and cornstarch. Marinate the beef for 20 minutes.

2. In a small bowl, combine 1 tablespoon rice wine or sherry, dark soy sauce, rice vinegar, water, sesame oil, and white pepper. Set aside.

3. Heat a wok or skillet until it is nearly smoking. Add 2 tablespoons oil. When the oil is hot, add the minced ginger. Stir-fry for 10 seconds.

4. Add half the beef, laying it flat in the pan. Let sear (brown) briefly, then stir-fry the meat, stirring and tossing for 2 minutes or until it is no longer pink. Remove and drain in a colander or on paper towels.

5. Clean out the pan and add 1½ tablespoons oil. When the oil is hot, add the garlic, chilies, and chili paste. Stir-fry for about 30 seconds, then add the beef back into the pan.

6. Add the sauce. Heat to boiling, stirring to combine the meat with the sauce and chili paste. Stir in the sugar. Serve hot.

PER SERVING | Calories: 221 | Fat: 9.8g | Protein: 24.6g | Sodium: 530mg | Fiber: 0.4g | Carbohydrates: 5.3g | Sugar: 1.6g

Crispy Ginger Beef

Adding a small amount of cornstarch to the marinade helps the beef slices separate more easily during stir-frying. If you like your chili hot, increase the chili powder to 2 tablespoons.

INGREDIENTS | SERVES 4

½ cup warm water

2 tablespoons cornstarch

2 large eggs

½ teaspoon black pepper

½ teaspoon kosher salt

1 pound sirloin beef, thinly sliced

½ cup vegetable oil

1 small carrot, julienned

2 scallions, cut into 1" pieces

2 tablespoons minced ginger

1 teaspoon minced garlic

1 red chili pepper, sliced

3 tablespoons soy sauce

2 tablespoons Chinese rice wine or dry sherry

1 teaspoon sesame oil

Storing Fresh Ginger

To maintain freshness and flavor, store unpeeled ginger in a resealable bag that has had all of the air pressed out. The refrigerated ginger can be kept for several weeks.

1. In a large bowl, whisk together the water and cornstarch until dissolved. Beat in the eggs, black pepper, and salt. Add in the beef and toss well to coat.

2. Add the oil to a wok and heat over medium-high heat. In batches, fry the beef for 2–3 minutes or until crispy and transfer to a paper-towel-lined plate to drain. Repeat with the remainder of the beef.

3. Carefully drain all but 1 tablespoon oil from the wok. Add in carrots, scallions, ginger, garlic, and chili pepper. Stir-fry the items for 1 minute.

4. Add in the soy sauce, rice wine, and sesame oil. Cook for an additional 2 minutes, then return the beef to the wok. Once the beef has heated, transfer the beef with sauce to a platter and serve hot.

PER SERVING | Calories: 494 | Fat: 36g | Protein: 28g | Sodium: 1,085mg | Fiber: 1.3g | Carbohydrates: 10g | Sugar: 2g

Mongolian Beef

Lamb is quite popular in China and can be substituted for beef in this dish.

INGREDIENTS | SERVES 4

1 pound flank steak, cut into ¼"-thick bite-size slices

1 tablespoon light soy sauce

1 tablespoon Chinese rice wine or dry sherry

1½ teaspoons cornstarch

2 tablespoons vegetable or peanut oil

2 cloves garlic, minced

2 scallions, cut into 1" pieces

¼ cup Peking Sauce (see Chapter 2)

½ teaspoon black pepper

1. Place the beef in a bowl and add the soy sauce, rice wine or sherry, and cornstarch. Marinate the beef for 15 minutes.

2. Heat a wok or skillet over medium-high heat until it is nearly smoking. Add the oil. When the oil is hot, add the garlic and scallions. Stir-fry for 10 seconds.

3. Add the beef and stir-fry for 1 minute.

4. Add the Peking Sauce and bring to a boil. Stir-fry for 1 additional minute, until the beef is cooked. Season with black pepper and serve hot.

PER SERVING | Calories: 236 | Fat: 11g | Protein: 24g | Sodium: 387mg | Fiber: 0.4g | Carbohydrates: 6g | Sugar: 3g

Beef in Black Bean Sauce

Adding in Chinese broccoli to this stir-fry provides a great crunchy texture and pairs well with the beef.

INGREDIENTS | SERVES 4

1 pound flank steak

1 tablespoon dark soy sauce

2 tablespoons Chinese rice wine or dry sherry, divided

3 tablespoons vegetable or peanut oil, divided

1½ teaspoons cornstarch

1 teaspoon minced ginger

1 teaspoon minced garlic

1 small fresh chili pepper, seeded and finely chopped

½ medium green bell pepper, seeded and cut into thin strips

½ medium red bell pepper, seeded and cut into thin strips

1 tablespoon black bean sauce

1 teaspoon granulated sugar

1. Cut the flank steak across the grain into thin strips about 1½" long. Place the beef strips in a bowl and add the dark soy sauce, 1 tablespoon rice wine or sherry, 1½ teaspoons oil, and cornstarch. Marinate the beef for 15 minutes.

2. Heat a wok or skillet over medium-high heat until it is nearly smoking. Add 1½ tablespoons oil. When the oil is hot, add the ginger. Stir-fry for 10 seconds.

3. Add the beef. Let sear (brown) briefly, then stir-fry the beef, stirring and moving it around the pan for 2 minutes or until it is nearly cooked. Remove and drain in a colander or on paper towels.

4. Heat 1 tablespoon oil in the wok or skillet. When the oil is hot, add the garlic and the chopped chili. Stir-fry for 10 seconds.

5. Add the green bell pepper. Stir-fry for 1 minute, then add the red bell pepper. Stir in 1 tablespoon rice wine or sherry while the peppers are stir-frying. Stir in the black bean sauce.

6. Add the beef back into the pan. Stir in the sugar. Stir-fry for 1–2 more minutes to blend all the flavors. Serve hot.

PER SERVING | Calories: 203 | Fat: 8g | Protein: 24g | Sodium: 286mg | Fiber: 0.6g | Carbohydrates: 4g | Sugar: 2g

Crisped Szechuan Beef

If you like beef jerky, you'll love this Szechuan specialty, made by stir-frying strips of marinated beef until they are crisp and chewy.

INGREDIENTS | SERVES 4

¾ pound flank steak

1 tablespoon soy sauce

5 teaspoons Chinese rice wine or dry sherry, divided

½ cup vegetable or peanut oil

1 tablespoon minced ginger

2 scallions, chopped

2 teaspoons chili paste

1 tablespoon dark soy sauce

1 teaspoon granulated sugar

½ teaspoon ground white pepper

Dry-Frying

Beef isn't the only food that can be cooked using the dry-frying method. Chinese green beans, a popular restaurant dish, are also cooked by frying the beans until they are dried out. This gives the beans a browned skin and softer texture. Other foods that can be dry-fried include chicken, fish, and denser vegetables such as eggplant.

1. Cut the flank steak across the grain into thin strips 1½"–2" long. Place the steak in a bowl and add the soy sauce and 2 teaspoons Chinese rice wine or dry sherry. Marinate the beef for 20 minutes.

2. Heat a wok or skillet over medium-high heat until it is nearly smoking. Add oil. When the oil is hot, add the beef, laying it flat in the pan. Let sear (brown) briefly, then stir-fry the meat for 10 minutes, or until the beef darkens and starts sizzling. (This is called dry-frying.) Remove the meat from the pan. Drain in a colander or on paper towels.

3. Remove all but 2 teaspoons oil from the wok or skillet. Add the minced ginger, scallions, and the chili paste. Stir-fry for 30 seconds.

4. Add the beef back into the pan. Splash the beef with the dark soy sauce, 3 teaspoons rice wine or dry sherry, and sugar. Stir in the freshly ground white pepper. Serve hot.

PER SERVING | Calories: 156 | Fat: 6g | Protein: 18g | Sodium: 534mg | Fiber: 0.5g | Carbohydrates: 4g | Sugar: 1.8g

Black Bean Beef with Asparagus

In this recipe, you can substitute 2 tablespoons Chinese fermented black beans for the black bean sauce. Rinse the fermented black beans and mash them together with the garlic and ginger. Both fermented black beans and Chinese black bean sauce are available at Asian grocery stores.

INGREDIENTS | SERVES 3

1 pound flank or sirloin steak

¼ cup Oyster-Flavored Marinade for Beef (see Chapter 2)

3½ tablespoons vegetable or peanut oil, divided

½ teaspoon minced ginger, divided

½ teaspoon minced garlic, divided

2 tablespoons Chinese black bean sauce

½ pound asparagus, cut on the diagonal into thin slices

¼ cup chicken broth

1 teaspoon granulated sugar

1. Cut the steak across the grain into thin strips 1½"–2" long. Place the beef strips in a bowl and add the marinade. Marinate the beef for 15 minutes.

2. Heat a wok or skillet over medium-high heat until it is nearly smoking and add 2 tablespoons oil. When the oil is hot, add half the ginger and garlic. Stir-fry for 10 seconds.

3. Add half the beef. Stir-fry the beef for 2 minutes or until it is no longer pink and is nearly cooked. Remove and drain in a colander or on paper towels. Stir-fry the remainder of the beef.

4. Heat 1½ tablespoons oil in the wok or skillet. When the oil is hot, add the remainder of the garlic and ginger. Stir-fry for 10 seconds.

5. Add the black bean sauce. Stir-fry for about 15 seconds, mixing with the garlic and ginger.

6. Add the asparagus to the wok or skillet. Stir-fry for 1 minute, then add the chicken broth and bring to a boil. Cover and cook until the asparagus turns a bright green and is tender but still crisp (about 2 more minutes).

7. Uncover and add the beef back into the pan. Stir in the sugar. Stir-fry for 1–2 more minutes to mix everything together. Serve hot.

PER SERVING | Calories: 330 | Fat: 14g | Protein: 35g | Sodium: 1,685mg | Fiber: 2g | Carbohydrates: 14g | Sugar: 4g

Cashew Beef

Instead of the water chestnuts or bamboo shoots, baby corn or straw mushrooms can be substituted.

INGREDIENTS | SERVES 4

1 pound top sirloin steak

1½ tablespoons oyster sauce

1 tablespoon soy sauce

½ teaspoon black pepper

1½ teaspoons cornstarch

½ cup raw, unsalted cashews

3 tablespoons vegetable or peanut oil, divided

1 teaspoon minced garlic

½ cup canned sliced water chestnuts, drained

½ cup canned sliced bamboo shoots, drained

½ teaspoon salt

1. Cut the steak across the grain into thin strips. Place the beef in a bowl and add the oyster sauce, soy sauce, black pepper, and cornstarch. Marinate the beef for 20 minutes.

2. Roast the cashews in a heavy frying pan over medium heat, shaking the pan continuously so that the nuts do not burn. Roast until the cashews are browned (about 5 minutes). Remove the cashews from the pan to cool.

3. Heat a wok or skillet over medium-high heat until it is nearly smoking. Add 2 tablespoons oil. When the oil is hot, add the beef, laying it flat in the pan. Let sear (brown) briefly, then stir-fry the meat, stirring and tossing for 2 minutes or until it is no longer pink. Remove and drain in a colander or on paper towels.

4. Heat 1 tablespoon oil in the wok or skillet. When the oil is hot, add the garlic. Stir-fry for 10 seconds.

5. Add the water chestnuts, bamboo shoots, and the salt. Stir-fry for 1 minute.

6. Add the beef back to the pan. Add the cashews. Stir-fry for another minute to combine all the ingredients. Serve hot.

PER SERVING | Calories: 177 | Fat: 5g | Protein: 26g | Sodium: 770mg | Fiber: 0.8g | Carbohydrates: 5g | Sugar: 0.8g

Beef Curry

Because of the strong flavor of beef, it is frequently paired with strongly flavored vegetables such as onion and garlic in stir-fries like this one.

INGREDIENTS | SERVES 4

1 pound flank steak

2 tablespoons soy sauce

1 teaspoon black or white pepper

1½ teaspoons cornstarch

3 tablespoons vegetable or peanut oil, divided

2 garlic cloves, chopped

1 large yellow onion, sliced

1 small green bell pepper, seeded and cut into thin strips

1 small red bell pepper, seeded and cut into thin strips

1 tablespoon water, optional

¾ cup Curry Sauce (see Chapter 2)

1. Cut the steak across the grain into thin strips about 1½" long. Place the beef in a bowl and add the soy sauce, pepper, and cornstarch. Marinate the beef for 15 minutes.

2. Heat a wok or heavy skillet on medium-high heat and add 2 tablespoons oil. When the oil is hot, add half the beef, laying it flat in the pan. Let sear (brown) briefly, then stir-fry the meat, stirring and tossing for 2 minutes or until it is no longer pink. Remove and drain in a colander or on paper towels. Repeat with the remainder of the beef.

3. Heat 1 tablespoon oil in the wok or skillet. When the oil is hot, add the chopped garlic and stir-fry for a few seconds, until it is fragrant. (Leave the garlic in the pan or remove as desired.)

4. Add the sliced onion and stir-fry for about 2 minutes, until it begins to soften. Add the green bell pepper. Stir-fry for 1 minute, then add the red bell pepper. Stir-fry for about 1 more minute. Add 1 tablespoon water if the vegetables begin to dry out during stir-frying.

5. Add the sauce into the pan and heat to boiling. Add the beef back in and cook for 1–2 more minutes to blend the flavors, stirring continually. Serve hot.

PER SERVING | Calories: 251 | Fat: 9g | Protein: 26g | Sodium: 872mg | Fiber: 3.6g | Carbohydrates: 15g | Sugar: 6g

Sizzling Beef with Teriyaki Sauce

Mirin, the Japanese version of rice wine, gives teriyaki dishes their rich flavor. If you can't find mirin, try substituting an equal amount of sake and increasing the amount of sugar in the marinade to 2 teaspoons.

INGREDIENTS | SERVES 4

1 pound flank steak

4½ teaspoons low-sodium soy sauce

3 teaspoons Japanese mirin

1 teaspoon granulated sugar

1 pound broccoli florets

3 tablespoons vegetable oil, divided

1 tablespoon minced garlic

2 teaspoons minced ginger

¼ cup Teriyaki Sauce (see Chapter 2)

Slicing Beef

If you find it difficult to make thin slices of beef, place the meat in the freezer for 10–15 minutes. The chilled beef makes it easier to slice.

1. Cut the beef into thin strips. In a medium bowl, combine the soy sauce, mirin, and sugar. Add the beef strips. Marinate the beef for 20 minutes.

2. Blanch the broccoli florets in boiling water for 2–3 minutes, until the broccoli turns bright green. Plunge the broccoli into cold water to stop the cooking process. Drain thoroughly.

3. Heat a wok or skillet until it is nearly smoking. Add 1½ tablespoons oil. When the oil is hot, add the garlic. Stir-fry for 10 seconds.

4. Add the steak, laying it flat in the pan. Let sear (brown) briefly, then stir-fry the meat, stirring and tossing for 2 minutes or until it is no longer pink. Remove and drain in a colander or on paper towels.

5. Heat 1½ tablespoons oil in the wok or skillet. When the oil is hot, add the ginger. As soon as the ginger starts sizzling, add the broccoli florets. Stir-fry for 1 minute.

6. Add the Teriyaki Sauce. Bring to a boil. Add the beef back into the pan. Cook for another minute, stirring to mix everything together, then serve hot.

PER SERVING | Calories: 331 | Fat: 18g | Protein: 28g | Sodium: 1,124mg | Fiber: 3g | Carbohydrates: 13g | Sugar: 5g

Stir-Fry Beef and Potatoes

Mushrooms add an extra earthy flavor to this dish. Try substituting with a variety of shiitake, portobello, or oyster mushrooms.

INGREDIENTS | SERVES 6

1 pound rib eye steak, thinly sliced

1 tablespoon minced garlic

1½ teaspoons cornstarch

½ teaspoon black pepper

2 cups plus 3 tablespoons vegetable oil, divided

2 large Russet potatoes, peeled and cut into ¼"-wide strips

1 small yellow onion, quartered

1½ cups white mushrooms, sliced

2 Roma tomatoes, sliced into wedges

1 tablespoon unsalted butter

2 tablespoons Maggi Seasoning or low-sodium soy sauce

¼ cup cilantro leaves

Maggi Seasoning

Although found in many Asian kitchens, Maggi Seasoning is actually owned by Nestlé and is often used in place of soy sauce. It can be used during cooking, in marinades, or in dipping sauces.

1. In a bowl, mix together the beef, garlic, cornstarch, black pepper, and 1 tablespoon vegetable oil. Set aside.

2. Heat 2 cups oil in a heavy pot until it reaches 375°F. Carefully add a handful of the potatoes into the pot and cook, stirring occasionally, until they are golden brown—about 7–8 minutes. Drain the potatoes on paper towels and keep warm on a baking sheet in a 200°F oven while frying remaining batches.

3. Heat 2 tablespoons oil in a large wok over medium heat. Add onion and mushrooms and cook until both have softened but not browned, approximately 3–4 minutes.

4. Add the tomatoes and cook for an additional 2 minutes.

5. Push the items to the side of your wok (or remove to a plate if your wok is not large enough) and add the beef. Quickly stir-fry the beef for 2–3 minutes or until lightly browned. Stir in the onion, tomato, and mushroom mixture to combine well.

6. Remove from heat and stir in the butter and Maggi Seasoning.

7. To serve, place the potatoes in a layer on a rimmed plate. Pour beef stir-fry over the top and garnish with cilantro. Serve immediately.

PER SERVING | Calories: 944 | Fat: 87g | Protein: 18g | Sodium: 357mg | Fiber: 3.7g | Carbohydrates: 23g | Sugar: 3g

Vietnamese Shaking Beef

This beloved Vietnamese dish is named after the "shaking" motion used to move the beef around the wok while it cooks. Serve it with jasmine rice.

INGREDIENTS | SERVES 4

1 pound filet mignon or rib eye steak, cut into ½" cubes

1 tablespoon minced garlic

1 small shallot, thinly sliced

½ teaspoon black pepper

2 tablespoons vegetable oil, divided

1 tablespoon unsalted butter

1 tablespoon Maggi Seasoning or low-sodium soy sauce

¼ cup fresh cilantro

1. In a large bowl, mix the beef, garlic, shallots, black pepper, and 1 tablespoon oil.

2. Heat a large wok over medium-high heat. Add 1 tablespoon oil to the wok and when it begins to slightly smoke, carefully toss in the beef mixture. Quickly stir-fry for 2–3 minutes and remove from heat.

3. Stir in the butter and Maggi Seasoning. Remove to a plate and top with cilantro.

PER SERVING | Calories: 370 | Fat: 30g | Protein: 22g | Sodium: 281mg | Fiber: 0.1g | Carbohydrates: 1g | Sugar: 0.1g

Korean Beef Tacos

Korean tacos have become a huge phenomena in the modern food truck industry with delicious trucks popping up all over the United States.

INGREDIENTS | SERVES 6

1 cup Korean-Inspired Marinade (see Chapter 2)

1 pound rib eye steak, thinly sliced

2 tablespoons vegetable oil

12 corn tortillas

2 cups kimchee, chopped

1 teaspoon toasted sesame seeds

1 cup seasoned and toasted seaweed, cut into thin strips

1. In a large bowl, massage the marinade into the beef. Cover the bowl with plastic wrap and refrigerate for at least 1 hour.

2. Heat wok over medium-high heat and add the vegetable oil. Once the oil has come to temperature, add in the beef and stir-fry for 3–4 minutes until browned. Transfer the beef to a platter.

3. Warm the tortillas in a cast-iron skillet. Divide the beef and kimchee among the tortillas. Top each taco with the toasted sesame seeds and seaweed strips.

PER SERVING | Calories: 657 | Fat: 16g | Protein: 18g | Sodium: 686mg | Fiber: 21g | Carbohydrates: 117g | Sugar: 76g

Beef Tataki with Ponzu Sauce

When searing, make sure you evenly rotate the beef so that when it is sliced there is an even ring of browned beef around the edges.

INGREDIENTS | SERVES 2

6 ounces beef tenderloin

2 teaspoons kosher salt

½ teaspoon black pepper

2 tablespoons vegetable oil

2 scallions, finely minced

1 red chili pepper, finely minced

½ cup microgreens or baby arugula leaves

1 cup Ponzu Sauce (see Chapter 2)

1. Season the beef with salt and pepper.

2. Heat a wok or skillet over medium-high heat until it is nearly smoking. Add the oil. Add the beef and sear it for 30 seconds on each side. Remove the beef to a cutting board and allow to rest for 10 minutes.

3. Slice the beef into ¼"–⅛" pieces. Fan the slices on a platter. Sprinkle the tops with the scallions, chili peppers, and microgreens. Drizzle the Ponzu Sauce on top of the beef and serve immediately.

PER SERVING | Calories: 335 | Fat: 22g | Protein: 22g | Sodium: 6,015mg | Fiber: 1.6g | Carbohydrates: 12g | Sugar: 4.7g

Cheese Steak Sandwiches

For a bit of acidity and spice, top your cheese steak sandwiches with pickled hot peppers.

INGREDIENTS | SERVES 4

1 pound rib eye steak, thinly sliced

2 teaspoons kosher salt

1 teaspoon black pepper

2 tablespoons vegetable oil

1 medium yellow onion, thinly sliced

1 pint white mushrooms, sliced

1 small red bell pepper, seeded and sliced lengthwise

4 slices provolone cheese

4 (6") hoagie rolls, split and lightly toasted

1. Season the beef with salt and pepper.

2. Heat wok over medium heat and add the oil. Once the oil is hot, add onion, mushrooms, and bell peppers and cook approximately 3–4 minutes.

3. Push the items to the side of your wok and add the beef. Quickly stir-fry the beef for 3–4 minutes or until brown.

4. Lay the cheese over the beef, cover, and allow the cheese to melt. Divide the meat and cheese amongst the rolls; top with vegetables. Serve immediately.

PER SERVING | Calories: 360 | Fat: 23g | Protein: 30g | Sodium: 1,497mg | Fiber: 1g | Carbohydrates: 5g | Sugar: 2.5g

Quick and Easy Flank Steak

Can't find flank steak? Try using either skirt steak or hanger steak.

INGREDIENTS | SERVES 2

½ pound flank steak

2 teaspoons tomato paste

1 tablespoon Worcestershire sauce

2 teaspoons soy sauce

1 tablespoon water

1 teaspoon brown sugar

2 tablespoons vegetable or peanut oil

2 cloves garlic, chopped

1 medium yellow onion, chopped

1. Cut the steak across the grain into thin strips 1½"–2" long, ⅛" wide, and ⅛" thick.

2. In a small bowl, combine the tomato paste, Worcestershire sauce, soy sauce, water, and brown sugar. Set aside.

3. Heat a wok or skillet over medium-high heat until it is nearly smoking. Add the oil. When the oil is hot, add the garlic. Stir-fry for 10 seconds.

4. Add the onion. Stir-fry until it begins to soften (about 2 minutes).

5. Add the steak. Sear briefly, then stir-fry for 2 minutes or until the beef is no longer pink and is nearly cooked.

6. Add the sauce and bring to a boil. Stir-fry for 2–3 more minutes, to blend the flavors. Serve hot.

PER SERVING | Calories: 222 | Fat: 8g | Protein: 25g | Sodium: 490mg | Fiber: 1g | Carbohydrates: 11g | Sugar: 6g

Pepper Steak

*Using a variety of bell peppers will not only offer a color pop to your dish,
but each color pepper has its own unique flavor. Serve Pepper Steak over rice.*

INGREDIENTS | SERVES 4

¾ cup beef broth

2 tablespoons soy sauce

1 teaspoon brown sugar

2 teaspoons cornstarch

2 tablespoons water

3½ tablespoons olive oil, divided

2 cloves garlic, chopped

1¼ pounds sirloin steak or sirloin tips,
cut into thin strips 1½"–2" long

1 medium onion, sliced

1 medium green bell pepper, seeded
and cut into thin strips

1 medium red bell pepper, seeded and
cut into thin strips

2 medium tomatoes, cut in half
lengthwise and thinly sliced

2 scallions, finely chopped

¼ teaspoon freshly ground black pepper

1 teaspoon kosher salt

1. Combine the beef broth with the soy sauce and brown sugar in a bowl and set aside.

2. In a separate small bowl, dissolve the cornstarch into the water and set aside.

3. Heat a wok or skillet over medium-high heat until it is nearly smoking. Add 2 tablespoons olive oil and the chopped garlic. When the oil is hot, add half the beef, laying it flat in the pan. Let sear (brown) briefly, then stir-fry the meat, stirring and tossing for 2 minutes or until it is no longer pink. Remove and drain in a colander or on paper towels. Repeat with the remainder of the beef.

4. Heat 1½ tablespoons oil in the wok or skillet. When the oil is hot, add the onion. Stir-fry for 2 minutes or until it begins to soften.

5. Add the green and red bell peppers. Stir-fry for 1 minute, then add the tomatoes, gently stirring and pressing down on them with a spatula so that they release their juices.

6. Push the vegetables to the sides of the wok or skillet. Pour the broth mixture in the middle and heat to boiling.

7. Quickly stir the cornstarch and water mixture and add into the middle of the pan, stirring to thicken. Once the sauce has thickened, mix with the rest of the ingredients in the wok.

8. Add the beef back into the pan, stirring to mix it with the vegetables. Stir in the scallions, black pepper, and salt.

PER SERVING | Calories: 353 | Fat: 19g | Protein: 32g |
Sodium: 1,274mg | Fiber: 2g | Carbohydrates: 12g | Sugar: 6g

Steak Diane

This dish was named after the Roman goddess Diana, who was the goddess of the hunt. At restaurants, the sauce is sometimes flambéed before serving.

INGREDIENTS | SERVES 4

4 (3-ounce) filet mignon medallions, pounded to ½" thick
1½ teaspoons kosher salt, divided
1 teaspoon black pepper, divided
2 tablespoons unsalted butter
1 tablespoon vegetable oil
2 tablespoons minced shallots
1 teaspoon minced garlic
1 cup sliced crimini mushrooms
2 tablespoons cognac
¾ cup low-sodium beef stock
2 teaspoons Dijon mustard
⅓ cup heavy cream
1 tablespoon chopped parsley

1. Season both sides of the beef medallions with 1 teaspoon salt and ½ teaspoon black pepper.

2. Bring a wok to medium-high heat. Melt the butter and oil together. Add the beef and cook for 1 minute on each side. Transfer the medallions to a plate and tent with aluminum foil.

3. Lower the heat to medium and add shallot, garlic, and mushrooms. Cook the mushrooms for 3–4 minutes or until softened and then deglaze the pan with cognac.

4. Once the cognac has nearly evaporated, add in the beef stock and Dijon mustard. When the liquid comes to a boil, whisk in the heavy cream. Allow the sauce to reduce for another 2–3 minutes and season with the remaining salt and pepper.

5. Return the beef and any juices to the wok and thoroughly cover the steak with the sauce.

6. Plate the steaks and mushrooms and spoon the sauce over the top. Sprinkle the tops with parsley and serve immediately.

PER SERVING | Calories: 386 | Fat: 32g | Protein: 17g | Sodium: 1,112mg | Fiber: 0.2g | Carbohydrates: 2g | Sugar: 0.06g

Sloppy Joes

Although these delightfully messy sandwiches are traditionally made with beef,
ground turkey can be substituted for a lighter version.

INGREDIENTS | SERVES 6

1 pound lean ground beef

1½ teaspoons kosher salt, divided

1¼ teaspoons black pepper, divided

2 teaspoons cornstarch

½ cup water

½ cup beef broth

3½ tablespoons olive oil, divided

2 cloves garlic, crushed

½ cup chopped onion

1 small red bell pepper, seeded and diced

1 cup tomato sauce

½ teaspoon red pepper flakes

½ teaspoon ground cumin

1 tablespoon brown sugar

1 tablespoon Worcestershire sauce

6 hamburger buns, lightly toasted

1. In a large bowl, combine the ground beef with ½ teaspoon salt, ¼ teaspoon pepper, and cornstarch. Let the ground beef stand for 15 minutes.

2. In a small bowl, combine the water with the beef broth. Set aside.

3. Heat a wok or skillet over medium-high heat and add 2 tablespoons oil. When the oil is hot, add the ground beef. Stir-fry the meat, stirring and moving it around the pan with a spatula for 3 minutes or until it is no longer pink and is nearly cooked through. Remove the meat and discard the liquids. Clean out the pan.

4. Heat remaining oil in the wok and add the crushed garlic. Stir-fry for 10 seconds, then add the onion. Stir-fry the onion for 2 minutes or until it begins to soften. Add the bell pepper. Stir-fry for 2 minutes.

5. Stir in the broth mixture, tomato sauce, and red pepper flakes. Stir in the cumin, brown sugar, and Worcestershire sauce. Bring to a boil.

6. Stir in the cooked beef. Stir-fry for 2–3 more minutes to combine all the ingredients and make sure the ground beef is cooked through. Season the mixture with remaining salt and pepper.

7. Divide the filling among the hamburger buns and serve hot.

PER SERVING | Calories: 212 | Fat: 11g | Protein: 17g | Sodium: 949mg | Fiber: 1g | Carbohydrates: 9g | Sugar: 5g

Chimichurri Skirt Steak

Chimichurri is a delicious herb-based sauce from Argentina that is typically served with grilled meats. It works just as well with stir-fried meat. This dish can be served with roasted potatoes or grilled bread.

INGREDIENTS | SERVES 4

1 pound skirt steak, thinly sliced crosswise

½ tablespoon kosher salt

¼ tablespoon black pepper

2 tablespoons vegetable oil

1 cup Chimichurri Sauce (see Chapter 2)

1. Season the beef with salt and pepper.

2. Heat wok over medium-high heat and add the vegetable oil. Once the oil is hot, add in the beef and stir-fry for 3–4 minutes until browned.

3. Transfer the beef to a platter and drizzle the Chimichurri Sauce over the steak. Serve immediately.

PER SERVING | Calories: 558 | Fat: 48g | Protein: 23g | Sodium: 1,852mg | Fiber: 1g | Carbohydrates: 7g | Sugar: 5g

Beef Fajitas

These fajitas would pair well with black beans, shredded cheese, guacamole, and salsa.

INGREDIENTS | SERVES 4

1 pound skirt steak

¼ cup Fajita Marinade (see Chapter 2)

2 tablespoons vegetable or peanut oil

1 teaspoon minced garlic

1 medium white onion, sliced

1 medium red bell pepper, seeded and cut into thin strips

1 medium green bell pepper, seeded and cut into thin strips

¼ cup chopped cilantro

8 flour tortillas, warmed

8 lime wedges

1. Cut the steak in half, and then cut crosswise into thin strips. Combine the beef in a bowl with the marinade. Marinate the beef in the refrigerator for 2 hours.

2. Heat wok over medium heat and add the oil. Once the oil is hot, add the garlic, onions, and bell peppers and cook until lightly browned, approximately 3–4 minutes.

3. Push the items to the side of your wok and add the beef. Quickly stir-fry the beef for 3–4 minutes or until brown.

4. Transfer the beef and vegetables to a platter and sprinkle with cilantro. Serve with tortillas and lime wedges.

PER SERVING | Calories: 486 | Fat: 23g | Protein: 28g | Sodium: 1,127mg | Fiber: 4g | Carbohydrates: 41g | Sugar: 5g

Beef Tostadas

If you can't find tostada shells, you can make them by deep-frying whole tortillas until crispy. Serve tostadas with hot sauce or your favorite salsa.

INGREDIENTS | SERVES 4

1 pound lean ground beef

1 teaspoon kosher salt

½ teaspoon pepper

¼ teaspoon cumin powder

½ teaspoon chili powder

2 tablespoons vegetable oil

2 cloves garlic, crushed

1 small white onion, diced

8 tostada shells, toasted

16 ounces refried beans, warmed

2 cups shredded lettuce

1 cup diced tomatoes

1 cup shredded Cheddar cheese

1. In a bowl, combine the ground beef with the salt, pepper, cumin, and chili powder. Let the beef stand for 10 minutes.

2. Heat a wok or skillet over medium-high heat and add the oil. When the oil is hot, add the garlic and onions. Cook for 2 minutes or until they are softened.

3. Add the ground beef. Cook the beef, stirring and tossing for 2 minutes in the wok until there is no trace of pink. Using a slotted spoon, remove the beef mixture to a large plate.

4. One at a time, spread 2 ounces of refried beans in an even layer on top of a tostada shell. Place several spoonfuls of the beef mixture over the beans and top with the lettuce, tomatoes, and cheese. Repeat with the remaining shells. Serve warm.

PER SERVING | Calories: 575 | Fat: 28g | Protein: 29g | Sodium: 1,456mg | Fiber: 8g | Carbohydrates: 38g | Sugar: 3g

Beef Flautas

Serve these crispy flautas with Roasted Tomato Salsa (see Chapter 2)
or Fresh Pico de Gallo (see Chapter 2)

INGREDIENTS | SERVES 4

¼ cup Fajita Marinade (see Chapter 2)

½ pound skirt steak

2 cups plus 2 tablespoons peanut or
   vegetable oil, divided

1 cup queso fresco

2 tablespoons chopped cilantro

12 small flour tortillas

1. Pour the marinade into a large resealable bag and add the beef. Massage the marinade into the steak and seal the bag. Refrigerate for 1 hour.

2. Heat 2 tablespoons oil in a wok over medium heat. Add the marinated steak and sear on both sides for 2 minutes. Transfer to a plate and allow the beef to cool. Once cooled, chop up the steak into ½" pieces and place in bowl. Mix in the queso fresco and cilantro.

3. Place 1 tortilla on a cutting board and place a few spoonfuls of the beef mixture in a line toward the bottom of the tortilla. Tightly roll up the tortilla and insert 1–2 toothpicks to secure the flauta. Repeat with the remaining beef mixture and tortillas.

4. Heat the remaining oil in a wok to 375°F. Working in batches, deep-fry the flautas until golden brown, 3–4 minutes, turning halfway through. Carefully remove the flautas and drain on plates lined with paper towels. Serve hot.

PER SERVING | Calories: 701 | Fat: 58g | Protein: 38g | Sodium: 895mg | Fiber: 7g | Carbohydrates: 13g | Sugar: 3g

Veal Marsala

Thinly pounded chicken breasts can be used instead of veal cutlets.

INGREDIENTS | SERVES 4

4 veal cutlets, pounded to ¼"–⅛" thickness

½ teaspoon black pepper, divided

½ tablespoon kosher salt, divided

½ teaspoon garlic powder

⅛ teaspoon paprika

4 tablespoons vegetable oil, divided

1 tablespoon minced garlic

1 large shallot, minced

1 pint crimini mushrooms, sliced

¼ cup Marsala wine

1 cup chicken stock

2 sprigs fresh thyme

2 tablespoons unsalted butter

2 tablespoons chopped fresh Italian parsley

1. Season the veal with ¼ teaspoon pepper, ¼ teaspoon salt, garlic powder, and paprika.

2. Heat wok over medium heat and add 2 tablespoons vegetable oil. Once the oil is hot, cook the cutlets in batches for about 1–2 minutes on each side or until golden. Transfer the cooked veal to a plate and tent with aluminum foil. Repeat with the remaining cutlets.

3. Add 2 tablespoons oil to the wok and add the garlic and shallot. Cook until fragrant (about 2 minutes) and then add the mushrooms. Cook for 5 minutes, until mushrooms are tender.

4. Add the wine. Reduce heat to low and simmer for 2 minutes.

5. Add in the chicken stock and thyme and cook for 3 minutes, until the liquids are reduced by half. Stir in the butter. Slide the veal back into the wok and season with the remaining salt and pepper.

6. Transfer the veal to plates and spoon the sauce over the cutlets. Sprinkle with parsley and serve.

PER SERVING | Calories: 221 | Fat: 20g | Protein: 1.8g | Sodium: 973mg | Fiber: 0.2g | Carbohydrates: 5g | Sugar: 2g

Veal Parmesan

Serve this dish with pasta tossed in marinara sauce or a side of mixed vegetables.

INGREDIENTS | SERVES 8

8 veal cutlets, pounded to ¼"–⅛" thickness
1 tablespoon Italian seasoning
½ teaspoon black pepper
1 tablespoon kosher salt
½ cup grated Parmesan cheese
¾ cup all-purpose flour
3 large eggs, beaten
1 cup Italian bread crumbs
4 tablespoons vegetable oil, divided
2 cups Marinara Sauce (see Chapter 2)
8 slices mozzarella or provolone cheese
¼ cup chopped fresh Italian parsley

1. Season the veal with Italian seasoning, pepper, and salt.

2. In a shallow dish, mix together the Parmesan cheese and flour. In a separate dish, place the beaten eggs. In a third dish, place the Italian bread crumbs.

3. Working with one piece of veal at a time, dredge the cutlet into the flour mixture, then the beaten eggs, and finally the bread crumbs. Use fingers to gently adhere the bread crumbs to the cutlet and place on a baking sheet. Repeat with the remaining cutlets.

4. Heat wok over medium heat and add 2 tablespoons oil. Once the oil is hot, cook the cutlets in batches for 1–2 minutes on each side or until golden. Transfer the cooked veal to a plate and tent with aluminum foil. Repeat with the remaining cutlets, adding the remaining oil as needed.

5. Preheat the oven broiler. Place the veal cutlets in a baking dish. Cover the tops with the Marinara Sauce and place 1 slice of cheese on top of each cutlet. Broil until the cheese has bubbled and browned, about 5 minutes. Top with parsley and serve immediately.

PER SERVING | Calories: 324 | Fat: 19g | Protein: 14g | Sodium: 1,511mg | Fiber: 1.8g | Carbohydrates: 19g | Sugar: 3g

Balsamic-Glazed Lamb

The rich flavors of balsamic vinegar and bright citrus notes match well with the gaminess of lamb.

INGREDIENTS | SERVES 2

½ pound lamb loin medallions

½ teaspoon kosher salt

¼ teaspoon black pepper

½ cup balsamic vinegar

½ cup orange juice

1½ tablespoons fresh rosemary, finely diced

1 tablespoon minced garlic

1 tablespoon minced shallots

2 tablespoons Dijon mustard

1 tablespoon agave nectar or honey

2 tablespoons vegetable oil

Balsamic Vinegar to the Rescue

In earlier times, balsamic vinegar was used as a medicine to treat ailments such as headaches.

1. Generously season lamb with salt and pepper.

2. In a small bowl, whisk together balsamic vinegar, orange juice, rosemary, garlic, shallots, mustard, and agave nectar. Pour the marinade into a resealable bag and add lamb. Seal bag and refrigerate for a minimum of 2 hours.

3. Remove lamb from the refrigerator at least 15 minutes before cooking. Take lamb from marinade and strain the liquid into a small saucepan. Bring the liquid to a boil and then reduce heat to low. Continue reducing until thickened—about 10–15 minutes.

4. Dry off the lamb to eliminate any excess moisture. Heat a wok to medium high and add the oil.

5. Add the lamb to the wok and sear it on each side for 1–2 minutes until golden brown. Place the lamb on a plate and drizzle the reduced balsamic marinade over the top. Serve hot.

PER SERVING | Calories: 987 | Fat: 91g | Protein: 8.9g | Sodium: 821mg | Fiber: 1g | Carbohydrates: 30g | Sugar: 23g

Rosemary-Garlic Lamb Chops

Lamb should be served rare to medium-rare to avoid becoming chewy.
Serve these delicious chops over Mushroom Risotto (see Chapter 8) or as an appetizer.

INGREDIENTS | SERVES 2

1 rack of lamb (6 or 7 chops)
2 tablespoons chopped fresh rosemary
1 tablespoon minced garlic
½ teaspoon kosher salt
¼ teaspoon red pepper flakes
¼ teaspoon black pepper
Zest of 1 lemon
¼ cup olive oil
2 tablespoons vegetable oil

1. Using a sharp knife, trim the rack by cutting off the top layer of fat and discard. Slice down in between each rib to create individual lamb chops.

2. In a small bowl, whisk the rosemary, garlic, salt, pepper flakes, black pepper, zest, and olive oil together. Pour marinade into a resealable bag. Add the lamb chops and massage the marinade into the meat. Seal the bag and allow the chops to marinate for at least 8 hours or overnight.

3. Heat vegetable oil in a wok to medium-high heat. Add the chops and sear them until they have developed a nice brown color—about 2 minutes on each side. To avoid overcrowding, this can be done in batches. Remove the chops and allow to rest for 3–5 minutes before serving.

PER SERVING | Calories: 377 | Fat: 40g | Protein: 0.7g | Sodium: 591mg | Fiber: 1g | Carbohydrates: 4.7g | Sugar: 0.7g

CHAPTER 5

Chicken and Turkey

Quick and Easy Chicken Stir-Fry

Stir-fry sauce and a prepackaged stir-fry vegetable mix make this recipe a great choice for busy weeknights. Cooking wine can be used in place of the rice wine or dry sherry.

INGREDIENTS | SERVES 4

1 pound boneless, skinless chicken breasts

1 tablespoon soy sauce

1 tablespoon Chinese rice wine or dry sherry

2 teaspoons cornstarch

3 tablespoons vegetable or peanut oil, divided

1 clove garlic, minced

1 slice ginger, minced

3 cups packaged fresh stir-fry vegetable mix

½ cup store-bought stir-fry sauce

Stir-Fry Sauce

Bottled stir-fry sauce is a great choice for those nights when you don't have ingredients on hand to prepare a sauce. Stir-fry sauce can be found in the international or ethnic cuisine section of most supermarkets.

1. Cut the chicken into bite-sized cubes. Place the chicken in a bowl and add the soy sauce, rice wine or sherry, and cornstarch. Marinate the chicken in the refrigerator for 30 minutes.

2. Heat a wok or skillet over medium-high heat until it is nearly smoking. Add 2 tablespoons oil.

3. When the oil is hot, add the garlic. Stir-fry for 30 seconds or until it is aromatic.

4. Add the chicken. Let brown briefly, then stir-fry, stirring and tossing the chicken for 3–4 minutes until it turns white and is nearly cooked. Remove the chicken from the pan. Drain on a plate lined with paper towels.

5. Add 1 tablespoon oil to the wok or skillet. When the oil is hot, add the ginger. Stir-fry for 30 seconds or until aromatic, then add the vegetables. Stir-fry for 1–2 minutes, until the vegetables are tender but still crisp.

6. Add the stir-fry sauce and bring to a boil. Add the chicken back into the pan. Stir-fry for 2 more minutes to heat through and thoroughly cook the chicken. Serve hot.

PER SERVING | Calories: 172 | Fat: 3g | Protein: 26g | Sodium: 1,734mg | Fiber: 0g | Carbohydrates: 7.5g | Sugar: 5g

Chicken with Almonds

To make this stir-fry even easier, you can replace the vegetables with 3 cups of a packaged stir-fry vegetable mix.

INGREDIENTS | SERVES 4

1 pound boneless, skinless chicken breasts

¼ cup Quick Chicken Marinade (see Chapter 2)

3 tablespoons vegetable or peanut oil, divided

2 cloves garlic, chopped

2 slices ginger, chopped

½ small zucchini, cut on the diagonal into ½" slices

1 tablespoon soy sauce

¼ pound fresh mushrooms, thinly sliced

1 small red bell pepper, seeded and cut into chunks

1–2 tablespoons water, if needed

½ cup Simple Stir-Fry Sauce (see Chapter 2)

½ cup almonds

1. Cut the chicken breasts into 1" cubes (it's easiest to do this if the chicken is partially frozen). Place the chicken in a medium bowl and add the marinade. Marinate the chicken for 20 minutes.

2. Heat a wok or skillet over medium-high heat until it is almost smoking. Add 2 tablespoons oil. When the oil is hot, add the garlic. Stir-fry for 10 seconds.

3. Add the chicken cubes. Stir-fry the chicken for 3–4 minutes until it turns white and is nearly cooked. Remove the chicken and drain in a colander or on paper towels.

4. Heat 1 tablespoon oil in the wok or skillet. Add the ginger and stir-fry for 10 seconds.

5. Add the zucchini and stir-fry for 1 minute. Stir in the soy sauce.

6. Add the mushrooms. Stir-fry for 1 minute, then add the red bell pepper. Add 1–2 tablespoons water if the vegetables begin to dry out during stir-frying.

7. Add the stir-fry sauce and bring to a boil. Add in the chicken and stir in the almonds. Stir-fry for 2 more minutes to mix the ingredients together and make sure the chicken is cooked through.

PER SERVING | Calories: 268 | Fat: 9.6g | Protein: 29g | Sodium: 2,196mg | Fiber: 3g | Carbohydrates: 14.5g | Sugar: 6g

Hoisin-Glazed Chicken with Cashews

Cashews are a good source of healthy, monounsaturated fats.

INGREDIENTS | SERVES 4

¾ pound boneless, skinless chicken breasts

1½ tablespoons oyster sauce

2 teaspoons Chinese rice wine or dry white sherry

1½ teaspoons sesame oil

¼ teaspoon salt

¼ teaspoon black pepper

1½ teaspoons cornstarch

½ cup raw, unsalted cashews

3 tablespoons vegetable or peanut oil, divided

1 thin slice fresh ginger

1 tablespoon minced garlic

2½ tablespoons hoisin sauce

Handling Raw Poultry

Raw poultry can carry salmonella bacteria. To prevent cross-contamination between raw meat and food that isn't going to be cooked, always thoroughly wash the cutting board, knife, and other utensils in hot, soapy water after handling raw poultry. If possible, use a separate cutting board and knife for raw poultry.

1. Cut the chicken breasts into 1" cubes and place in a large bowl. Add the oyster sauce, Chinese rice wine or dry sherry, sesame oil, salt, pepper, and cornstarch (adding the cornstarch last). Cover and marinate in the refrigerator for 30 minutes.

2. While the chicken is marinating, roast the cashews in a wok or skillet over medium heat, shaking the pan continuously so that the nuts do not burn. Roast until the cashews are browned (about 5 minutes). Remove the cashews from the pan to cool.

3. Turn the heat up to medium high and add 2 tablespoons oil to the wok or skillet. When the oil is almost smoking, add the slice of ginger. Let it cook for 2–3 minutes, until browned, then remove it with a spatula. (This is to flavor the oil.)

4. Add the marinated chicken cubes to the wok or skillet. Let brown briefly, then stir-fry, stirring and tossing the chicken for 3–4 minutes until it turns white and is nearly cooked. Remove the chicken from the pan. Drain in a colander or on paper towels.

5. Heat 1 tablespoon oil in the pan. When the oil is hot, add the chopped garlic. Stir in the hoisin sauce. Add the chicken. Stir-fry for 1 minute or until the chicken is nicely glazed with the hoisin sauce.

6. Stir in the cashews. Remove and serve immediately.

PER SERVING | Calories: 147 | Fat: 4g | Protein: 18g | Sodium: 591mg | Fiber: 0.4g | Carbohydrates: 7g | Sugar: 2.7g

Thai-Style Cashew Chicken

Palm sugar is a commonly used sweetener in Southeast Asian cuisine and can be found in most Asian grocery stores. Light brown sugar can be used as a substitute if you can't find palm sugar.

INGREDIENTS | SERVES 4

1 pound boneless, skinless chicken breasts

¾ cup unsalted cashews

2 tablespoons vegetable or peanut oil

6–10 small Thai red chili peppers

1½ tablespoons oyster sauce

1 medium white onion, chopped

2 scallions, finely chopped

¼ cup chicken broth

1½ tablespoons fish sauce

1 tablespoon palm sugar

Cooking with Nuts

When cooking with nuts, it is best to toast them before adding to a dish. Toasting the nuts will allow the oils to release and deepen their flavors

1. Cut the chicken into bite-sized cubes.

2. Roast the cashews in a heavy skillet over medium heat, shaking the pan continuously so that the nuts do not burn. Roast until the cashews are browned (about 5 minutes). Remove the cashews from the pan to cool.

3. Turn up the heat to medium high and add the oil. When the oil is hot, add the red chili peppers. Cook for 1 minute or until they begin to darken. Use a slotted spoon to remove the chilies.

4. Add the chicken to the wok and stir-fry until it is nearly cooked through—about 3–4 minutes. Stir in the oyster sauce while the chicken is stir-frying.

5. Add the onion and scallions. Stir-fry for 2 minutes, until the onion begins to soften.

6. Add the chicken broth. Stir in the fish sauce.

7. Add the chilies back into the pan. Stir in the roasted cashews.

8. Sprinkle the palm sugar over the mixture. Stir to mix everything together until heated through. Serve hot.

PER SERVING | Calories: 162 | Fat: 3g | Protein: 24g | Sodium: 382mg | Fiber: 0.5g | Carbohydrates: 7.7g | Sugar: 4.7g

Kung Pao Chicken

While white rice vinegar works best in the marinade for this recipe, feel free to experiment with using other types of rice vinegar when preparing the sauce.

INGREDIENTS | SERVES 4

¾ pound boneless, skinless chicken breasts

5 teaspoons rice vinegar, divided

2 teaspoons soy sauce

1½ teaspoons cornstarch

1½ tablespoons dark soy sauce

1 tablespoon water

1 teaspoon granulated sugar

2 tablespoons vegetable or peanut oil

3 dried chili peppers

2 slices ginger

1 tablespoon chopped garlic

1 cup unsalted peanuts

1. Cut the chicken into 1" cubes. Place the chicken cubes in a bowl and add 3 teaspoons rice vinegar, soy sauce, and cornstarch. Marinate the chicken for 20 minutes.

2. In a small bowl, combine the dark soy sauce, water, sugar, and 2 teaspoons rice vinegar. Set aside.

3. Heat a wok or skillet over medium-high heat until it is almost smoking. Add the oil. When the oil is hot, add chili peppers and ginger slices. Let brown for 2–3 minutes, and then remove.

4. Add the chicken. Let brown briefly, then stir-fry, stirring and tossing the chicken until it turns white and is nearly cooked—about 3–4 minutes. Remove the chicken from the pan.

5. Add the garlic to the wok or skillet. Stir-fry 30 seconds, then add the sauce. Bring to a boil.

6. Add the chicken back into the pan. Stir-fry, stirring to mix the chicken with the sauce. Stir in the peanuts. Serve hot.

PER SERVING | Calories: 331 | Fat: 20g | Protein: 28g | Sodium: 594mg | Fiber: 3.7g | Carbohydrates: 12g | Sugar: 4.4g

Broccoli Chicken

Chinese broccoli can also be substituted in this dish and can be found easily in Asian markets.

INGREDIENTS | SERVES 4

1 pound boneless, skinless chicken breasts

1 teaspoon salt, divided

½ teaspoon black pepper

1 tablespoon Chinese rice wine or dry sherry

1 pound broccoli florets

2 tablespoons oyster sauce

3 tablespoons water

1 teaspoon brown sugar

2 cups vegetable or peanut oil

1 tablespoon minced ginger

1. Cut the chicken into bite-sized cubes. In a large bowl, add the chicken, ½ teaspoon salt, pepper, and rice wine. Marinate in the refrigerator for 30 minutes.

2. Chop the broccoli into bite-sized pieces. Blanch in boiling water for 2–3 minutes, until the broccoli turns bright green. Plunge the broccoli into cold water to stop the cooking process. Drain thoroughly.

3. In a small bowl, combine the oyster sauce, water, and brown sugar. Set aside.

4. Heat a wok or skillet over medium-high heat. Add oil. When the oil is hot, add the chicken. Stir-fry the chicken cubes until they turn white (about 1 minute), using a spatula to separate the cubes. Remove from the wok and drain on a plate lined with paper towels.

5. Remove all but 1½ tablespoons oil from the wok or skillet. Reheat the oil over medium-high heat until hot, then add the minced ginger. Stir-fry for 10 seconds.

6. Add the broccoli and ½ teaspoon salt. Stir-fry for 1 minute.

7. Add the chicken. Stir-fry the chicken for 1 minute, then add the oyster sauce mixture. Cook for another minute, mixing everything together. Serve hot.

PER SERVING | Calories: 184 | Fat: 3g | Protein: 27g | Sodium: 1,003mg | Fiber: 3g | Carbohydrates: 10g | Sugar: 3g

Mongolian Chicken

While the breast is the most popular part of the chicken for stir-frying, thighs can be used as well. This is a good recipe for people who enjoy the dark meat of the chicken.

INGREDIENTS | SERVES 4

1 pound boneless, skinless chicken thighs, cut into 1½"–2" strips

1 tablespoon soy sauce

1 tablespoon dry sherry

3 teaspoons cornstarch, divided

2 tablespoons plus 2 teaspoons water, divided

1½ tablespoons hoisin sauce

1 tablespoon red wine vinegar

3½ tablespoons vegetable or peanut oil, divided

1 teaspoon minced garlic

1 teaspoon minced ginger

2 green onions, cut on the diagonal into quarters

½ teaspoon chili paste

¼ pound fresh mushrooms, thinly sliced

1 cup canned bamboo shoots, drained and rinsed

1. Place the chicken in a bowl with soy sauce, sherry, and 2 teaspoons cornstarch. Marinate for 20 minutes.

2. In a small bowl, combine 2 tablespoons water, hoisin sauce, and red wine vinegar.

3. In a separate small bowl, dissolve 1 teaspoon cornstarch in 2 teaspoons water.

4. Heat a wok or skillet over medium-high heat until it is nearly smoking. Add 2 tablespoons oil. When the oil is hot, add the garlic. Stir-fry for 10 seconds. Add the chicken. Let sit briefly, then stir-fry until it turns white and is nearly cooked through—about 3–4 minutes. Remove from the pan and drain on paper towels.

5. Heat 1½ tablespoons oil in the wok or skillet. When the oil is hot, add the ginger, green onions, and chili paste. Stir-fry for 30 seconds.

6. Add the mushrooms. Stir-fry the mushrooms for 1 minute, then add the bamboo shoots. Stir-fry for 1 minute, or until the mushrooms have darkened.

7. Push the vegetables to the side and add the hoisin sauce mixture in the middle. Stir the cornstarch and water mixture together and then add to the sauce, stirring quickly to thicken. After about 1 minute when the sauce has thickened, add the chicken back into the pan. Stir-fry for 2 more minutes to mix everything together and make sure the chicken is cooked through. Serve hot.

PER SERVING | Calories: 180 | Fat: 4.8g | Protein: 24g | Sodium: 433mg | Fiber: 1g | Carbohydrates: 8g | Sugar: 3.5g

Chicken with Snow Peas

Snow peas turn a beautiful dark green when stir-fried and provide a wonderful crunchy texture with the chicken in this dish.

INGREDIENTS | SERVES 4

1 pound boneless, skinless chicken breasts

1 tablespoon soy sauce

1 tablespoon oyster sauce

2 teaspoons cornstarch

3½ tablespoons vegetable oil, divided

2 slices ginger

8 ounces snow peas, edges trimmed

¼ teaspoon salt

1 teaspoon black pepper

Nutritional Benefits of Chicken

Chicken is high in protein and low in fat, and it is a good source of the B vitamin niacin and important minerals such as selenium. Stir-frying is one of the leaner ways to prepare chicken.

1. Cut the chicken breasts into thin strips 1½"–2" long. (It's easier to do this if the chicken breasts are partially frozen.) Place the chicken strips in a bowl and add the soy sauce, oyster sauce, and cornstarch. Marinate the chicken for 20 minutes.

2. Heat a wok or frying pan on medium-high heat until it is almost smoking. Add 2 tablespoons oil. When the oil is hot, add the ginger slices. Let brown for 2–3 minutes, then remove. (This is to flavor the oil.)

3. Add the chicken strips. Let them brown briefly, then stir-fry, stirring and tossing the chicken until it turns white and is nearly cooked—about 3–4 minutes. Remove the chicken from the pan.

4. Heat 1½ tablespoons oil in the wok or skillet. When the oil is hot, add the snow peas and the salt. Stir-fry the snow peas for 2 minutes or until they turn bright green.

5. Add the chicken back into the pan. Add a bit of water if the stir-fry is too dry. Season with black pepper. Stir to mix everything together and serve hot.

PER SERVING | Calories: 267 | Fat: 15g | Protein: 25g | Sodium: 627mg | Fiber: 1.6g | Carbohydrates: 6.5g | Sugar: 2g

Chicken with Bean Sprouts

Mung bean sprouts are low in calories and also contain a high amount of vitamin K. Their mild flavor pairs well with most Asian-inspired sauces.

INGREDIENTS | SERVES 4

1 pound boneless, skinless chicken breasts

1 tablespoon white rice vinegar

1 tablespoon soy sauce

2 teaspoons cornstarch

2 tablespoons dark soy sauce

2 tablespoons water

1 teaspoon sugar

3 tablespoons vegetable oil, divided

2 slices ginger

¼ teaspoon salt

2½ cups mung bean sprouts, trimmed

1. Cut the chicken breasts into thin strips approximately 1½"–2" long. Place the chicken strips in a bowl and add the white rice vinegar, soy sauce, and cornstarch. Marinate the chicken for 20 minutes.

2. In a small bowl, combine the dark soy sauce, water, and sugar. Set aside.

3. Heat a wok or skillet on medium-high heat until it is almost smoking. Add 2 tablespoons oil. When the oil is hot, add the ginger slices. Let brown for 2–3 minutes, then remove. (This is to flavor the oil.)

4. Add the chicken strips. Let them brown briefly, then stir-fry, stirring and tossing the chicken for 3–4 minutes, until it turns white and is nearly cooked. Remove the chicken from the pan.

5. Heat 1 tablespoon oil in the wok or skillet. When the oil is hot, add the salt and the mung bean sprouts. Stir-fry for 1 minute, then add the soy sauce mixture.

6. Add the chicken back into the pan. Stir-fry for 2 more minutes to heat everything through. Serve hot.

PER SERVING | Calories: 266 | Fat: 13g | Protein: 29g | Sodium: 958mg | Fiber: 0.1g | Carbohydrates: 7.8g | Sugar: 1g

Sweet-and-Sour Chicken

Serve this quick and easy stir-fry dish with cooked rice and a green vegetable for a complete meal.

INGREDIENTS | SERVES 4

1½ pounds boneless, skinless chicken breasts

1 tablespoon soy sauce

1 tablespoon oyster sauce

2 teaspoons cornstarch

¼ cup pineapple juice

2 tablespoons vinegar

2 tablespoons brown sugar

2 tablespoons olive oil

3 slices fresh ginger

3 scallions, cut into thirds

1. Cut the chicken into bite-sized cubes. Place the chicken cubes in a bowl and add the soy sauce, oyster sauce, and cornstarch. Marinate the chicken for 20 minutes.

2. In a small bowl, combine the pineapple juice, vinegar, and brown sugar. Set aside.

3. Heat a wok or skillet on medium-high heat until it is nearly smoking. Add the oil. When the oil is hot, add the ginger slices. Let the ginger slices cook for 2–3 minutes, until they are browned. Remove the ginger.

4. Add the chicken cubes. Stir-fry, stirring and tossing the chicken for 3–4 minutes until it changes color and is nearly cooked through.

5. Add the pineapple sauce into the pan and bring to boil. Stir in the scallions. Stir-fry for 1–2 more minutes, until the chicken is thoroughly coated with the sauce and cooked through. Serve hot.

PER SERVING | Calories: 300 | Fat: 1g | Protein: 36g | Sodium: 546mg | Fiber: 0.2g | Carbohydrates: 11.5g | Sugar: 8.7g

Chicken with Leeks

Serve this dish over steamed rice or Garlic Rice (see Chapter 10).

INGREDIENTS | SERVES 4

1 pound boneless, skinless chicken breasts

1 tablespoon dark soy sauce

1 tablespoon Chinese rice wine or dry sherry

1 teaspoon ground white pepper

2 teaspoons cornstarch

3 tablespoons vegetable or peanut oil, divided

1 teaspoon minced ginger

½ teaspoon chili paste with garlic

½ teaspoon salt

½ pound leeks, cut diagonally into ½" pieces

¼ cup Peking Sauce (see Chapter 2)

Washing Leeks

Leeks are a wonderful aromatic and can be found in many Chinese dishes. However, they must be washed thoroughly as they can have a lot of grit. To wash, fill your sink with cool water, add the leeks, and swirl them around. Allow the leeks to soak for a few minutes so that the grit settles to the bottom of your sink and then remove to a colander.

1. Cut the chicken into thin strips 1½"–2" in length. Place the chicken in a bowl and add the dark soy sauce, rice wine or sherry, white pepper, and cornstarch. Marinate the chicken for 20 minutes.

2. Heat a wok or skillet over medium-high heat until it is nearly smoking. Add 2 tablespoons oil. When the oil is hot, add the ginger. Stir-fry for 10 seconds.

3. Add the chicken. Let brown briefly, then stir-fry for 3–4 minutes until the chicken turns white and is nearly cooked through. Remove the chicken from the pan and drain in a colander or on paper towels.

4. Heat 1 tablespoon oil in the wok or skillet. When the oil is hot, add the chili paste. Stir-fry for 20 seconds, then add the salt and the leeks. Stir-fry for 1 minute.

5. Add the Peking Sauce. Bring to a boil, then add the chicken back into the pan. Stir-fry for 1–2 more minutes to combine all the flavors and make sure the chicken is cooked through. Serve hot.

PER SERVING | Calories: 224 | Fat: 6.6g | Protein: 25g | Sodium: 761mg | Fiber: 1.4g | Carbohydrates: 14g | Sugar: 5g

Asparagus Chicken

When available, try using white asparagus in this recipe. The flavor of white asparagus is milder than its counterpart and offers a great alternative.

INGREDIENTS | SERVES 4

1 pound boneless, skinless chicken breasts

1 tablespoon lemon juice

1½ tablespoons soy sauce

½ teaspoon granulated sugar

2 teaspoons cornstarch

3 tablespoons chicken broth

1 tablespoon oyster sauce

½ teaspoon chili paste

3 tablespoons vegetable or peanut oil, divided

2 cloves garlic, chopped

¼ teaspoon salt

½ pound fresh asparagus, trimmed and cut into 1" pieces

1 small red bell pepper, seeded and cut into thin strips

1. Cut the chicken breasts into thin strips approximately 1½"–2" long. Place the chicken strips in a bowl and add the lemon juice, soy sauce, granulated sugar, and cornstarch. Marinate the chicken for 20 minutes.

2. In a small bowl, combine the chicken broth, oyster sauce, and chili paste. Set aside.

3. Heat a wok or frying pan over medium-high heat until it is almost smoking. Add 2 tablespoons oil. When the oil is hot, add the garlic. Stir-fry for 15 seconds or until the garlic is aromatic.

4. Add the chicken strips. Let them brown briefly, then stir-fry, stirring and tossing the chicken for 3–4 minutes until it turns white and is nearly cooked. Remove the chicken from the pan.

5. Heat 1 tablespoon oil in the wok or skillet. When the oil is hot, add the salt and the asparagus. Stir-fry the asparagus, stirring and moving it around the pan for 1 minute.

6. Add the red bell pepper. Stir-fry for 1 minute, then add the oyster sauce mixture.

7. Add the chicken back into the pan. Stir-fry for another 1–2 minutes to heat everything through. Serve hot.

PER SERVING | Calories: 169 | Fat: 3g | Protein: 26g | Sodium: 799mg | Fiber: 2g | Carbohydrates: 8g | Sugar: 3g

Plum Chicken Thighs

Plum sauce can be found in the international or ethnic section of most supermarkets. For extra flavor, stir 1 tablespoon Chinese dark soy sauce into the plum sauce and water mixture before adding it to the stir-fry.

INGREDIENTS | SERVES 4

1 pound boneless, skinless chicken thighs

1 egg white

¼ teaspoon salt

1 tablespoon Chinese rice wine or dry sherry

1½ teaspoons cornstarch

2 tablespoons plum sauce

3 tablespoons water

2 cups olive oil

1 tablespoon minced ginger

2 scallions, finely chopped

2 teaspoons chili paste with garlic

1. Cut the chicken into 1" cubes. In a large bowl combine the egg white, salt, rice wine or sherry, and cornstarch and mix in the chicken cubes. Marinate the chicken in the refrigerator for 30 minutes.

2. In a small bowl, combine the plum sauce and water. Set aside.

3. Heat a wok or skillet over medium-high heat. Add 2 cups oil. When the oil is hot, add the chicken. Cook the chicken cubes until they turn white (about 30 seconds–1 minute), using a spatula to separate the cubes. Remove the chicken from the wok to a plate lined with paper towels.

4. Drain all but 1 tablespoon oil in the wok or skillet. Add the minced ginger, scallions, and chili paste with garlic. Stir-fry for about 30 seconds.

5. Add the chicken. Stir-fry for 1 minute, then add the plum sauce. Heat the sauce to boiling. Stir-fry for 2 minutes to mix the chicken with the sauce and make sure the chicken is thoroughly cooked. Serve hot.

PER SERVING | Calories: 1,115 | Fat: 112g | Protein: 23g | Sodium: 272mg | Fiber: 0.2g | Carbohydrates: 4g | Sugar: 2g

Sesame Chicken

Toss the fried chicken in Orange Sauce (see Chapter 2) for an easy variation on this dish.

INGREDIENTS | SERVES 2

½ pound boneless, skinless chicken breast

1 tablespoon soy sauce

1 egg white

3 teaspoons cornstarch, divided

⅓ cup plus 4 teaspoons water, divided

1 tablespoon vinegar

1 tablespoon granulated sugar

½ teaspoon chili paste

2 tablespoons vegetable or peanut oil, divided

1 thin slice ginger

2 cloves garlic, chopped

1 scallion, finely chopped

1 tablespoon toasted sesame seeds

1. Cut the chicken into bite-sized cubes and place in a bowl. Combine with the soy sauce, egg white, and 1 teaspoon cornstarch. Marinate the chicken in the refrigerator for 30 minutes.

2. In a medium bowl, combine ⅓ cup water, vinegar, sugar, and the chili paste.

3. In a separate bowl, dissolve 2 teaspoons cornstarch in 4 teaspoons water. Set aside.

4. Heat a wok or skillet over medium-high heat until it is nearly smoking. Add 1½ tablespoons oil. When the oil is hot, add the ginger. Let brown for 2–3 minutes, then remove from the pan.

5. Add the chicken. Cook the chicken cubes until they turn white and are nearly cooked through—about 3–4 minutes. Remove the chicken from the pan and drain on a plate lined with paper towels.

6. Heat ½ tablespoon oil in the same wok or skillet. When the oil is hot, add the garlic and scallion. Stir-fry for 10 seconds.

7. Add the vinegar sauce. Bring to a boil. Add the cornstarch and water mixture, stirring to thicken.

8. After a minute when the sauce has thickened, add the chicken back into the pan. Stir-fry until it is browned and cooked through. Garnish with the toasted sesame seeds.

PER SERVING | Calories: 214 | Fat: 5g | Protein: 27g | Sodium: 629mg | Fiber: 0.8g | Carbohydrates: 13g | Sugar: 7g

Garlic Chicken

This quick and flavorful dish pairs well with rice.
Or you can toss the chicken with Garlic Noodles (see Chapter 9)

INGREDIENTS | SERVES 4

1 pound boneless, skinless chicken breasts

1 egg white

1 teaspoon sesame oil

½ teaspoon salt

1 tablespoon plus 1 teaspoon cornstarch, divided

¼ cup chicken broth

1 tablespoon dark soy sauce

2 teaspoons brown sugar

4 teaspoons water

2 cups vegetable or peanut oil

4 garlic cloves, crushed

1 scallion, chopped

¼ teaspoon chili paste

1. Cut the chicken breasts into bite-sized cubes. In a large bowl, combine the egg white, sesame oil, salt, and 1 tablespoon cornstarch. Add the chicken cubes and marinate the chicken in the refrigerator for 30 minutes.

2. In a medium bowl, combine the chicken broth, dark soy sauce, and brown sugar. Set aside.

3. In a small bowl, dissolve the 1 teaspoon cornstarch into the water and set aside.

4. Heat a wok or skillet over medium-high heat and add the oil. When the oil is hot, add the chicken. Stir-fry the chicken cubes until they turn white (about 30 seconds–1 minute), using a spatula to separate the cubes. Remove from the wok and drain in a colander or on paper towels.

5. Remove all but 1 tablespoon oil from the wok or skillet. Heat the oil over medium-high heat. When the oil is hot, add the garlic, scallions, and the chili paste. Add the soy sauce mixture and bring to a boil. Stir in the cornstarch and water mixture.

6. Add the chicken. Stir-fry for 2–3 minutes or until the chicken is cooked through. Serve hot.

PER SERVING | Calories: 174 | Fat: 4g | Protein: 25g | Sodium: 735mg | Fiber: 0.1g | Carbohydrates: 7g | Sugar: 2.5g

Five-Spiced Chicken

If you are new to the strong flavors of five-spice powder, use ½ teaspoon in this recipe and slowly increase the amount once you are accustomed to the taste.

INGREDIENTS | SERVES 4

1 pound boneless, skinless chicken breasts

1 large egg white

½ teaspoon salt

1 teaspoon five-spice powder

4 teaspoons cornstarch, divided

½ cup chicken broth

1½ tablespoons dark soy sauce

2 teaspoons brown sugar

½ teaspoon chili paste

4 teaspoons water

2 cups vegetable or peanut oil

2 cloves garlic, chopped

1 small zucchini, sliced into ¼" pieces

¼ teaspoon salt

¼ teaspoon black pepper

1. Cut the chicken into bite-sized cubes. In a bowl, stir together the egg white, salt, five-spice powder, and 3 teaspoons cornstarch. Add the chicken cubes, cover, and marinate in the refrigerator for 30 minutes.

2. In a small bowl, combine the chicken broth, dark soy sauce, brown sugar, and chili paste. Set aside.

3. In a separate small bowl, dissolve 1 teaspoon cornstarch into the water.

4. Heat 2 cups oil over medium-high heat in a wok or heavy, deep-sided skillet. When the oil is hot, add the chicken. Cook the chicken for 30 seconds or until the cubes turn white, stirring gently to separate the pieces. Remove the chicken with a slotted spoon and drain on a plate lined with paper towels.

5. Drain all but 2 tablespoons oil from the wok or skillet. Add the garlic. Stir-fry the garlic for 10 seconds.

6. Add the zucchini. Stir-fry the zucchini, sprinkling the salt over it, until the zucchini turns a darker green and is tender but still crisp. Remove from the pan and drain.

7. Add the chicken cubes back into the pan. Stir-fry for 1 minute, then add the soy sauce mixture and bring to a boil. Add the cornstarch and water mixture to the sauce, stirring quickly to thicken.

8. After 1–2 minutes when the sauce has thickened, add the zucchini back into the pan. Stir in the black pepper. Stir-fry for 1–2 more minutes to heat everything through. Serve hot.

PER SERVING | Calories: 177 | Fat: 3.5g | Protein: 26g | Sodium: 1,068mg | Fiber: 0.6g | Carbohydrates: 8.8g | Sugar: 3.6g

Walnut Chicken

Brown bean sauce is available at Asian markets. If you find the walnut flavor in this dish a bit too strong, try blanching the walnut halves in boiling water for a minute before stir-frying.

INGREDIENTS | SERVES 4

1 pound boneless, skinless chicken breasts

2 tablespoons oyster sauce

2 teaspoons cornstarch

3 tablespoons chicken broth

1 tablespoon soy sauce

1 tablespoon rice wine or dry sherry

3½ tablespoons vegetable or peanut oil, divided

1 teaspoon minced ginger

1 teaspoon minced garlic

2 tablespoons Chinese brown bean sauce

1 cup toasted walnut halves

1. Chop the chicken into thin strips 1½"–2" long. Place the chicken in a bowl and add the oyster sauce and cornstarch. Marinate the chicken for 20 minutes.

2. In a small bowl, combine the chicken broth, soy sauce, and rice wine or sherry. Set aside.

3. Heat a wok or skillet over medium-high heat until it is nearly smoking. Add 2 tablespoons oil. When the oil is hot, add the ginger. Stir-fry for 10 seconds.

4. Add the chicken. Let sit briefly, then stir-fry the chicken, stirring and moving it around the pan until it turns white and is nearly cooked through—about 3–4 minutes. Remove the chicken and drain in a colander or on paper towels.

5. Heat 1½ tablespoons oil in the wok or skillet. When the oil is hot, add the garlic and the brown bean sauce. Stir-fry for 10 seconds.

6. Add the walnut halves. Stir-fry for 1 minute, mixing them in with the bean sauce.

7. Add the chicken broth mixture and bring to a boil.

8. Add the chicken back into the pan. Stir-fry for 2 more minutes to mix everything together and make sure the chicken is cooked through. Serve hot.

PER SERVING | Calories: 349 | Fat: 22g | Protein: 29g | Sodium: 674mg | Fiber: 2.5g | Carbohydrates: 9g | Sugar: 1g

General Tso's Chicken

Chicken thighs are combined with hot chilies and a spicy sauce in this famous dish that is named after a nineteenth-century Chinese military officer.

INGREDIENTS | SERVES 4

1 pound boneless, skinless chicken thighs

1 large egg white

2 teaspoons Chinese rice wine or dry sherry

½ teaspoon salt

1 tablespoon cornstarch

2 tablespoons plus 1 teaspoon dark soy sauce

1 tablespoon white wine vinegar

3 tablespoons water

1 teaspoon hoisin sauce

2 teaspoons granulated sugar

2 cups vegetable or peanut oil

1 teaspoon minced garlic

6 small dried red chili peppers

1. Cut the chicken into 1" cubes. In a bowl, stir together the egg white, rice wine or sherry, salt, and the cornstarch. Add the chicken and marinate in the refrigerator for 30 minutes.

2. In a small bowl, combine the dark soy sauce, white wine vinegar, water, hoisin sauce, and sugar. Set aside.

3. Heat a wok or skillet over medium-high heat until it is nearly smoking. Add 2 cups oil. When the oil is hot, add the chicken. Stir-fry the chicken cubes until they turn white (about 30 seconds), using a spatula to separate the cubes. Remove from the wok and drain in a colander or on paper towels.

4. Remove all but 1 tablespoon oil from the wok or skillet. When the oil is hot, add the garlic and chili peppers. Stir-fry for 10 seconds.

5. Add the chicken back into a pan. Stir-fry the chicken for 1 minute, then push to the sides of the pan and add the soy sauce mixture in the middle. Bring the sauce to a boil. Stir-fry for 1–2 more minutes to mix the sauce with the chicken. Serve hot.

PER SERVING | Calories: 165 | Fat: 4g | Protein: 23g | Sodium: 951mg | Fiber: 0.1g | Carbohydrates: 5.6g | Sugar: 2.6g

Chicken Chop Suey

*Chop suey is a great dish to make when it's time to clean
out the vegetable crisper section of your refrigerator.*

INGREDIENTS | SERVES 2

½ pound boneless, skinless chicken
breast

2 teaspoons soy sauce

2 teaspoons rice wine or dry sherry

¼ teaspoon black pepper

2 teaspoons cornstarch, divided

¼ cup chicken broth

2½ teaspoons oyster sauce

3 tablespoons vegetable or peanut oil,
divided

1 teaspoon minced garlic

1 teaspoon minced ginger

1 small onion, chopped

1 small green bell pepper, seeded, thinly
sliced

¼ pound thinly sliced mushrooms

2 ribs celery, thinly sliced

1 teaspoon salt (optional)

1 teaspoon granulated sugar (optional)

1 cup mung bean sprouts

1. Cut the chicken into thin strips about 1½" long. Place the chicken in a bowl and add the soy sauce, rice wine or sherry, black pepper, and 1 teaspoon cornstarch. Marinate the chicken for 20 minutes.

2. In a small bowl, combine the chicken broth and oyster sauce. Whisk in 1 teaspoon cornstarch. Set aside.

3. Heat a wok or skillet over medium-high heat until it is nearly smoking. Add 1½ tablespoons oil. When the oil is hot, add the garlic and ginger. Stir-fry for 10 seconds.

4. Add the chicken. Let brown briefly, then stir-fry the chicken until it turns white and is nearly cooked through—about 3–4 minutes. Remove and drain in a colander or on paper towels.

5. Heat 1½ tablespoons oil in the wok or skillet. Add the onion. Stir-fry for 2 minutes or until it begins to soften.

6. Add the green bell pepper and the mushrooms. Stir-fry for 1 minute, then add the celery. Stir-fry for 1 minute or until the mushrooms have darkened and the green vegetables are tender but still crisp. (Stir in up to 1 teaspoon salt and 1 teaspoon sugar while stir-frying the vegetables, if desired.)

7. Stir in the mung bean sprouts and stir-fry for another 30 seconds.

8. Push the vegetables to the sides of the wok or skillet. Stir the chicken broth mixture and add in the middle. Bring to a boil, stirring to thicken. After 1 minute, stir-fry for 1 minute to blend all the flavors. Serve hot.

PER SERVING | Calories: 250 | Fat: 4g | Protein: 31g |
Sodium: 1,957mg | Fiber: 2.8g | Carbohydrates: 22g | Sugar: 7g

Almond Gai Ding

*Diced chicken and vegetables are combined with almonds in this popular takeout dish.
You can replace the almonds with cashews if you prefer.*

INGREDIENTS | SERVES 3

¾ pound boneless, skinless chicken breast

1 tablespoon oyster sauce

1 tablespoon dry sherry

½ teaspoon ground white pepper

1 teaspoon cornstarch

½ cup almonds

2 tablespoons vegetable or peanut oil

1 teaspoon garlic

1 teaspoon ginger

1 small onion, finely chopped

2 ribs celery, diced

¼ pound thinly sliced mushrooms

½ teaspoon salt

2 tablespoons chicken broth

1 tablespoon soy sauce

½ teaspoon granulated sugar

Almonds in Ancient Times

You'll find several references to almonds in ancient writings. In Greek mythology, the gods take pity on Phyllis and turn her into an almond tree after she is deserted by her lover, Demophon. In the Bible, the famous rod used by Aaron is made from the wood of an almond tree.

1. Dice the chicken into bite-sized cubes. Place the diced chicken in a bowl and add the oyster sauce, dry sherry, white pepper, and cornstarch. Marinate the chicken for 20 minutes.

2. Toast the almonds in a wok or skillet over medium heat, shaking the pan continuously so that the nuts do not burn. Toast until the almonds are golden (about 5 minutes). Remove the almonds from the pan to cool.

3. Heat a wok or skillet over medium-high heat until it is nearly smoking. Add the oil. When the oil is hot, add the garlic and ginger. Stir-fry for 10 seconds.

4 Add the chicken. Stir-fry the chicken until it turns white and is nearly cooked—about 3–4 minutes.

5. Push the chicken to the sides of the wok or skillet. Add the onion in the middle and stir-fry for about 2 minutes, until it begins to soften. Add the celery, mushrooms, and salt and stir-fry for about 2 minutes, until the mushrooms darken and the celery has turned a darker green and is tender but still crisp.

6. Stir in the chicken broth, soy sauce, and sugar. Stir-fry for another minute. Garnish with the almonds.

PER SERVING | Calories: 142 | Fat: 8g | Protein: 5g |
Sodium: 904mg | Fiber: 3g | Carbohydrates: 12g | Sugar: 4g

Teriyaki Chicken

Beef or pork is a wonderful substitute in this recipe and can be combined with broccoli florets for added texture.

INGREDIENTS | SERVES 4

1 pound boneless, skinless chicken breasts

⅔ cup Teriyaki Sauce (see Chapter 2)

4 scallions, finely chopped

2 teaspoons granulated sugar

¼ cup minced ginger

2 tablespoons vegetable or peanut oil

2 cloves garlic, crushed

¼ teaspoon red pepper flakes

1. Cut the chicken breasts into thin strips approximately 1½"–2" long. In a large bowl, combine the Teriyaki Sauce, scallions, sugar, and ginger. Store half the teriyaki sauce mixture in a sealed container in the refrigerator. Combine the chicken in the bowl with the remainder of the teriyaki sauce mixture and marinate in the refrigerator for 30 minutes.

2. Heat a wok or skillet on medium-high heat until it is almost smoking. Add the oil. When the oil is hot, add the garlic and red pepper flakes. Stir-fry for 30 seconds.

3. Add the chicken. Let brown briefly, then stir-fry, moving the chicken around the pan until it turns white and is nearly cooked—about 3–4 minutes.

4. Add the reserved marinade into the pan. Reduce the heat and cook, stirring occasionally for an additional 2 minutes or until the chicken is fully cooked and nicely glazed with the sauce. Serve hot.

PER SERVING | Calories: 227 | Fat: 3g | Protein: 27g | Sodium: 2,534mg | Fiber: 1.4g | Carbohydrates: 20g | Sugar: 12.5g

Chicken Adobo

Coconut vinegar is popular in Southeast Asia, and in particular the Philippines.
The vinegar is highly acidic and takes on a cloudy appearance.

INGREDIENTS | SERVES 4

2 tablespoons vegetable oil

4 pounds skinless, bone-in chicken thighs

1 cup low-sodium soy sauce

1 cup water

½ cup coconut vinegar or white vinegar

6 cloves garlic, smashed

1 teaspoon whole peppercorns

2 slices fresh ginger

2 dried bay leaves

1. Heat oil in a wok to medium heat. In batches, brown the chicken for 2–3 minutes on each side.

2. Return all the chicken to the wok and add soy sauce, water, vinegar, garlic, peppercorns, ginger, and bay leaves.

3. Allow the liquids to come up to a slight boil. Lower the heat and cover the wok. Allow the chicken to simmer for 25–30 minutes, occasionally stirring. Serve hot.

PER SERVING | Calories: 641 | Fat: 24g | Protein: 92g | Sodium: 3,982mg | Fiber: 0.7g | Carbohydrates: 6.8g | Sugar: 1g

Lemongrass Chicken

In many Asian grocery stores, you can find lemongrass that has been already
minced in the freezer section. Alternatively, you can use fresh lemongrass.
You'll need to peel the exterior tough portions to get to the tender white bulb.

INGREDIENTS | SERVES 4

2 tablespoons fish sauce

½ tablespoon sugar

¼ teaspoon turmeric powder

4 tablespoons vegetable oil, divided

1 pound boneless, skinless chicken thighs, cut into 1" pieces

1 tablespoon minced garlic

¼ cup minced shallots

2 tablespoons minced lemongrass

2 chilies, minced, or ½ teaspoon red pepper flakes

2 scallions, cut into 1" pieces

1. In a large bowl, mix the fish sauce, sugar, turmeric powder, and 2 tablespoons oil. Add the chicken and stir to coat well. Allow the chicken to marinate for 15 minutes.

2. Heat a wok over medium heat. Add the remaining oil and cook the garlic, shallots, lemongrass, and chilies until fragrant, about 1 minute.

3. Add in the marinated chicken and increase the heat to medium high. Stir-fry the chicken for 3–4 minutes until browned. Toss in the scallions and serve hot.

PER SERVING | Calories: 281 | Fat: 18g | Protein: 22g | Sodium: 100mg | Fiber: 0.5g | Carbohydrates: 6g | Sugar: 3g

Thai Basil Turkey

In this dish, ground turkey is used for a leaner option. However, feel free to substitute with sliced or ground chicken. Serve this dish over white rice.

INGREDIENTS | SERVES 4

1 tablespoon peanut oil
2 tablespoons minced garlic
3 red Thai chilies, minced
¼ cup chopped scallions
1 pound lean ground turkey
¼ teaspoon black pepper
2 tablespoons fish sauce
1½ cups chopped Thai basil

1. Heat a wok over medium heat and add the oil.

2. Add the garlic and cook until fragrant, about 30 seconds.

3. Add chilies and cook for 1 minute before adding in scallions. Cook for an additional minute or until the scallions have softened.

4. Add in the ground turkey. Cook the turkey until it is no longer pink, approximately 3–4 minutes.

5. Remove the wok from heat. Stir in pepper, fish sauce, and basil. Serve immediately.

PER SERVING | Calories: 222 | Fat: 12g | Protein: 21g | Sodium: 110mg | Fiber: 0.9g | Carbohydrates: 5g | Sugar: 2g

Chicken Fajitas

Serve these fajitas with Spanish Rice (see Chapter 10).

INGREDIENTS | SERVES 4

1 pound boneless, skinless chicken thighs, sliced into strips
¼ cup Fajita Marinade (see Chapter 2)
2 tablespoons vegetable or peanut oil
1 teaspoon minced garlic
1 medium white onion, sliced
1 medium red bell pepper, seeded and cut into thin strips
1 medium green bell pepper, seeded and cut into thin strips
¼ cup chopped cilantro
8 flour tortillas, warmed
8 lime wedges

1. In a large bowl, combine the chicken with the marinade. Marinate the chicken in the refrigerator for 1 hour.

2. Heat wok over medium heat and add the oil. Once the oil is hot, add garlic, onions, and bell peppers. Cook until lightly browned, approximately 3–4 minutes. Push the vegetables to the side of your wok.

3. Add the chicken. Stir-fry until chicken is cooked through.

4. Transfer the chicken and vegetables to a platter and sprinkle with cilantro. Serve with tortillas and lime wedges.

PER SERVING | Calories: 381 | Fat: 12g | Protein: 28g | Sodium: 1,151mg | Fiber: 3.8g | Carbohydrates: 37g | Sugar: 4g

Tofu and Soba Noodles • Chapter 8

Belgian Beer Mussels • Chapter 7

Beef Fajitas • Chapter 4

Korean Chap Chae • Chapter 9

Fresh Pico de Gallo • Chapter 2

Chicken and Pepper Rolls • Chapter 5

Saag Aloo • Chapter 8

Uni (Sea Urchin Roe) Pasta • Chapter 9

Ahi on Wonton Chips • Chapter 3

Crispy Fried Shrimp Balls • Chapter 3

Cucumber-Mint Raita • Chapter 2

Chinese Broccoli with Oyster Sauce • Chapter 8

Clams with Ginger and Lemongrass • Chapter 7

Pork Larb-Gai Lettuce Wraps • Chapter 3

Kimchee Fried Rice • Chapter 10

Ginger Peanut Noodles • Chapter 9

Tofu Lettuce Wraps • Chapter 3

Chicken Tostadas • Chapter 5

Korean Spicy Pork Tacos • Chapter 6

Fried Rice with Shrimp • Chapter 10

Tonkatsu • Chapter 6

Vietnamese Shaking Beef • Chapter 4

Salt and Pepper Shrimp • Chapter 7

Agedashi Tofu • Chapter 3

Chicken Tostadas

Serve these tostadas with Tomatillo Salsa (see Chapter 2) or with your favorite hot sauce.

INGREDIENTS | SERVES 4

1 pound ground chicken

1 teaspoon kosher salt

½ teaspoon pepper

¼ teaspoon cumin powder

½ teaspoon chili powder

2 tablespoons vegetable oil

2 cloves garlic, crushed

1 small white onion, diced

8 tostada shells, toasted

16 ounces refried beans, warmed

2 cups shredded lettuce

1 cup diced tomatoes

1 cup shredded pepper jack cheese

1. In a bowl, combine the ground chicken with the salt, pepper, cumin, and chili powder. Let stand for 20 minutes in the refrigerator.

2. Heat a wok or skillet over medium-high heat and add the oil. When the oil is hot, add in the garlic and onions. Cook for 3–4 minutes, until softened.

3. Add the chicken. Cook the chicken, stirring and crumbling up the meat until there is no trace of pink— about 3–4 minutes. Using a slotted spoon, remove the mixture to a large plate.

4. Spread 2 ounces refried beans in an even layer on top of a tostada shell. Place several spoonfuls of the chicken mixture over the beans and top with the lettuce, tomatoes, and cheese. Repeat with the remaining shells. Serve warm.

PER SERVING | Calories: 650 | Fat: 39g | Protein: 35g | Sodium: 1,444mg | Fiber: 8g | Carbohydrates: 38g | Sugar: 3g

Tequila Lime Chicken

Serve this chicken alongside black beans, tortillas, and a few
Cadillac margaritas for a fun and easy weeknight meal.

INGREDIENTS | SERVES 4

½ cup Tequila Lime Marinade (see Chapter 2)

1 pound boneless, skinless chicken thighs, chopped into quarters

2 tablespoons vegetable oil

1 small red onion, sliced thinly

½ jalapeño pepper, seeded and diced

2 garlic cloves, minced

¼ cup chopped cilantro

Lime wedges

1. Pour the marinade into a large resealable bag and add the chicken. Massage the marinade into the chicken and seal the bag. Refrigerate for 15–20 minutes.

2. Heat oil in a wok over medium heat and add the onion, jalapeño, and garlic. Add in the marinated chicken and stir-fry until browned and cooked through—about 4–5 minutes. Serve with cilantro on top and lime wedges on the side.

PER SERVING | Calories: 319 | Fat: 21g | Protein: 22g | Sodium: 245mg | Fiber: 0.5g | Carbohydrates: 5g | Sugar: 3g

Chicken and Pepper Rolls

For a bit of acidity and spice, top your chicken and pepper rolls with pickled hot peppers.

INGREDIENTS | SERVES 4

1 pound boneless, skinless chicken breasts, sliced in thin strips

⅛ teaspoon cayenne pepper

1 teaspoon black pepper

2 teaspoons kosher salt

2 tablespoons vegetable oil

1 small yellow onion, thinly sliced

1 pint white mushrooms, sliced

1 medium red bell pepper, seeded and sliced lengthwise

4 slices provolone cheese

4 (6") hoagie rolls, split and lightly toasted

1. Season chicken with cayenne, black pepper, and salt.

2. Heat a wok over medium heat and add the vegetable oil. Once the oil is hot, add the onion, mushrooms, and bell peppers. Cook for 3–4 minutes.

3. Push the vegetables to the side of your wok and add the chicken. Stir-fry the chicken for 4–5 minutes or until brown.

4. In a single layer, lay the cheese over the chicken. Cover and allow cheese to melt. Divide the chicken, cheese, and vegetables amongst the rolls. Serve immediately.

PER SERVING | Calories: 307 | Fat: 17g | Protein: 31g | Sodium: 1,556mg | Fiber: 1.2g | Carbohydrates: 5g | Sugar: 2.5g

Chicken Flautas

Short on time? Pick up a rotisserie chicken from your local grocery store and shred the meat to use in the filling.

INGREDIENTS | SERVES 4

¼ cup Fajita Marinade (see Chapter 2)

½ pound chicken tenders

2 tablespoons plus 2 cups peanut or vegetable oil, divided

1 cup queso fresco

2 tablespoons chopped cilantro

12 small flour tortillas

2½ cups Fresh Pico de Gallo (see Chapter 2)

Chicken Tenders

Chicken tenders are the tenderloin portion of chicken breast. If packaged chicken tenders are unavailable, feel free to cut boneless, skinless chicken breast into 2"-wide strips.

1. Pour the marinade into a large resealable bag and add the chicken. Massage the marinade into the chicken and seal the bag. Refrigerate for 15–20 minutes.

2. Heat 2 tablespoons oil in a wok over medium heat. Add the marinated chicken and stir-fry for 3–4 minutes or until cooked through. Transfer to a plate and allow the chicken to cool. Once cooled, shred the chicken and place in bowl. Mix in the queso fresco and cilantro.

3. Place 1 tortilla on a cutting board and place a few spoonfuls of the chicken mixture in a line toward the bottom of the tortilla. Tightly roll up the tortilla and insert 1 or 2 toothpicks to secure the flauta. Repeat with the remaining chicken mixture and tortillas.

4. Heat the remaining oil in a wok to 375°F. Working in batches, deep-fry the flautas until golden brown, 3–4 minutes, turning halfway through. Carefully remove the flautas and drain on plates lined with paper towels. Serve hot with Fresh Pico de Gallo.

PER SERVING | Calories: 612 | Fat: 51g | Protein: 28g | Sodium: 1,455mg | Fiber: 8g | Carbohydrates: 19g | Sugar: 6.5g

Chicken Cacciatore

To avoid bruising fresh herbs, tear the leaves instead of using a knife to chop them.

INGREDIENTS | SERVES 4

1 pound boneless, skinless chicken breasts

5 tablespoons dry white wine, divided

½ teaspoon salt

½ teaspoon ground black pepper

2 teaspoons cornstarch

3 tablespoons chicken broth

3½ tablespoons olive oil, divided

2 shallots, chopped

¼ pound thinly sliced fresh mushrooms

2 tablespoons tomato sauce

¼ cup fresh basil leaves, roughly torn

1 teaspoon fresh thyme leaves

1. Cut the chicken breasts into thin strips approximately 1½"–2" long. Place the chicken in a bowl and add 2 tablespoons dry white wine, salt, black pepper, and cornstarch. Marinate the chicken for 20 minutes.

2. In a small bowl, combine the chicken broth and 3 tablespoons white wine. Set aside.

3. Heat a wok or skillet on medium-high heat until it is almost smoking. Add 2 tablespoons oil. When the oil is hot, add the chicken strips. Let them brown briefly, then stir-fry, stirring and tossing the chicken for 4–5 minutes until it turns white and is nearly cooked. Remove the chicken from the pan.

4. Heat 1½ tablespoons oil in the pan. When the oil is hot, add the shallots. Stir-fry for 1 minute or until they begin to soften, then add the sliced mushrooms. Stir-fry for about 10 seconds.

5. Add the chicken broth and white wine mixture. Stir in the tomato sauce. Bring to a boil, then add the chicken back into the pan. Stir in the chopped basil and thyme. Stir-fry for 2 more minutes to blend all the ingredients and make sure the chicken is cooked. Serve hot.

PER SERVING | Calories: 266 | Fat: 15g | Protein: 25g | Sodium: 516mg | Fiber: 0.5g | Carbohydrates: 3.8g | Sugar: 1g

Chicken with Marsala Wine

You can experiment with different combinations of fresh mushrooms in this recipe—oyster, porcini, and fresh shiitake mushrooms all add subtle variations in flavor and texture.

INGREDIENTS | SERVES 4

1 pound boneless, skinless chicken breasts

6 tablespoons dry Marsala wine, divided

½ teaspoon salt

½ teaspoon black pepper

2 teaspoons cornstarch

¼ cup chicken broth

3½ tablespoons olive oil, divided

2 thin slices ginger, chopped

2 cloves garlic, chopped

2 shallots, chopped

¼ pound fresh mushrooms, thinly sliced

1 tablespoon chopped fresh basil leaves

1 tablespoon chopped Italian parsley, for garnish

Marvelous Marsala Wine

Originating in Sicily, Marsala wine is fortified with ethyl alcohol, giving it an alcohol level of over 15 percent. Marsala wine was introduced to the rest of the world in the eighteenth century by Englishman John Woodhouse, who realized that the fortification process meant that the wine would survive the voyage to England without going bad.

1. Cut the chicken breasts into thin strips approximately 1½"–2" long. Place the chicken strips in a bowl and add 2 tablespoons wine, salt, black pepper, and cornstarch. Marinate the chicken for 20 minutes.

2. In a small bowl, combine the chicken broth and 4 tablespoons wine. Set aside.

3. Heat a wok or skillet on medium-high heat until it is almost smoking. Add 2 tablespoons oil. When the oil is hot, add the chicken strips. Let them sit briefly, then stir-fry, stirring and tossing the strips for 4–5 minutes until they turn white and are nearly cooked. Remove the chicken from the pan.

4. Heat 1½ tablespoons oil in the pan. When the oil is hot, add the ginger and garlic. Stir-fry for 10 seconds.

5. Add the shallots. Stir fry for 1 minute or until they begin to soften, then add the sliced mushrooms. Stir-fry for about 2 minutes.

6. Add the broth and wine mixture. Bring to a boil, then add the chicken back into the pan. Stir in the chopped basil. Stir-fry for 2 more minutes to blend all the ingredients and make sure the chicken is cooked through. Garnish with the fresh parsley.

PER SERVING | Calories: 287 | Fat: 15g | Protein: 25g | Sodium: 494mg | Fiber: 0.4g | Carbohydrates: 6.5g | Sugar: 2g

Chicken Parmesan

Serve this dish on top of pasta for a delicious, hearty meal.

INGREDIENTS | SERVES 8

8 chicken breast cutlets, pounded to ¼"–⅛" thickness

1 tablespoon Italian seasoning

½ teaspoon black pepper

1 tablespoon kosher salt

½ cup grated Parmesan cheese

¾ cup all-purpose flour

3 large eggs, beaten

1 cup Italian bread crumbs

4 tablespoons vegetable oil

2 cups Marinara Sauce (see Chapter 2)

8 slices mozzarella cheese

¼ cup chopped fresh Italian parsley

1. Season the chicken with Italian seasoning, pepper, and salt.

2. In a shallow dish, mix together the Parmesan cheese and flour.

3. In a second separate dish, place the beaten eggs.

4. In a third dish, place the Italian bread crumbs.

5. Working with 1 piece of chicken at a time, dredge the cutlet into the flour mixture, then the beaten eggs, and finally the bread crumbs. Use fingers to gently adhere the bread crumbs to the cutlet and place on a baking sheet. Repeat with the remaining cutlets.

6. Heat wok over medium heat and add 2 tablespoons vegetable oil. Once the oil is hot, cook 2 cutlets at a time for 2 minutes on each side or until golden. Transfer the cooked chicken to a plate and tent with aluminum foil. Repeat with the remaining cutlets.

7. Preheat the oven broiler. Place the cutlets in a baking dish. Cover the tops with the Marinara Sauce and place 1 piece of cheese on top of each cutlet. Broil until the cheese has bubbled and browned. Top with parsley and serve immediately.

PER SERVING | Calories: 324 | Fat: 19g | Protein: 14g | Sodium: 1,511mg | Fiber: 1.8g | Carbohydrates: 22g | Sugar: 3g

Chicken Piccata

Serve this chicken with its sauce over cooked angel hair pasta or alongside garlic mashed potatoes.

INGREDIENTS | SERVES 4

8 chicken breast cutlets, pounded to ¼"–⅛" thickness

¼ teaspoon black pepper

1 teaspoon garlic salt

⅛ teaspoon paprika

½ cup plus 1 tablespoon all-purpose flour, divided

3 tablespoons olive oil, divided

2 garlic cloves, minced

¼ teaspoon red pepper flakes

1 tablespoon caper berries, drained

1 teaspoon lemon zest

½ cup dry white wine

1 cup chicken broth

1 tablespoon unsalted butter

½ teaspoon kosher salt

½ cup diced Roma tomatoes

2 tablespoons fresh basil, torn

1. Season the chicken with pepper, garlic salt, and paprika.

2. Place ½ cup flour in a shallow dish. Roll a chicken cutlet in the flour, using your fingers to assist in adhering it to the meat. Carefully shake off excess flour and set cutlet aside. Repeat with the remaining cutlets.

3. Heat 2 tablespoons oil in a wok over medium-high heat. In batches, fry cutlets until golden brown, approximately 2–3 minutes on each side. Remove from wok and transfer to a plate and tent with aluminum foil. Repeat with the remaining cutlets.

4. Add the remaining oil and reduce heat to medium. Cook garlic until fragrant but not browned, about 30 seconds.

5. Add in the chili flakes, caper berries, lemon zest, wine, and chicken broth. Use a wooden spoon to scrape off the tasty brown bits from the bottom of the wok.

6. Raise the heat to medium high and cook for 2–3 minutes, until the liquids are reduced by half.

7. While the liquids are reducing, use a fork to mash together the remaining 1 tablespoon flour and butter together in a small bowl.

8. Whisk the flour paste into the sauce and allow to cook and thicken for 1–2 minutes. Whisk out any lumps of flour. Remove from the heat and stir in salt and tomatoes.

9. Place chicken on plates and spoon the sauce over the top. Sprinkle with basil and serve immediately.

PER SERVING | Calories: 235 | Fat: 14g | Protein: 3.4g | Sodium: 1,213mg | Fiber: 1g | Carbohydrates: 18g | Sugar: 1g

Chicken Saltimbocca

Serve your saltimbocca with mashed potatoes or on top of cooked pasta.

INGREDIENTS | SERVES 4

4 chicken breast cutlets, pounded to ¼"–⅛" thickness

½ teaspoon kosher salt

¼ teaspoon black pepper

½ cup all-purpose flour

¼ teaspoon cayenne powder

2 tablespoons vegetable oil

3 tablespoons unsalted butter, divided

8 fresh sage leaves

4 thin slices prosciutto

4 slices mozzarella cheese

½ cup dry white wine

½ teaspoon dry sage

1. Use paper towels and blot excess moisture from chicken. Season with salt and pepper.

2. In a shallow dish, whisk together the flour and cayenne.

3. Heat the oil in a wok over medium heat and add 1 tablespoon butter. Place each cutlet into the flour mixture. Use your fingers to adhere the flour on both sides. Shake off excess flour and add to the wok. Repeat with the remaining chicken. Cook the cutlets for 2 minutes on each side until golden and transfer to a baking sheet.

4. On top of each cutlet, place 2 fresh sage leaves, 1 slice prosciutto, and 1 slice mozzarella.

5. Set the oven to broil. Transfer the baking sheet to the oven and allow the cheese to melt and brown. Remove and cover with foil.

6. Using the same wok, add the white wine and cook for 2–3 minutes to allow the liquids to reduce by half. Use a wooden spoon to scrape up the brown bits. Whisk in the dry sage and remaining 2 tablespoons butter.

7. Place the chicken on a platter and top with the sauce.

PER SERVING | Calories: 303 | Fat: 21g | Protein: 8g | Sodium: 474mg | Fiber: 0.5g | Carbohydrates: 13g | Sugar: 0.6g

Chicken Roulade

Turkey cutlets can also be used in this dish.

INGREDIENTS | SERVES 2

2 (5-ounce) skinless, boneless chicken breasts, pounded to ⅛" thickness

½ tablespoon kosher salt

½ teaspoon black pepper

½ teaspoon dried thyme

2 slices Swiss cheese

4 blanched asparagus spears

2 tablespoons chopped sundried tomatoes

2 tablespoons vegetable oil

1 cup chicken stock or dry white wine

1 tablespoon unsalted butter

1 tablespoon Dijon mustard

1 teaspoon fresh thyme leaves

1. Season the chicken with salt, pepper, and thyme. Lay the chicken pieces on a flat surface. Place 1 slice cheese on top, followed by 2 spears asparagus and 1 tablespoon sundried tomatoes.

2. Roll up the chicken cutlet, starting at one long end, and secure with toothpicks. Repeat with the other chicken breast.

3. Heat the oil in the wok over medium heat. Carefully add the chicken rolls to the wok and cook for 1–2 minutes on each side, rotating until roulades are golden brown. Remove the roulades and cover with aluminum foil to keep warm.

4. Add the chicken stock or wine to the wok and turn the heat to medium high. Scrape up the bottom of the wok to loosen the flavorful brown bits. Cook for 2–3 minutes until the liquids are reduced by half and whisk in the butter, mustard, and thyme.

5. Return the chicken roulades to the wok and spoon the sauce over the tops. Lower the heat and simmer the chicken for 3–4 minutes. Serve hot..

PER SERVING | Calories: 501 | Fat: 32g | Protein: 41g | Sodium: 2,316mg | Fiber: 1.4g | Carbohydrates: 9.5g | Sugar: 4g

Chicken Cutlets with Mustard Cream Sauce

In this dish, whole-grain mustard not only offers a rich flavor to the sauce but also provides great texture.

INGREDIENTS | SERVES 8

8 chicken breast cutlets, pounded to ¼"–⅛" thickness

¼ teaspoon black pepper

1 teaspoon kosher salt

1 tablespoon olive oil

2 tablespoons unsalted butter

2 tablespoons minced shallots

½ tablespoon minced garlic

1 cup dry white wine

¼ cup chicken stock

1 tablespoon whole-grain mustard

1 teaspoon fresh thyme leaves

¼ cup heavy cream

1. Season the chicken with pepper and salt.

2. Heat a wok over medium-high heat, add the oil, and then add the butter and melt it into the olive oil. In batches, slide in the chicken and fry until golden brown, approximately 2–3 minutes on each side. Remove from wok and transfer to a plate and tent with aluminum foil. Repeat with the remaining cutlets.

3. Reduce the heat to medium and add the shallots and garlic and cook for 1 minute.

4. Add the wine and chicken stock and cook for 3–4 minutes to allow the liquids to reduce by half.

5. Whisk in the mustard, thyme leaves, and cream. Return the chicken to the wok and spoon the sauce over the tops to coat. Simmer for 1 minute before serving.

PER SERVING | Calories: 97 | Fat: 7g | Protein: 0.5g | Sodium: 332mg | Fiber: 0.1g | Carbohydrates: 2g | Sugar: 0.4g

CHAPTER 6

Pork

Pork with Pepper and Bean Sprouts

To make a meal out of this simple pork dish, serve it with
Basic Stir-Fry Noodles (see Chapter 9) and sliced fresh tomato.

INGREDIENTS | SERVES 2

½ pound boneless pork

2 tablespoons dark soy sauce, divided

4 teaspoons cider vinegar, divided

1 teaspoon brown sugar

½ teaspoon freshly cracked black or white pepper

2 tablespoons vegetable or peanut oil, divided

½ teaspoon minced ginger

½ teaspoon minced garlic

1 small green bell pepper, seeded and cut into bite-sized chunks

½ teaspoon salt

½ pound mung bean sprouts

1 tablespoon water or soy sauce, optional

1 teaspoon granulated sugar

Using Pork in Stir-Fries

Pork shoulder is an excellent choice for stir-fries; it's lean but with just enough fat to lend flavor and moisture to the dish.

1. Cut the pork into thin strips. Place the pork strips in a bowl and add 1 tablespoon dark soy sauce, 2 teaspoons cider vinegar, brown sugar, and cracked pepper. Marinate the pork in the refrigerator for 20 minutes.

2. Heat a wok or skillet over medium-high heat until it is nearly smoking. Add 1 tablespoon oil. When the oil is hot, add the minced ginger. Stir-fry for 10 seconds.

3. Add the pork. Stir-fry the pork for about 2 minutes, or until it is no longer pink and is nearly cooked. Remove the pork from the pan and drain in a colander or on paper towels.

4. Heat 1 tablespoon oil in the same wok or skillet. When the oil is hot, add the minced garlic. Stir-fry for 10 seconds.

5. Add the green pepper and the salt. Stir-fry for 1 minute, then add the mung bean sprouts. Stir-fry for 30–60 seconds, taking care not to overcook the sprouts. Splash the vegetables with 1 tablespoon water or soy sauce during stir-frying if desired.

6. Push the vegetables to the sides and add the pork back into the pan. Stir in 1 tablespoon dark soy sauce, 2 teaspoons cider vinegar, and the granulated sugar. Stir-fry for 1–2 more minutes to heat everything, and serve hot.

PER SERVING | Calories: 217 | Fat: 4.5g | Protein: 31g | Sodium: 1,552mg | Fiber: 1.3g | Carbohydrates: 13g | Sugar: 6g

Spicy Orange Pork Chops

Adjust the spiciness of this dish according to your own preference by using hotter or milder chili peppers. Serve these chops with Stir-Fried Bok Choy (see Chapter 8) and cooked rice or noodles for a complete meal.

INGREDIENTS | SERVES 4

1 pound boneless pork chops

¼ cup Orange Marinade (see Chapter 2)

2 tablespoons vegetable or peanut oil

1 tablespoon minced ginger

2 red chili peppers, chopped

1 teaspoon granulated sugar

3 scallions, green parts only, cut into thirds

1 teaspoon sesame oil

1. Chop the pork into bite-sized pieces. Place the pork in a bowl and add the marinade. Marinate the pork in the refrigerator for 30 minutes.

2. Heat a wok or skillet over medium-high heat until it is nearly smoking. Add the oil. When the oil is hot, add the pork. Let it brown for 1 minute, then stir-fry, stirring and moving the pork around the pan for an additional 1–2 minutes or until it is no longer pink and is nearly cooked through.

3. Push the pork to the sides of the wok and tilt the wok so that the remaining oil runs to the middle. Add the minced ginger and chopped chilies into the oil. Let cook for about 30 seconds, then mix together with the pork.

4. Stir in the sugar and scallions. Continue stir-frying until the pork is cooked through, about 5 minutes.

5. Remove from the heat and stir in the sesame oil. Serve hot.

PER SERVING | Calories: 172 | Fat: 5g | Protein: 25g | Sodium: 58mg | Fiber: 0.6g | Carbohydrates: 4.5g | Sugar: 2.7g

Pork with Mushrooms

Instead of button mushrooms, you can use a combination of dried Chinese black mushrooms and fresh mushrooms in this dish.

INGREDIENTS | SERVES 4

4 boneless pork chops

1½ tablespoons oyster sauce

1 tablespoon dry sherry

1½ teaspoons sesame oil

1 tablespoon cornstarch

⅓ cup chicken broth

2 tablespoons dark soy sauce

1½ teaspoons granulated sugar

4 tablespoons vegetable or peanut oil, divided

2 teaspoons minced ginger

1 teaspoon minced garlic

½ teaspoon chili paste

6 ounces button mushrooms, thinly sliced

Freezing Chicken Broth

It's easy to freeze leftover chicken broth— just pour the unused broth into ice-cube trays and freeze until needed. For recipe measuring purposes, keep in mind that each frozen cube contains approximately 1 ounce of broth.

1. Cut the pork chops into bite-sized cubes. Place the pork cubes in a bowl and add the oyster sauce, sherry, sesame oil, and cornstarch. Marinate the pork for 15 minutes.

2. In a small bowl, combine the chicken broth, dark soy sauce, and sugar. Set aside.

3. Heat a wok or skillet over medium-high heat until it is nearly smoking. Add 3 tablespoons oil. When the oil is hot, add the ginger. Stir-fry for 10 seconds.

4. Add the pork cubes. Let sit for 1 minute, then stir-fry, moving the pork around the pan for 1–2 minutes or until it is no longer pink and is nearly cooked. Remove and drain on a plate lined with paper towels.

5. Heat 1 tablespoon oil in the same wok or skillet. When the oil is hot, add the garlic and the chili paste. Stir-fry for 10 seconds.

6. Add the mushrooms. Stir-fry for about 3 minutes, until the mushrooms have darkened, then add the prepared sauce.

7. Add the pork back into the pan. Heat everything through and serve hot.

PER SERVING | Calories: 290 | Fat: 8g | Protein: 42g | Sodium: 822mg | Fiber: 0.2g | Carbohydrates: 7g | Sugar: 2g

Pork with Baby Bok Choy

If you like, thicken the sauce in this recipe by stirring in 1 teaspoon cornstarch mixed with 2 teaspoons water at the end of cooking. Stir quickly until the sauce has thickened, and serve immediately.

INGREDIENTS | SERVES 3

¾ pound lean pork

1 tablespoon soy sauce

1 tablespoon rice wine or dry sherry

1 teaspoon granulated sugar

1 teaspoon sesame oil

¼ teaspoon black pepper

1½ teaspoons cornstarch

1 pound bok choy

3 tablespoons chicken broth

1 tablespoon oyster sauce

4 tablespoons vegetable or peanut oil, divided

1 teaspoon minced ginger

2 cloves garlic, crushed

½ teaspoon salt

2 scallions cut on the diagonal into 1" pieces

1. Cut the pork into cubes. Place the pork in a bowl and add the soy sauce, rice wine, sugar, sesame oil, black pepper, and cornstarch. Marinate the pork for 20 minutes.

2. Remove the base of the bok choy. Wash the bok choy and drain thoroughly. Separate the leaves from the stalks. Cut the stalks diagonally into 2" pieces. Cut the leaves crosswise into 2" pieces.

3. In a small bowl, combine the chicken broth with the oyster sauce. Set aside.

4. Heat a wok or skillet over medium-high heat until it is almost smoking. Add 2 tablespoons oil. When the oil is hot, add the ginger. Stir-fry for 10 seconds.

5. Add the pork. Let sit briefly, then stir-fry the pork, stirring and moving it around the pan for 1–2 minutes or until it is no longer pink and is nearly cooked. Remove the pork and drain in a colander or on paper towels.

6. Add 2 tablespoons oil to the wok or skillet. When the oil is hot, add the crushed garlic. Stir-fry for 10 seconds, then add the bok choy stalks. Add the salt. Stir-fry for 1 minute, then add the leaves. Stir-fry for 1 more minute, or until the bok choy turns bright green.

7. Add the chicken broth/oyster sauce mixture into the wok and bring it to a boil.

8. Add the pork back into the pan. Stir in the green onions. Stir-fry for 1 minute and serve hot.

PER SERVING | Calories: 211 | Fat: 6g | Protein: 28g | Sodium: 1,075mg | Fiber: 1.8g | Carbohydrates: 9.5g | Sugar: 3.6g

Mu Shu Pork

Traditionally, mu shu pork is made with colorful Chinese vegetables such as dried mushrooms, cloud ear fungus, and lily buds. Canned bamboo shoots and fresh mushrooms make quick and easy alternatives while still providing color and texture.

INGREDIENTS | SERVES 2

½ pound pork tenderloin, cut into thin shreds

1 tablespoon light soy sauce

2 teaspoons Chinese rice wine or dry sherry

½ teaspoon sesame oil

1 teaspoon cornstarch

½ cup canned bamboo shoots

2 scallions

¼ cup water

1 tablespoon hoisin sauce

2 teaspoons dark soy sauce

1 teaspoon granulated sugar

3 large eggs

¼ teaspoon kosher salt

¼ teaspoon black pepper

4½ tablespoons vegetable or peanut oil, divided

½ teaspoon minced ginger

½ cup thinly sliced fresh mushrooms

Serving Mu Shu Pork

In restaurants, this dish would be served with thin mandarin pancakes, green onion "brushes," and sweet and spicy hoisin sauce. Diners use the brushes to spread hoisin sauce on the pancake, add some mu shu pork, and roll up the pancake like a tortilla.

1. Place the pork in a bowl and add the light soy sauce, rice wine or sherry, sesame oil, and cornstarch. Marinate the pork for 20 minutes.

2. Rinse the bamboo shoots under cold running water and drain thoroughly. Cut the slices into thin shreds. Rinse the green onions, drain, and shred.

3. In a small bowl, combine the water, hoisin sauce, dark soy sauce, and sugar. Set aside.

4. In a separate small bowl, lightly beat the eggs, stirring in the salt and pepper.

5. Heat a wok or skillet over medium-high heat until it is nearly smoking. Add 2 tablespoons oil. When oil is hot, turn the heat down to medium and add the beaten eggs. Scramble quickly and remove. Clean out the pan.

6. Heat 1 tablespoon oil in the wok or skillet. When the oil is hot, add the minced ginger and the scallions. Stir-fry for 10 seconds.

7. Add the pork. Stir-fry for 3–4 minutes or until the pork is no longer pink and is nearly cooked through. Remove and drain in a colander or on paper towels.

8. Heat 1½ tablespoons oil in the wok. Add the bamboo shoots and ¼ teaspoon salt. Stir-fry for 1 minute and then add the mushrooms. Stir-fry for 1 more minute.

9. Add the hoisin sauce mixture. Bring to a boil, then add the pork back into the pan. Stir in the eggs. Cook for another minute to mix everything together and serve hot.

PER SERVING | Calories: 299 | Fat: 11g | Protein: 35g | Sodium: 1,343mg | Fiber: 1.3g | Carbohydrates: 11g | Sugar: 6.5g

Plum Pork

Allspice is made from the dried, unripe berries of the tropical Pimenta dioica tree. The English gave it the name, because they thought it combined the flavors of cinnamon, nutmeg, and cloves.

INGREDIENTS | SERVES 4

1 pound lean pork

1 tablespoon dark soy sauce

1 tablespoon Chinese rice wine or dry sherry

1 teaspoon sesame oil

2 teaspoons cornstarch

3½ tablespoons vegetable or peanut oil, divided

2 teaspoons minced garlic

1 tablespoon minced ginger

1 small red bell pepper, cut into bite-sized cubes

3 small plums, pits removed and cut in half

¼ cup water

¼ cup orange, peach, or plum juice

1 tablespoon granulated sugar

¼ teaspoon allspice

¼ teaspoon salt

1. Cut the pork into cubes. Place the pork cubes in a bowl and add the dark soy sauce, rice wine or dry sherry, sesame oil, and cornstarch. Marinate the pork for 20 minutes.

2. Heat a wok or skillet over medium-high heat until it is nearly smoking. Add 2 tablespoons oil. When the oil is hot, add the minced garlic. Stir-fry for 10 seconds.

3. Add the pork. Stir-fry the pork for 3–4 minutes until it is no longer pink and is nearly cooked through. Remove the pork from the pan and drain in a colander or on paper towels.

4. Add 1½ tablespoons oil in the wok or skillet. When the oil is hot, add the ginger. Stir-fry for 10 seconds, then add the red bell pepper. Stir-fry for 1 minute, or until the bell pepper is tender but still firm.

5. Add the plums and stir-fry for 1 minute.

6. Add the water, fruit juice, and the sugar. Bring to a boil, stirring to dissolve the sugar.

7. Add the pork into the pan. Stir in the allspice and the salt. Stir-fry for 1–2 more minutes to mix everything together.

PER SERVING | Calories: 220 | Fat: 5g | Protein: 26g | Sodium: 429mg | Fiber: 1.8g | Carbohydrates: 15g | Sugar: 10g

Sweet-and-Sour Pork

Deep-frying the pork before stir-frying seals in the flavor and makes it extra crispy. The amount of oil needed will depend on the size and shape of the pan—make sure there is enough oil to cover the pork.

INGREDIENTS | SERVES 4

½ cup cornstarch, divided

4 tablespoons water

1 pound boneless pork

4 cups oil, or as needed

2 cloves garlic, crushed

1 small carrot, cut on the diagonal into ½" slices

1 small green bell pepper, seeded and cut into bite-sized chunks

1 cup Sweet-and-Sour Sauce (see Chapter 2)

½ cup canned pineapple chunks, drained

¼ teaspoon kosher salt

¼ teaspoon black pepper

Extra Crispy Sweet-and-Sour Pork

It takes only a few simple adjustments to make this recipe taste like it came straight from your favorite Chinese restaurant. Instead of dredging the pork in cornstarch, dip it in a batter consisting of egg and equal parts flour, cornstarch, and water. After deep-frying the pork, reheat the oil and deep-fry the pork a second time to make it extra crispy.

1. In a small bowl, dissolve 1 tablespoon cornstarch in the water and set aside.

2. Cut the pork into bite-sized cubes.

3. Heat oil for deep-frying in a deep-fat fryer or wok to 360°F–375°F. Dredge the pork in the remaining cornstarch. Deep-fry the pork for about 2 minutes or until it is browned and crispy. Carefully remove the pork from the deep-fat fryer. Drain in a colander or on paper towels.

4. Heat a wok or skillet over medium-high heat. Add 2 tablespoons oil. When the oil is hot, add the garlic. Stir-fry for about 30 seconds or until it is aromatic, then add the carrot and green bell pepper. Stir-fry for 2 minutes or until they are tender but still crisp.

5. Add the Sweet-and-Sour Sauce and bring to a boil. Add the cornstarch and water mixture to the sauce, stirring to thicken.

6. After 1–2 minutes when the sauce thickens, add the pork, pineapple, salt, and pepper. Stir-fry for 2 more minutes or until all the ingredients are heated through. Serve hot.

PER SERVING | Calories: 2226 | Fat: 221g | Protein: 25g | Sodium: 303mg | Fiber: 1.5g | Carbohydrates: 38g | Sugar: 19g

Teriyaki-Marinated Pork Chops

Teriyaki marinade works well in pork dishes. To increase the flavor, marinate the pork for 30 minutes.

INGREDIENTS | SERVES 4

4 boneless pork chops, cut into cubes

½ cup Teriyaki Sauce (see Chapter 2)

2 tablespoons water

2 tablespoons vegetable or peanut oil

1 tablespoon minced ginger

2 tablespoons Chinese or Japanese rice wine

3 scallions, chopped on the diagonal into 1" sections

1. In a large bowl, whisk together Teriyaki Sauce and water. Toss in the pork and marinate for 20 minutes.

2. Heat a wok or skillet over medium-high heat and add the oil. When the oil is hot, add the minced ginger. Stir-fry for 30 seconds or until it is aromatic.

3. Add the pork. Let it brown for 1 minute, then stir-fry for 1–2 minutes or until it is no longer pink.

4. Stir in rice wine and scallions. Continue stir-frying for 1 minute or until pork is cooked through.

PER SERVING | Calories: 302 | Fat: 6g | Protein: 43g | Sodium: 1,892mg | Fiber: 0.7g | Carbohydrates: 12g | Sugar: 7.7g

Korean Spicy Pork Tacos

If you prefer not to use kimchee with your tacos, try substituting with the quick coleslaw used with the Asian Pork Burgers (see recipe in this chapter)

INGREDIENTS | SERVES 4

1 cup Korean-Inspired Marinade (see Chapter 2)

3 tablespoons gojuchang paste

½ teaspoon red pepper flakes

¾ pound pork loin, cut into ½" cubes

2 tablespoons vegetable oil

¼ cup chopped scallions

½ small white onion, sliced

12 corn tortillas

2 cups kimchee, chopped

1 teaspoon toasted sesame seeds

1 cup seasoned and toasted seaweed, cut into thin strips

1. In a large bowl, whisk together the marinade, gojuchang paste, and red pepper flakes. Add the pork and refrigerate for at least 1 hour.

2. Heat wok over medium-high heat and add the oil. Once the oil is hot, stir-fry scallions and onion for 30 seconds. Add in the pork and stir-fry for 3–4 minutes until browned. Transfer to a plate.

3. Warm the tortillas in a cast-iron skillet. Divide the pork and kimchee among the tortillas. Top each taco with toasted sesame seeds and seaweed strips. Serve warm.

PER SERVING | Calories: 1,059 | Fat: 35g | Protein: 19g | Sodium: 1,199mg | Fiber: 32g | Carbohydrates: 180g | Sugar: 117g

Miso-Glazed Pork Belly

The pork belly in this dish has a wonderful toothiness to it and pairs beautifully with the salty miso marinade.

INGREDIENTS | SERVES 2

2 tablespoons low-sodium soy sauce

1 tablespoon miso paste

1 tablespoon honey

1 tablespoon mirin

1 tablespoon water

1 teaspoon sesame oil

1 garlic clove, minced

1 tablespoon vegetable oil

½ pound pork belly, sliced into ¼" pieces

1 cup cooked white rice

1 teaspoon toasted sesame seeds

1 scallion, green part only, diced

1. In a small bowl, whisk together the soy sauce, miso paste, honey, mirin, water, sesame oil, and garlic. Set aside.

2. Heat a wok over medium heat and add the oil. Swirl the pan and add the pork belly. Cook for 1–2 minutes on each side until both sides of the pork belly have turned golden brown and some of the fat has rendered out. You may need to use paper towels to blot out excess fat.

3. Pour the soy sauce glaze into the wok and lower the heat. Cover and simmer the pork for 6–8 minutes, flipping the pork halfway through.

4. Serve the pork belly over bowls of rice and drizzle glaze on top. Sprinkle toasted sesame seeds and scallion over the bowls and serve immediately.

PER SERVING | Calories: 851 | Fat: 69g | Protein: 15g | Sodium: 1,256mg | Fiber: 1.2g | Carbohydrates: 39g | Sugar: 9.8g

Korean-Style Pork Stir-Fry

*This stir-fry would also serve as a great alternative filling for
Korean Spicy Pork Tacos (see recipe in this chapter)*

INGREDIENTS | SERVES 4

¼ cup Korean-Inspired Marinade (see Chapter 2)

2 tablespoons gojuchang paste

2 tablespoons soy sauce

1 teaspoon sesame oil

½ tablespoon honey

½ tablespoon rice wine vinegar

1 pound lean pork

2 tablespoons vegetable oil

½ small white onion, sliced

2 cloves garlic, crushed

2 scallions, cut into 1" pieces

1 tablespoon toasted sesame seeds

1. In a medium bowl, whisk together the marinade, gojuchang, soy sauce, sesame oil, honey, and vinegar. Set aside.

2. Cut the pork into thin strips, about 1½" long and ⅛" wide. Place the pork strips in a large resealable plastic bag. Pour in the marinade and add the pork. Seal the bag and allow to marinate for at least 2 hours, turning the bag occasionally so that all the pork is evenly coated.

3. Heat a wok or skillet over medium-high heat until it is nearly smoking and add the oil. When the oil is hot, stir-fry the onion and garlic for 30 seconds.

4. Add the pork. (Discard the marinade.) Stir-fry the pork for 3–4 minutes or until it is no longer pink, then add the scallions. Remove from the pan and garnish with the toasted sesame seeds.

PER SERVING | Calories: 437 | Fat: 15g | Protein: 27g | Sodium: 848mg | Fiber: 9g | Carbohydrates: 50g | Sugar: 32g

Ginger Soy Pork Chops

Instead of honey, feel free to substitute with agave nectar.

INGREDIENTS | SERVES 4

4 tablespoons low-sodium soy sauce

2 tablespoons mirin

1 tablespoon honey

2 tablespoons vegetable oil, divided

1" fresh ginger, grated

1 tablespoon minced shallots

¼ teaspoon black pepper

4 boneless pork chops, ½" thick

1. In a small bowl, whisk together soy sauce, mirin, honey, 1 tablespoon oil, ginger, shallots, and pepper. Pour the marinade into a large resealable bag and add the pork. Massage the marinade into the pork and seal the bag. Refrigerate for 15–20 minutes.

2. Heat the remaining oil in a wok over medium-high heat. Cook the pork chops on each side for 1–2 minutes.

3. Lower the heat to medium and pour the marinade into the wok. Cover and cook for an additional 4–5 minutes, flipping the chops halfway through the cooking process.

4. Serve immediately.

PER SERVING | Calories: 321 | Fat: 13g | Protein: 42g | Sodium: 989mg | Fiber: 0.1g | Carbohydrates: 6g | Sugar: 4.6g

Tonkatsu

Tonkatsu is a popular Japanese dish that was first introduced by the Portuguese. Tonkatsu is a close cousin to chicken katsu as both are thin cuts of meat that have been breaded and fried.

INGREDIENTS | SERVES 4

1 cup panko bread crumbs

½ cup all-purpose flour

2 large eggs

2 tablespoons milk

¼ teaspoon kosher salt

¼ teaspoon black pepper

4 pork loin pieces, pounded to ½" thickness

½ cup vegetable oil

½ cup Tonkatsu Sauce (see Chapter 2)

4 lemon wedges

1. Place bread crumbs in a shallow dish, and place the flour in another dish.

2. In a small bowl, whisk together the eggs and milk.

3. Season the pork with salt and pepper. Working in batches, dredge a few pieces of the pork in the flour, then the egg mixture, and finally the bread crumbs to coat, shaking off the excess between each step. Repeat with the remaining pork.

4. Heat the oil in a wok to medium-high heat. In batches, slide in 2 pieces of pork and fry until golden brown, approximately 2–3 minutes on each side. Remove from pan and drain the cutlets on plates lined with paper towels. Repeat with remaining pork.

5. To serve, drizzle the Tonkatsu Sauce over the pork and serve with lemon wedges and rice.

PER SERVING | Calories: 386 | Fat: 30g | Protein: 5.7g | Sodium: 788mg | Fiber: 1g | Carbohydrates: 24g | Sugar: 8g

Teriyaki Meatball Submarine Sandwiches

These meatballs can also serve as a delicious appetizer.

INGREDIENTS | SERVES 4

½ pound lean ground pork

½ tablespoon grated ginger

2 garlic cloves, minced

2 scallions, diced

1 tablespoon low-sodium soy sauce

1 teaspoon sesame oil

½ teaspoon black pepper

2 tablespoons vegetable oil

¾ cup Teriyaki Sauce (see Chapter 2)

¾ cup beef broth or vegetable broth

½ cup onion slices

¼ teaspoon red pepper flakes

4 hoagie rolls, split and toasted

1. In a large bowl, mix together the ground pork, ginger, garlic, scallions, soy sauce, sesame oil, and pepper. It's easiest to do this with your hands. Once combined, roll about 2 tablespoons of the mixture into a ball. Repeat with the remaining pork.

2. Heat a wok over medium heat. Add the oil and swirl it around the wok. In batches, evenly brown the meatballs, approximately 3–4 minutes.

3. While the meatballs brown, whisk together the Teriyaki Sauce and beef broth in a medium bowl.

4. Once all the meatballs have browned, add them all back to the wok with the onions, teriyaki sauce mixture, and red pepper flakes. Spoon the sauce over the tops to glaze. Cover the wok and lower the heat. Simmer for 5–7 minutes or until the meatballs have cooked through and the onions have softened.

5. Divide the meatballs amongst the rolls. Top each roll with the sauce and onions. Serve immediately.

PER SERVING | Calories: 313 | Fat: 20g | Protein: 13g | Sodium: 3,104mg | Fiber: 1.2g | Carbohydrates: 18g | Sugar: 12g

Pork and Apple Stir-Fry

Paprika lends a vivid red color and strong flavor to this quick and easy stir-fry. Be sure to use fresh paprika that you've purchased within the last six months, because stale paprika can develop a bitter taste.

INGREDIENTS | SERVES 4

¾ pound boneless pork, cut into small cubes

1 tablespoon soy sauce

1 tablespoon Chinese rice wine or dry sherry

¼ teaspoon black pepper

2 teaspoons cornstarch

4½ tablespoons vegetable or peanut oil, divided

2 thin slices ginger, chopped

2 cloves garlic, chopped

1 small onion, chopped

1 tablespoon paprika

1½ cups cooked rice

1 cup chopped apple

1 tablespoon brown sugar

1 cup apple juice

1 teaspoon chopped fresh thyme

1 teaspoon chopped fresh parsley

¼ teaspoon kosher salt

Pungent Paprika

Paprika, the spice that defines Hungarian cuisine, comes from the chili pepper plant. The taste and strength of paprika varies depending on the type of chili pepper used to make it and whether the seeds (the hottest part of the chili pepper) are included. In North America, paprika is normally brighter red and has a sweeter flavor than Hungarian paprika, which can be quite hot.

1. Place pork in a large bowl. Add the soy sauce, rice wine or dry sherry, black pepper, and cornstarch. Marinate for 15 minutes.

2. Heat a wok or skillet on medium-high heat until it is nearly smoking, and add 2 tablespoons oil. When the oil is hot, add the ginger. Stir-fry for 10 seconds.

3. Add the cubed pork. Stir-fry, stirring and tossing it in the pan for 3–4 minutes or until the pork is no longer pink and is nearly cooked through. Remove the pork and drain in a colander or on paper towels.

4. Heat 1½ tablespoons oil. When the oil is hot, add the garlic. Stir-fry for 10 seconds and add the onion. Stir-fry the onion until it begins to soften (about 2 minutes), sprinkling the paprika over the onion while you are stir-frying.

5. Add 1 tablespoon oil in the middle of the pan. Add the rice and stir-fry, stirring it in the oil for 1 minute until it turns golden brown.

6. Push the items in the wok to the sides and add the apple in the middle of the pan, stir-frying for 1 minute or until it begins to brown.

7. Stir in the brown sugar. Stir to mix the apple with the onion and rice. Add the apple juice and bring to a boil.

8. Stir in the pork, thyme, parsley, and salt. Continue stir-frying for 2–3 minutes to mix all the ingredients together. Serve hot.

PER SERVING | Calories: 238 | Fat: 3.4g | Protein: 21g | Sodium: 418mg | Fiber: 2g | Carbohydrates: 39g | Sugar: 13g

Stuffed Green Peppers

In this dish, make sure to use green bell peppers, which are firmer than red bell peppers and hold their shape better during stir-frying.

INGREDIENTS | SERVES 4

½ pound lean ground pork

1 teaspoon sugar

1 tablespoon light soy sauce

2 teaspoons dark soy sauce

1 teaspoon minced ginger

1 teaspoon cornstarch plus 1 teaspoon

4 green bell peppers, cut in half and seeded

2 tablespoons vegetable or peanut oil, divided

½ cup chicken broth

1. Place the ground pork in a large bowl. Stir in the sugar, light soy sauce, dark soy sauce, ginger, and 1 teaspoon cornstarch. Marinate the pork for 15 minutes.

2. Sprinkle cornstarch on the inside of the pepper halves (this will help the pork mixture stick to the pepper).

3. Heat a wok or skillet over medium-high heat until it is nearly smoking. Add 1 tablespoon oil. When the oil is hot, add the ground pork. Stir-fry the ground pork for 2–3 minutes or until it is no longer pink and is nearly cooked through. Remove from the pan.

4. Spoon a heaping portion of ground pork into each of the green pepper halves.

5. Heat 1 tablespoon oil in the wok. When the oil is hot, add the stuffed green peppers, meat-side down. Let cook for 1 minute, then add the chicken broth.

6. Bring to a boil. Turn down the heat, cover, and simmer for 5 minutes, adding more broth if needed. Serve hot with jasmine rice.

PER SERVING | Calories: 195 | Fat: 12g | Protein: 11g | Sodium: 540mg | Fiber: 2g | Carbohydrates: 9g | Sugar: 4g

Pork and Paprika Stir-Fry

*To simplify the process, feel free to use a stir-fry vegetable mix
from the produce section of the supermarket.*

1. Cut the pork into 1½"–2" cubes. Place the pork cubes in a large bowl and toss with the salt, black pepper, and cornstarch. Let the pork stand for 15 minutes.

2. Heat a wok or skillet over medium-high heat until it is nearly smoking. Add 2 tablespoons oil. When the oil is hot, add half of the garlic. Stir-fry for 10 seconds.

3. Add the pork. Let it sit briefly to brown, then stir-fry the pork, stirring and tossing for 2–3 minutes or until it is no longer pink and it is nearly cooked through. Remove the meat and drain in a colander or on paper towels.

4. Heat 1½ tablespoons oil in the wok or skillet. When the oil is hot, add the remaining garlic. Stir-fry for 10 seconds, then add the onion. Sprinkle the paprika over the onion and stir-fry for 2 minutes or until the onion begins to soften.

5. Add the mushrooms. Stir-fry for 1 minute, then add the red bell pepper and the snow peas. Stir-fry for another minute or until the mushrooms have darkened and the snow peas and red bell pepper are tender but still crisp. Splash the vegetables with a bit of the beef broth if they begin to dry out during stir-frying.

6. Add the beef broth into the pan and bring to a boil. Add the pork back into the pan, stirring to mix it with the other ingredients.

7. Stir in the Worcestershire sauce and the sugar. Stir-fry for 1–2 more minutes to mix everything together. Serve hot.

PER SERVING | Calories: 297 | Fat: 16g | Protein: 27g | Sodium: 641mg | Fiber: 2g | Carbohydrates: 10g | Sugar: 5g

Chile Verde Stir-Fry

Pork is paired with tomatillos, onion, and garlic in this easy stir-fried version of chile verde stew. Instead of chili powder, you may add either hot red jalapeño peppers or milder green Anaheim chilies.

INGREDIENTS | SERVES 4

1 pound boneless pork
1 teaspoon salt
½ teaspoon black pepper
1 tablespoon cornstarch
3 tablespoons chicken broth
1 tablespoon soy sauce
1 tablespoon dry sherry
3 tablespoons olive oil, divided
3 cloves garlic, chopped, divided
1 small onion, chopped
1 teaspoon chili powder
¼ teaspoon ground cumin
6 tomatillos, thinly sliced
¼ teaspoon black pepper

1. Cut the boneless pork into cubes. Place the pork cubes in a large bowl and add the salt, pepper, and cornstarch. Let the pork stand for 20 minutes.

2. Combine the chicken broth, soy sauce, and dry sherry in a small bowl. Set aside.

3. Heat a wok or skillet over medium-high heat until it is nearly smoking. Add 2 tablespoons oil. When the oil is hot, add half the garlic. Stir-fry for 10 seconds.

4. Add the pork. Lay flat for 1 minute, then stir-fry, moving the pork around the pan for 2–3 minutes or until it is no longer pink and is nearly cooked. Remove and drain in a colander or on paper towels.

5. Heat 1 tablespoon oil in the wok or skillet. When the oil is hot, add the remaining garlic. Stir-fry for 10 seconds, then add the onion. Stir-fry for about 2 minutes or until the onion begins to soften, then stir in the chili powder and ground cumin.

6. Add the tomatillos. Stir-fry for 2 minutes, or until the tomatillos are tender but not too soft.

7. Add the pork back into the pan. Stir in the chicken broth mixture and black pepper. Stir-fry for 1–2 more minutes to combine all the flavors. Serve hot.

PER SERVING | Calories: 269 | Fat: 14g | Protein: 26g | Sodium: 926mg | Fiber: 0.8g | Carbohydrates: 7g | Sugar: 1.5g

French-Herbed Pork

Serve with rice and Double Nutty Fiddlehead Greens with Sesame Seeds (see Chapter 8) for a complete meal.

INGREDIENTS | SERVES 4

1 pound pork tenderloin

2½ tablespoons balsamic vinegar, divided

1 teaspoon dried rosemary

½ teaspoon garlic salt

¼ teaspoon black pepper

2 tablespoons olive oil

2 cloves garlic, crushed

1. Cut the pork into bite-sized cubes. Place the pork cubes in a large bowl and add 1½ tablespoons balsamic vinegar, rosemary, garlic salt, and black pepper. Marinate the pork for 15 minutes.

2. Heat a wok or skillet over medium-high heat and add the oil. When the oil is hot, add the crushed garlic. Stir-fry for 10 seconds.

3. Add the pork. Let brown for 1 minute, then stir-fry the pork, moving it around the pan for 6–8 minutes until it is thoroughly cooked through. Splash the pork chops with 1 tablespoon balsamic vinegar during stir-frying. Serve hot.

PER SERVING | Calories: 194 | Fat: 9g | Protein: 23g | Sodium: 356mg | Fiber: 0.1g | Carbohydrates: 2.4g | Sugar: 1.5g

Skillet Chili

This quick chili can be served with an assortment of condiments such as sour cream, shredded Cheddar cheese, diced scallions, and tortilla chips.

INGREDIENTS | SERVES 4

1½ pounds boneless pork

1¼ teaspoon salt, divided

½ teaspoon black pepper

1 tablespoon chili powder

1 tablespoon cornstarch

3 tablespoons olive oil, divided

1 teaspoon minced ginger

2 tablespoons chopped jalapeño peppers

1 teaspoon minced garlic

1 small onion, chopped

1 medium green bell pepper, seeded and diced

1 (15-ounce) can black beans, rinsed and drained

1 (15-ounce) can diced tomatoes, drained

2 tablespoons chopped chipotle peppers, plus 1 tablespoon of the adobo sauce

1 teaspoon cumin

½ cup chicken stock

1. Cut the pork into cubes. Place the pork cubes in a large bowl and add 1 teaspoon salt, black pepper, chili powder, and cornstarch. Set aside.

2. Heat a wok or skillet over medium-high heat and add 2 tablespoons oil. When the oil is hot, add the minced ginger. Stir-fry for 30 seconds or until aromatic.

3. Add the pork. Let sit for 1 minute, then stir-fry the pork for 2–3 minutes or until it is no longer pink and is nearly cooked through. Remove from the pan and drain on a plate lined with paper towels.

4. Heat 1 tablespoon oil. When the oil is hot, add the chopped jalapeño peppers. Stir-fry for a few seconds, then add the minced garlic. Add the onion and stir-fry for about 2 minutes, until it is softened.

5. Add the diced bell pepper. Stir-fry for 1 minute, adding remaining ¼ teaspoon salt.

6. Stir in the black beans, diced tomatoes, and the chipotle peppers and adobo sauce.

7. Stir in the cumin and chicken stock and bring to a boil.

8. Stir in the cooked pork. Turn down the heat, cover, and simmer for about 10–15 minutes. Serve hot.

PER SERVING | Calories: 458 | Fat: 17g | Protein: 45g | Sodium: 1,345mg | Fiber: 8g | Carbohydrates: 28g | Sugar: 7g

Breakfast Burritos

Serve these hearty burritos with tomato salsa or Fresh Pico de Gallo (see Chapter 2).

INGREDIENTS | SERVES 4

6 large eggs

½ teaspoon kosher salt

½ teaspoon black pepper

¼ teaspoon cumin powder

2 scallions, diced

2 tablespoons vegetable oil

½ pound Mexican chorizo

1½ cups boiled and cubed potatoes

4 large flour tortillas, warmed

4 tablespoons low-fat sour cream

¼ cup shredded Monterey jack cheese

¼ cup chopped cilantro

1. In a medium bowl, lightly beat the eggs. Whisk in the salt, pepper, cumin, and scallions.

2. Heat wok over medium heat and add 1 tablespoon oil. Once the oil is hot, add the chorizo. Stir-fry, stirring and moving the chorizo around the pan until it is cooked through, about 5 minutes.

3. Add in the potatoes and continue cooking for 1 minute. Remove the chorizo-potato mixture from the pan.

4. Add the remaining oil in the wok and pour in the egg mixture. Scramble the eggs and cook about 3 minutes, until the eggs are set but still moist. Remove from the heat and gently fold in the chorizo-potato mixture.

5. Lay a tortilla on a flat surface. Spoon ¼ of the egg mixture lengthwise in the center of the tortilla. Spoon 1 tablespoon of the sour cream over the filling, and then sprinkle ¼ of the cheese and ¼ of the cilantro on top. Fold the sides of the tortilla in and roll upward tightly. Repeat with the remaining tortillas and serve warm.

PER SERVING | Calories: 510 | Fat: 39g | Protein: 26g | Sodium: 1,140mg | Fiber: 1.5g | Carbohydrates: 11g | Sugar: 1.5g

Parmesan Pork Chops

On the go? Grab 2 hoagie rolls and place one pork chop in each. Top with marinara sauce and a slice of mozzarella cheese and you've got a delicious, mobile meal.

INGREDIENTS | SERVES 2

½ cup Italian bread crumbs

½ cup plus 1 tablespoon grated Parmesan cheese

¼ teaspoon dried thyme leaves

1 large egg

2 boneless pork chops, pounded to ½" thickness

¼ teaspoon kosher salt

¼ teaspoon black pepper

½ cup vegetable oil

2 cups Marinara Sauce (see Chapter 2), heated

1 tablespoon chopped Italian parsley

1. Place the bread crumbs in a shallow dish. Place ½ cup Parmesan cheese in a separate dish.

2. In a small bowl, whisk together the thyme and egg.

3. Season the pork with salt and pepper.

4. Working in batches, dredge a few pieces of the pork in the Parmesan cheese, then the egg mixture, and finally the bread crumbs to coat, shaking off the excess between each step. Repeat with the remaining pork.

5. Heat the oil in a wok to medium-high heat. Slide in the pork chops and fry until golden brown, about 3–4 minutes on each side. Remove from pan and drain the pork chops on plates lined with paper towels.

6. Take two plates and place several spoonfuls of Marinara Sauce on the bottoms. Place 1 pork chop on top of each plate and sprinkle the tops with the remaining Parmesan cheese and parsley. Serve hot.

PER SERVING | Calories: 1,091 | Fat: 79g | Protein: 61g | Sodium: 1,960mg | Fiber: 4g | Carbohydrates: 32g | Sugar: 8g

Asian Pork Burgers

These burgers not only pack a punch of flavor but also have a wonderful crunchy texture from the slaw.

INGREDIENTS | SERVES 2

1 cup shredded purple cabbage

½ cup shredded carrots

½ cup Chili Ponzu Marinade (see Chapter 2)

½ pound lean ground pork

½ tablespoon minced garlic

1 teaspoon minced ginger

1 teaspoon minced lemongrass

1 tablespoon fish sauce

1 teaspoon sesame oil

½ teaspoon black pepper

¼ teaspoon red pepper flakes

2 scallions, minced

2 tablespoons vegetable oil

2 tablespoons Wasabi Aioli (see Chapter 2)

2 hamburger buns, toasted

Puffed-Up Patties?

Do your burger patties puff up in the center once cooked? To help prevent that, create a small indentation in the center of the patty while you're forming them.

1. To make the cabbage slaw, toss the cabbage and carrots in a medium bowl with the marinade. Cover and refrigerate for 1 hour.

2. In another bowl, mix together the pork, garlic, ginger, lemongrass, fish sauce, sesame oil, black pepper, red pepper flakes, and scallions. Divide the mixture into 2 equal patties. Using your hands, make a small indentation in the center.

3. Heat the vegetable oil in a wok over medium heat Add both pork patties, side by side. Cook the patties for 2 minutes on each side until the pork is golden brown and cooked through. Remove from wok.

4. Assemble the burgers by spreading the Wasabi Aioli inside both sides of the toasted buns. Layer with a pork patty and a heaping mound of the cabbage slaw. Serve immediately.

PER SERVING | Calories: 737 | Fat: 67g | Protein: 22g | Sodium: 2,038mg | Fiber: 3g | Carbohydrates: 13g | Sugar: 5g

Italian Sausage Sandwiches

Not a fan of pork? Feel free to substitute with chicken or turkey sausages.

INGREDIENTS | SERVES 3

3 tablespoons vegetable oil, divided

1 tablespoon minced garlic

1 medium red bell pepper, sliced

1 medium green bell pepper, sliced

1 small white onion, sliced

2 sweet Italian sausage links

½ cup chicken or beef broth

2 cups Marinara Sauce (see Chapter 2)

¼ teaspoon red pepper flakes

¼ teaspoon kosher salt

2 tablespoons Italian parsley, chopped

2 slices mozzarella cheese

2 hoagie rolls, toasted

1. In a wok, heat 2 tablespoons oil over medium heat. Add garlic, bell peppers, and onions and cook until softened—about 3–4 minutes. Remove the items to a plate.

2. Add remaining oil, swirling the wok. Brown the sausages 2 minutes on each side. Add the broth and cook for 3–4 minutes or until the liquid has nearly evaporated.

3. Lower the heat and pour in the Marinara Sauce, salt, and red pepper flakes. Simmer for 3–4 minutes.

4. Stir in the parsley, peppers, and onion, and continue simmering for 2–3 minutes or until the sauce has thickened and reduced to nearly half.

5. Place 1 slice mozzarella inside each roll. Top with sausage, vegetables, and sauce. Serve immediately.

PER SERVING | Calories: 285 | Fat: 22g | Protein: 6g | Sodium: 927mg | Fiber: 4g | Carbohydrates: 15g | Sugar: 8g

Mojo Pork Medallions

Serve alongside black beans and Fried Plantains (see Chapter 8).

INGREDIENTS | SERVES 2

½ pound pork medallions, pounded to ½" thickness

1 cup Cuban Mojo Marinade (see Chapter 2)

2 tablespoons vegetable oil

1. In a shallow dish, add the pork with all but 2 tablespoons of the marinade. Flip to coat and refrigerate for 2 hours.

2. Heat oil in a wok over medium high heat. Use paper towels to pat the pork dry. Add the pork to the wok and sear for 1–2 minutes on each side. Transfer the pork to plates and spoon the reserved marinade on top. Serve hot.

PER SERVING | Calories: 410 | Fat: 29g | Protein: 24g | Sodium: 65mg | Fiber: 1.6g | Carbohydrates: 11g | Sugar: 5.7g

Spiced-Rub Pork Chops

Serve these South Asian–flavored chops with dollops of Mango Chutney (see Chapter 2) and Stir-Fried Coconut Basmati (see Chapter 10)

INGREDIENTS | SERVES 2

½ tablespoon garam masala

2 garlic cloves, minced

1 teaspoon minced ginger

1 tablespoon lemon juice

½ tablespoon honey

1 scallion, minced

1 teaspoon kosher salt

¼ teaspoon black pepper

4 tablespoons vegetable oil, divided

2 boneless pork chops, ½" thick

1. In a large bowl, whisk together the garam masala, garlic, ginger, lemon juice, honey, scallion, salt, pepper, and 2 tablespoons oil. Add the pork chops and evenly coat with the marinade. Refrigerate for 30 minutes.

2. Heat the remaining oil in a wok over medium-high heat. Add the pork chops and cook for 2 minutes on each side until cooked through.

PER SERVING | Calories: 512 | Fat: 34g | Protein: 41g | Sodium: 1,273mg | Fiber: 0.7g | Carbohydrates: 7.8g | Sugar: 5g

Smothered Pork Chops

These pork chops would be delicious over buttermilk biscuits for a hearty brunch.

INGREDIENTS | SERVES 2

½ cup all-purpose flour

2 tablespoons garlic powder

½ teaspoon cayenne powder

2 boneless pork chops, ½" thickness

½ teaspoon kosher salt

¼ teaspoon black pepper

2 tablespoons vegetable oil

½ cup white wine or chicken stock

¼ cup heavy cream

2 tablespoons minced Italian parsley

1. In a shallow dish, whisk together the flour, garlic powder, and cayenne.

2. Use paper towels and blot excess moisture off the pork. Season with salt and pepper.

3. Heat the oil in a wok over medium heat. Place each pork chop into the flour mixture. Use your fingers to adhere the flour on both sides. Shake off excess flour and add to the wok. Repeat with the remaining pork chop. Cook the chops for 2 minutes on each side until golden and then transfer to a plate. Tent the plate with aluminum foil.

4. Whisk in the wine or chicken stock and turn the heat to high. Allow the liquids to reduce for 2 minutes while scraping up the brown bits from the bottom.

5. Lower the heat and whisk in the cream.

6. Return the pork chops to the wok and simmer for an additional 1–2 minutes.

7. Serve the pork chops topped with a few spoonfuls of sauce and garnished with the parsley.

PER SERVING | Calories: 652 | Fat: 31g | Protein: 26g | Sodium: 702mg | Fiber: 2g | Carbohydrates: 32g | Sugar: 1g

Pork Saltimbocca

Saltimbocca is traditionally made with veal; however, pork cutlets serve as a wonderful substitute.

INGREDIENTS | SERVES 2

4 boneless pork cutlets, pounded to
  ¼"–⅛" thickness

½ teaspoon kosher salt

¼ teaspoon black pepper

½ cup all-purpose flour

¼ teaspoon cayenne powder

2 tablespoons vegetable oil

3 tablespoons unsalted butter, divided

8 fresh sage leaves

4 thin slices prosciutto

4 slices mozzarella cheese

½ cup dry white wine

½ teaspoon dry sage

1. Use paper towels to blot excess moisture from the pork. Season with salt and pepper.

2. In a shallow dish, whisk together the flour and cayenne.

3. Heat the oil in a wok over medium heat and add 1 tablespoon butter.

4. Place each cutlet in the flour mixture. Use your fingers to adhere the flour on both sides. Shake off excess flour and add to the wok. Repeat with the remaining pork. Cook the cutlets for 1–2 minutes on each side until golden and transfer to a baking sheet.

5. On top of each cutlet, place 2 fresh sage leaves, 1 slice prosciutto, and one slice mozzarella. Transfer the baking sheet to the oven broiler and allow the cheese to melt and brown. Remove and cover loosely with foil.

6. Using the same wok, add the white wine and allow 2–3 minutes for the liquids to reduce by half. Use a wooden spoon to scrape up the brown bits. Whisk in the dry sage and remaining butter.

7. Serve the pork with a few spoonfuls of the sauce on top.

PER SERVING | Calories: 606 | Fat: 43g | Protein: 16g | Sodium: 950mg | Fiber: 1g | Carbohydrates: 27g | Sugar: 1g

Spinach and Goat Cheese–Stuffed Pork Chops

If you prefer, crumbled feta cheese would be a great alternative to the goat cheese.

INGREDIENTS | SERVES 2

4 tablespoons vegetable oil, divided

¼ cup minced shallots

½ tablespoon minced garlic

6 ounces frozen spinach, thawed and drained

5 ounces goat cheese

2 boneless pork chops, ½"–¾" thickness

½ teaspoon kosher salt

¼ teaspoon black pepper

1 cup white wine

1 tablespoon unsalted butter

½ tablespoon whole grain or Dijon mustard

½ teaspoon fresh thyme leaves

1. Heat 2 tablespoons oil in a wok over medium heat. Add the shallots and garlic and cook for 30 seconds.

2. Add the spinach and stir-fry for 1 minute. Remove from heat.

3. Mix the goat cheese with the spinach mixture in a small bowl. Set aside and allow to cool to room temperature.

4. Cut a small pocket into each pork chop, being careful not to cut all the way through. Season the pork with salt and pepper. Stuff each chop with a few spoonfuls of the cooled spinach mixture. If needed, use toothpicks to help keep chop closed.

5. Wipe the inside of the wok with paper towels. Heat the remaining oil over medium heat. Add the pork chops to the wok and cook for 3–4 minutes on each side until golden brown. Remove the chops and cover loosely with foil to keep warm.

6. Add the wine to the wok and turn the heat to medium high. Scrape up the bottom of the wok to loosen the flavorful brown bits. Allow 2–3 minutes for the wine to reduce by half, then whisk in the butter, mustard, and thyme. Cook for 1 minute and then spoon the sauce over the stuffed pork chops. Serve hot.

PER SERVING | Calories: 982 | Fat: 64g | Protein: 66g | Sodium: 994mg | Fiber: 2.5g | Carbohydrates: 12g | Sugar: 3g

Pork with Mustard Cream Sauce

Serve these pork medallions with vegetables or over penne pasta.

INGREDIENTS | SERVES 2

½ pound pork medallions, pounded to
  ¼"–½" thickness

1 teaspoon kosher salt

¼ teaspoon black pepper

2 tablespoons unsalted butter

1 tablespoon olive oil

2 tablespoons minced shallots

½ tablespoon minced garlic

1 cup dry white wine

¼ cup chicken stock

1 tablespoon whole-grain mustard

1 teaspoon fresh thyme leaves

¼ cup heavy cream

1. Season the pork with salt and pepper.

2. Heat a wok over medium-high heat and melt the butter into the olive oil. In batches, slide in pork and fry until golden brown, approximately 2 minutes on each side. Remove pork from wok, transfer to a plate, and tent loosely with foil. Repeat with the remaining medallions.

3. Reduce the heat to medium; add the shallots and garlic and cook for 1 minute.

4. Add the wine and chicken stock and allow 2–3 minutes for the liquids to reduce by half.

5. Whisk in the mustard, thyme leaves, and cream. Return the pork to the wok and spoon the sauce over the tops to coat. Allow to simmer for 1 minute before serving.

PER SERVING | Calories: 500 | Fat: 32g | Protein: 25g | Sodium: 1,347mg | Fiber: 0.4g | Carbohydrates: 7g | Sugar: 1g

Pork with Mushroom Sage Sauce

Sage has a deep, earthy flavor. If you only have dried sage on hand, use ¼ of what the fresh measurement states.

INGREDIENTS | SERVES 2

½ pound pork medallions, pounded to ¼"–½" thickness

½ teaspoon dried sage

1 teaspoon kosher salt

¼ teaspoon black pepper

2 tablespoons unsalted butter

1 tablespoon olive oil

2 tablespoons minced shallots

½ tablespoon minced garlic

1½ cups sliced crimini mushrooms

1 cup dry white wine

¼ cup chicken stock

2 tablespoons chopped fresh sage

¼ cup heavy cream

Medicinal Sage

Like many herbs, sage has had a long history for being used for treating ailments. It has been used to assist with sore throats, reduce inflammations, and treat intestinal infections.

1. Season the pork with the dried sage, salt, and pepper.

2. Heat a wok over medium-high heat and melt the butter into the olive oil. In batches, slide in the pork and fry until golden brown, approximately 2 minutes on each side. Remove pork from wok, transfer to a plate, and tent loosely with foil. Repeat with the remaining medallions.

3. Reduce the heat to medium; add the shallots and garlic and cook for 30 seconds.

4. Add in the mushrooms and stir-fry for 2 minutes.

5. Add the wine and chicken stock and allow 2–3 minutes for the liquids to reduce by half. Whisk in the fresh sage and cream.

6. Return the pork back to the wok and spoon the sauce over the tops to coat. Allow to simmer for 1 minute before serving.

PER SERVING | Calories: 494 | Fat: 31g | Protein: 24g | Sodium: 1,258mg | Fiber: 0.1g | Carbohydrates: 6.5g | Sugar: 1g

CHAPTER 7

Seafood and Shellfish

Stir-Fried Shrimp with Snow Peas

This is a simple shrimp stir-fry that would pair well with cooked jasmine or brown rice.

INGREDIENTS | SERVES 4

1 pound large shrimp, shelled and deveined

½ teaspoon kosher salt

2 tablespoons chicken broth

2 tablespoons soy sauce or fish sauce

1 teaspoon granulated sugar

3 tablespoons vegetable or peanut oil

2 teaspoons minced ginger

1 tablespoon Chinese rice wine or dry sherry

6 ounces snow peas, trimmed

1 scallion, finely chopped

Fish Sauce

As the name implies, fish sauce is made from small fresh fish, which are fermented in salt for about 18 months. The salty brown liquid is a staple ingredient in most Southeast Asian cooking, taking the place of salt as a seasoning.

1. Rinse the shrimp under cold running water and pat dry with paper towels. Place the shrimp in a large bowl and toss with the salt.

2. In a small bowl, combine the chicken broth with the soy sauce or fish sauce and the sugar.

3. Heat a wok or skillet over medium-high heat until it is nearly smoking and add the oil. When the oil is hot, add the ginger. Stir-fry for 10 seconds.

4. Add the shrimp. Stir-fry the shrimp briefly until they turn bright pink. Splash the shrimp with the rice wine or sherry while stir-frying.

5. Push the shrimp to the sides of the pan. Add the snow peas in the middle. Stir-fry in the hot oil for about 1 minute, until the snow peas turn a darker green and are tender but still crisp.

6. Add the chicken broth mixture into the pan and bring to a boil. Stir in the chopped scallion. Stir-fry for 1 more minute to heat everything through. Serve hot.

PER SERVING | Calories: 156 | Fat: 2g | Protein: 24g | Sodium: 944mg | Fiber: 1g | Carbohydrates: 7g | Sugar: 3g

Shrimp and Asparagus

For an extra touch, try garnishing the shrimp and asparagus with toasted white sesame seeds before serving.

INGREDIENTS | SERVES 4

1 pound large shrimp, shelled, deveined

1 tablespoon Chinese rice wine or dry sherry

1 teaspoon kosher salt, divided

2 teaspoons cornstarch

3 tablespoons vegetable or peanut oil

2 slices fresh ginger

½ pound fresh asparagus, sliced on the diagonal into 1" pieces

½ teaspoon kosher salt, optional

¼ cup Sesame Sauce (see Chapter 2)

Stir-Frying Shrimp

When stir-frying shrimp, it's important not to overcook them. If overcooked, shrimp become tough. Stir-fry the shrimp just until they turn pink and the edges begin to curl.

1. Rinse the shrimp under cold running water and pat dry. Place the shrimp in a large bowl and add the rice wine or sherry, ½ teaspoon salt, and cornstarch. Marinate the shrimp for 15 minutes.

2. Heat a wok or skillet over medium-high heat until it is nearly smoking. Add the oil. When the oil is hot, add the ginger. Let the ginger brown for 2–3 minutes, then remove it from the pan.

3. Add the shrimp into the wok or skillet. Stir-fry briefly until the shrimp turns pink and the edges begin to curl. Push the shrimp to the sides of the pan, and add the asparagus in the middle. Stir-fry for 1 minute, stirring in remaining salt. Stir-fry the asparagus until it is tender but still crisp (about 2 minutes total).

4. Stir the Sesame Sauce and add it to the middle of the pan, stirring to thicken. Stir-fry briefly for 30 seconds to combine all the ingredients and allow the flavors to blend, and serve hot.

PER SERVING | Calories: 183 | Fat: 5g | Protein: 24g | Sodium: 1,016mg | Fiber: 1g | Carbohydrates: 7g | Sugar: 2g

Salt and Pepper Shrimp

Leaving the shells on the shrimp enhances the flavor and provides an additional texture to the dish. It also helps prevent the shrimp from overcooking.

INGREDIENTS | SERVES 4

1 pound medium to large shrimp, shells on

2 tablespoons cornstarch

¾ teaspoon kosher or sea salt

¾ teaspoon freshly ground black pepper

2 cups vegetable or peanut oil

1 teaspoon minced ginger

½ teaspoon minced garlic

1 shallot, chopped

1 scallion, finely chopped

1. Rinse the shrimp under cold running water and pat dry with paper towels. Dredge the shrimp in the cornstarch. Place the dredged shrimp on a plate next to the stove.

2. In a small bowl, combine the salt and pepper.

3. Heat a wok or skillet over medium-high heat and add the oil. When the oil is hot, carefully add the shrimp. Cook until the shrimp turns pink and the edges begin to curl (about 1 minute). Remove the shrimp and drain in a colander or on paper towels.

4. Remove all but 1½ tablespoons oil from the wok or skillet. Add the ginger, garlic, and shallot. Stir-fry for 30 seconds or until the shallot begins to soften, then add the shrimp.

5. Stir in the salt and pepper mixture from step 2. Stir in the scallion. Stir-fry for 1 minute to combine the ingredients. Serve hot.

PER SERVING | Calories: 137 | Fat: 2g | Protein: 22g | Sodium: 609mg | Fiber: 0.2g | Carbohydrates: 5g | Sugar: 0.1g

Prawns with Water Chestnuts and Baby Corn

*When using canned baby corn and water chestnuts,
be sure to rinse them under running water and drain well.*

INGREDIENTS | SERVES 4

¾ pound large prawns, shelled and deveined

¼ cup chicken broth

1 tablespoon Chinese rice wine or dry sherry

1 teaspoon granulated sugar

2 tablespoons vegetable or peanut oil

½ teaspoon kosher salt

1 teaspoon minced ginger

1 cup baby corn, drained and halved

1 cup sliced water chestnuts

2 scallions, quartered

½ teaspoon ground black pepper

½ teaspoon sesame oil

Prawn or Shrimp?

Prawns and shrimp are two different species of crustacean. If you look closely, you'll see slight differences in their legs and pincers. Whenever a recipe calls for prawns, feel free to substitute large shrimp.

1. Rinse the prawns under cold running water and pat dry with paper towels.

2. In a small bowl, combine the chicken broth, rice wine or sherry, and sugar.

3. Heat a wok or skillet over medium-high heat until it is nearly smoking. Add the oil. When the oil is hot, add the salt and the prawns. Stir-fry the prawns until they turn pink and the edges begin to curl, about 1 minute.

4. Push the prawns to the sides of the wok or skillet. Add the ginger, baby corn, and water chestnuts in the middle. Stir-fry for 30 seconds and then stir in the scallions.

5. Add the chicken broth mixture and bring to a boil. Add the black pepper and stir-fry for 1 minute to blend the flavors. Remove from the heat and stir in the sesame oil. Serve hot.

PER SERVING | Calories: 143 | Fat: 2g | Protein: 17g | Sodium: 490mg | Fiber: 1g | Carbohydrates: 10g | Sugar: 2.8g

Shrimp in Black Bean Sauce

*Black bean sauce lends a rich flavor to shellfish dishes. If you like,
spice up this dish by adding a small amount of chili paste to the garlic and black bean sauce.*

INGREDIENTS | SERVES 4

1 pound large shrimp, shelled and
   deveined
2 teaspoons cornstarch
2 tablespoons vegetable or peanut oil
2 tablespoons Chinese black bean sauce
1 teaspoon minced garlic
2 slices ginger, minced
2 scallions, quartered
¼ cup chicken broth

1. Rinse the shrimp in cold running water and drain. Place the shrimp in a bowl and toss with the cornstarch.

2. Heat a wok or skillet over medium-high heat until it is nearly smoking. Add the oil. When the oil is hot, add the black bean sauce and the garlic. Stir-fry for 30 seconds, mixing the garlic and black bean sauce together.

3. Add the shrimp, minced ginger, and scallions. Stir-fry the shrimp until they turn pink and the edges begin to curl, about 1 minute, mixing in with the sauce.

4. Add the chicken broth and bring to a boil. Serve hot with rice.

PER SERVING | Calories: 139 | Fat: 2g | Protein: 23g | Sodium: 256mg | Fiber: 0.5g | Carbohydrates: 4g | Sugar: 0.4g

Shrimp with Broccoli in Garlic Sauce

To add extra heat to this dish, replace the chili sauce with 2 teaspoons chopped red chili peppers.

INGREDIENTS | SERVES 4

1 pound medium to large shrimp, shelled and deveined

½ teaspoon kosher salt

⅓ cup chicken broth

1½ teaspoons Chinese rice vinegar

2 teaspoons chopped garlic

½ teaspoon chili sauce

1 teaspoon cornstarch

4 teaspoons water

4 tablespoons vegetable or peanut oil, divided

2 thin slices ginger

½ teaspoon minced ginger

½ cup chopped yellow onion

2 cups chopped broccoli

½ teaspoon granulated sugar

1–2 tablespoons additional water, if needed

1. Rinse the shrimp and pat dry with paper towels. Place the shrimp in a bowl and toss with salt.

2. In a small bowl, combine the chicken broth, rice vinegar, garlic, and chili sauce. In a separate small bowl, dissolve the cornstarch in the water.

3. Heat a wok or skillet over medium-high heat until it is nearly smoking. Add 2 tablespoons oil. When the oil is hot, add the sliced ginger. Let the ginger brown for 2–3 minutes, then remove from the oil. Add the shrimp. Stir-fry until they turn pink, about 1 minute. Remove the shrimp and drain in a colander or on paper towels.

4. Heat 2 tablespoons oil in the wok or skillet over medium-high heat. Add the minced ginger. Stir-fry for 10 seconds, then add the onion. Stir-fry the onion for about 2 minutes, until it begins to soften.

5. Add the broccoli and sprinkle the sugar over the entire vegetable mixture. Stir-fry the broccoli until it turns a darker green and is tender but still crisp (about 3 minutes). Add 1–2 tablespoons water if the broccoli begins to dry out during stir-frying.

6. Push the vegetables to the sides of the wok or skillet. Add the broth mixture into the middle of the pan and bring to a boil. Stir the cornstarch and water mixture and add to the sauce, stirring quickly to thicken.

7. When the sauce has thickened, add the shrimp back into the pan. Stir-fry shrimp with the vegetables for 1 minute to blend the flavors. Serve hot.

PER SERVING | Calories: 158 | Fat: 2g | Protein: 24g | Sodium: 573mg | Fiber: 1.6g | Carbohydrates: 8g | Sugar: 2g

Spicy Shrimp with Peanuts

Cashews can be substituted for peanuts in this dish.

1 pound large shrimp, peeled and deveined

1 teaspoon kosher salt

1 tablespoon red wine vinegar

1 tablespoon soy sauce

1 tablespoon water

1 teaspoon granulated sugar

2 tablespoons vegetable or peanut oil

2 teaspoons minced ginger

2 scallions, finely chopped

6–8 small red chilies, seeded and chopped

½ cup peanuts

Enhancing Shrimp Flavor

To add extra flavor, let the shrimp stand in warm salted water for 10–15 minutes after rinsing. This firms up the shrimp and enhances its natural flavor. Pat the shrimp dry with paper towels before stir-frying.

1. Rinse the shrimp under cold running water. Place the shrimp in a bowl and soak in warm water with the salt for 15 minutes. Remove. Pat the shrimp dry with paper towels.

2. In a small bowl, combine the red wine vinegar, soy sauce, water, and sugar. Set aside.

3. Heat a wok or skillet over medium-high heat until it is nearly smoking and add the oil. When the oil is hot, add the ginger, scallions, and the chopped chilies. Stir-fry for about 30 seconds.

4. Add the shrimp. Stir-fry the shrimp for 1 minute or until they turn pink, then add the vinegar sauce.

5. Stir in the peanuts. Cook for another 2 minutes to heat through, then serve hot.

PER SERVING | Calories: 467 | Fat: 22g | Protein: 55g | Sodium: 1,968mg | Fiber: 3g | Carbohydrates: 12g | Sugar: 4g

Sweet-and-Sour Shrimp

The combination of red bell pepper with celery and baby corn in this dish provides an interesting contrast in color and texture.

INGREDIENTS | SERVES 4

1 pound jumbo shrimp, shelled and deveined

½ teaspoon kosher salt

2 ribs celery

3 tablespoons vegetable or peanut oil

2 slices ginger

½ cup chopped red bell pepper

1 cup canned baby corn, rinsed and drained

½ cup Sweet-and-Sour Sauce (see Chapter 2)

2 scallions, quartered

How to Devein Shrimp

Deveining shrimp isn't as difficult as you may imagine. Using a small sharp knife, make a shallow cut along the back of the shrimp. Remove the vein by hand or hold the shrimp under a strong stream of cold running water to rinse it out.

1. Rinse the shrimp under cold running water. Pat dry with paper towels, place in a bowl, and toss with the salt.

2. Cut the celery into ½" slices on the diagonal. Fill a medium saucepan with enough water to cover the celery and bring to a boil. Blanch the celery in boiling water for 2–3 minutes, until it is tender but still crisp. Rinse the celery in cold water and drain in a colander.

3. Heat a wok or skillet over medium-high heat until it is nearly smoking. Add the oil. When the oil is hot, add the ginger. Stir-fry for 10 seconds.

4. Add the shrimp. Stir-fry the shrimp until they turn pink, about 1 minute. Push the shrimp up the sides of the pan.

5. Add the celery. Stir-fry briefly, then add the red bell pepper. Stir in the baby corn. Stir-fry until the vegetables are tender but still crisp (total stir-frying time should be 2–3 minutes).

6. Push the vegetables to the sides and add the Sweet-and-Sour Sauce in the middle, stirring quickly to thicken. When the sauce has thickened, stir to mix the sauce with the other ingredients.

7. Stir in the scallions. Cook for 1 minute, mixing everything together. Serve hot.

PER SERVING | Calories: 159 | Fat: 2g | Protein: 23g | Sodium: 504mg | Fiber: 0.5g | Carbohydrates: 10.6g | Sugar: 8g

Curried Shrimp

The heat level can be adjusted by increasing or reducing the amounts of curry paste.

INGREDIENTS | SERVES 4

1 pound large shrimp, shelled and deveined

½ teaspoon kosher salt

3 tablespoons vegetable or peanut oil

1 teaspoon minced garlic

1½ tablespoons red curry paste

1 shallot, chopped

1 small green bell pepper, seeded and cut into bite-sized chunks

1 small red bell pepper, seeded and cut into bite-sized chunks

1 tablespoon soy sauce

1 tablespoon Chinese rice wine or dry sherry

½ teaspoon granulated sugar

Red or Green Curry Paste

Red chili peppers are the main ingredient in red curry paste, while green chilies are used to make green curry paste. The heat level of the paste will depend on the specific type of chili pepper used and whether the seeds (which are the hottest part of the pepper) are included.

1. Rinse the shrimp under cold running water and pat dry with paper towels. Place the shrimp in a bowl and toss with the salt.

2. Heat a wok or skillet over medium-high heat until it is nearly smoking. Add the oil. When the oil is hot, add the shrimp. Stir-fry briefly until they turn pink, about 1 minute.

3. Push the shrimp up the sides of the pan. Add the garlic and curry paste into the hot oil. Stir-fry for 30 seconds.

4. Add the shallot. Stir-fry, mixing the shallot in with the curry paste, for about 1 minute or until the shallot begins to soften.

5. Add the green bell pepper. Stir-fry briefly, then add the red bell pepper. Stir-fry for 2 minutes, or until the green bell pepper is tender but still crisp. Splash the peppers with the soy sauce while stir-frying.

6. Stir-fry for 1 minute, mixing the shrimp with the vegetables and stirring in the rice wine or sherry and the sugar. Serve hot.

PER SERVING | Calories: 143 | Fat: 2g | Protein: 23g | Sodium: 687mg | Fiber: 1g | Carbohydrates: 5g | Sugar: 2g

Butter Prawns

The indescribable aroma of fresh curry leaves is the secret behind many Indian dishes. You can either leave the curry leaves in the stir-fry or remove them before serving.

INGREDIENTS | SERVES 4

1 pound large prawns, shell on

1 sprig fresh curry leaves (about 15 leaves)

2 tablespoons vegetable or peanut oil

1 teaspoon minced ginger

2 teaspoons Chinese rice wine or dry sherry

2 tablespoons butter

2 large green chilies

2 teaspoons minced garlic

¼ cup coconut milk

1 teaspoon granulated sugar

1 teaspoon fish sauce

1 tablespoon sweetened coconut flakes

2 tablespoons chopped fresh cilantro

Curry Leaves

Curry leaves play a prominent role as a flavor enhancer in Indian cuisine in the same way that bay leaves do in the West. While dried curry leaves can be used in long-simmered dishes, it's best to stick with fresh curry leaves for stir-fries. If the fresh leaves are unavailable, you can substitute fresh basil.

1. Rinse the prawns under cold running water and pat dry with paper towels. (Do not remove the shells.) Strip the curry leaves from the stem.

2. Heat a wok or skillet over medium-high heat until it is nearly smoking and add the oil. When the oil is hot, add the minced ginger. Stir-fry for 10 seconds.

3. Add the prawns. Stir-fry the prawns for about 1 minute or until the shells turn a bright pink. Splash the prawns with the rice wine or sherry during stir-frying.

4. Push the prawns to the sides of the wok or skillet. Add the butter, green chilies, curry leaves, and the garlic in the middle of the pan. Stir-fry for about 1 minute, mixing the seasonings with the butter.

5. Add the coconut milk and bring to a boil. Stir in the sugar and fish sauce. Stir-fry for 1 minute to mix the prawns with the coconut milk and seasonings.

6. Garnish with the coconut flakes and cilantro before serving.

PER SERVING | Calories: 212 | Fat: 11g | Protein: 23g | Sodium: 169mg | Fiber: 0.2g | Carbohydrates: 3g | Sugar: 1g

Coconut Shrimp

For added texture and flavor, top this dish with toasted, unsweetened coconut flakes.

Why Devein Shrimp at All?

If you look closely at a shrimp, you'll see a gray thread running down its back. This is the shrimp's digestive tract or "vein." While eating the vein can't harm you, removing it improves the appearance of the dish. In addition, the veins of larger-sized shrimp may contain dirt or grit.

1. Rinse the shrimp and pat dry with paper towels. Place the shrimp in a bowl and toss with salt.

2. In a small bowl, combine the coconut milk, chicken broth, and palm or brown sugar. In a separate small bowl, dissolve the cornstarch into 4 teaspoons water.

3. Heat a wok or skillet over medium-high heat until it is nearly smoking. Add 2 tablespoons oil. When the oil is hot, add the ginger. Stir-fry for 10 seconds.

4. Add the shrimp. Stir-fry the shrimp until they turn pink, about 1 minute. Remove the shrimp from the pan and drain in a colander or on paper towels.

5. Heat 1 tablespoon oil in the wok or skillet. When the oil is hot, add the garlic and the chili paste. Stir-fry for 10 seconds.

6. Add the shallots. Stir-fry for 30 seconds or until the shallot until softened, then add the bell pepper. Stir-fry the bell pepper for 2 minutes, or until it is tender but still crisp.

7. Push the vegetables to the sides of the pan. Add the coconut milk and chicken broth mixture in the middle and bring to a boil. Stir the cornstarch and water mixture, and pour into the coconut milk and broth, stirring to thicken.

8. When the sauce has thickened, add the shrimp back into the pan. Stir-fry for 1–2 more minutes to combine all the ingredients. Serve hot.

PER SERVING | Calories: 164 | Fat: 5g | Protein: 23g | Sodium: 496mg | Fiber: 0.5g | Carbohydrates: 5g | Sugar: 1.8g

Five-Spiced Shrimp

Five-spice powder is a commonly used ingredient in Chinese cuisine and is a blend of spices, usually cinnamon, cloves, star anise, Szechuan pepper, and fennel seeds.

INGREDIENTS | SERVES 4

1 pound jumbo shrimp, shelled and deveined

2 tablespoons cornstarch

3 tablespoons vegetable or peanut oil, divided

1 teaspoon minced ginger

2 teaspoons chopped red chilies

1 tablespoon five-spice powder

1 scallion, cut into 1" pieces

Classifying Shrimp

The seafood industry uses a combination of size and number to classify shrimp. Whether shrimp are classified as medium, large, or jumbo depends on the number of that type of shrimp that is needed to make up 1 pound. A 1-pound bag of jumbo shrimp will contain only 16–20 shrimp, while a 1-pound bag of medium shrimp will hold 35–40 shrimp.

1. Rinse the shrimp under cold running water and pat dry with paper towels. Place the shrimp in a bowl and dust with the cornstarch.

2. Heat a wok or skillet over medium-high heat until it is nearly smoking. Add 2 tablespoons oil. When the oil is hot, add the minced ginger. Stir-fry for 10 seconds.

3. Add the shrimp. Stir-fry briefly until they turn pink, about 1 minute. Remove from the pan and drain in a colander or on paper towels.

4. Heat 1 tablespoon oil in the wok or skillet. When the oil is hot, add the chopped chilies and the five-spice powder. Stir-fry for 30 seconds.

5. Add the shrimp back into the pan. Stir-fry briefly, coating the shrimp with the five-spice powder. Stir in the scallion and transfer to a serving platter. Serve hot.

PER SERVING | Calories: 136 | Fat: 2g | Protein: 22g | Sodium: 166mg | Fiber: 0.1g | Carbohydrates: 5g | Sugar: 0.2g

Vietnamese Caramelized Shrimp

This classic Vietnamese dish is often made with thinly sliced pork belly. For that variation, stir-fry ¼ pound thinly sliced pork belly for 5–6 minutes before adding in the shrimp.

INGREDIENTS | SERVES 4

1 pound large shrimp, shell and head on

½ tablespoon fish sauce

2 scallions, diced

2 garlic cloves, minced

1 teaspoon minced ginger

¼ cup plus 1 tablespoon vegetable oil, divided

¼ cup granulated sugar

½ teaspoon ground black pepper

1. Rinse the shrimp under cold running water and pat dry with paper towels.

2. In a large bowl, combine the shrimp, fish sauce, scallions, garlic, and ginger. Allow to marinate in the refrigerator for at least 10 minutes.

3. In a small saucepan, heat ¼ cup oil over medium heat. Sprinkle in the sugar and swirl the saucepan around from time to time until the liquid takes on a dark golden caramel color. It is important to watch while the sugar is cooking to avoid burning. Once done, set aside.

4. Heat a wok or skillet to medium-high heat and add the remaining oil. Once the oil is hot, add the shrimp and stir-fry for 1–2 minutes.

5. Add a few spoonfuls of the caramelized sugar, tossing the shrimp to coat evenly. Cook for an additional 1–2 minutes until the shrimp is thoroughly cooked. Season with black pepper and serve immediately.

PER SERVING | Calories: 324 | Fat: 19g | Protein: 22g | Sodium: 167mg | Fiber: 0g | Carbohydrates: 14g | Sugar: 13g

Southwestern Shrimp

This dish is perfect served on top of fresh romaine lettuce or even wrapped inside warmed tortillas.

INGREDIENTS | SERVES 4

1 pound large shrimp, peeled and deveined

2 tablespoons fresh chopped cilantro

½ jalapeño pepper, finely diced and seeded

¼ teaspoon cumin powder

¼ teaspoon red pepper flakes

½ teaspoon garlic salt

¼ teaspoon black pepper

1 cup plus 2 tablespoons vegetable oil, divided

2 corn tortillas, sliced into thin strips

1 teaspoon kosher salt

2 garlic cloves, minced

1 large shallot, minced

1 cup corn kernels

1 cup black beans, rinsed and drained

1 small red bell pepper, seeded and diced

1 cup diced tomatoes, seeded

¼ cup Cotija cheese

Lime wedges

Cotija

Cotija is a dry, Mexican cheese that can be warmed but does not melt. If you cannot find Cotija, Parmesan or manchego cheese can be substituted.

1. In a large bowl, combine the shrimp, cilantro, jalapeño pepper, cumin, red pepper flakes, garlic salt, and pepper. Mix the items well and marinate for 10 minutes in the refrigerator.

2. While the shrimp marinates, fill a small pot with 1 cup vegetable oil (about 2 inches) and heat to 375°F. Working in batches, fry the tortilla strips for 45–60 seconds until crispy. Carefully transfer the fried tortilla strips to a paper-towel-lined plate and season with kosher salt. Continue until all of the tortilla strips have been fried and seasoned. Set aside.

3. Heat a wok or large skillet over medium-high heat and add remaining 2 tablespoons oil. Once the oil is hot, stir-fry the garlic and shallots for 30 seconds.

4. Add the shrimp and stir-fry until they are barely pink, about 1 minute.

5. Stir in the corn, black beans, bell pepper, and tomatoes and cook for another 2–3 minutes.

6. Transfer the contents to a large platter and sprinkle the top with the crispy tortilla strips and Cotija cheese. Serve immediately with lime wedges on the side.

PER SERVING | Calories: 788 | Fat: 64g | Protein: 29g | Sodium: 1,293mg | Fiber: 5.8g | Carbohydrates: 24g | Sugar: 5g

Shrimp Creole

Adding chopped green bell pepper or sliced okra makes a great variation to this Southern dish.

INGREDIENTS | SERVES 4

1 pound shelled, deveined large shrimp
1½ teaspoons kosher salt, divided
1 egg white
2 teaspoons cornstarch
1 cup canned diced tomatoes, undrained
3½ tablespoons tomato paste
3½ tablespoons olive oil, divided
3 slices ginger
½ cup chopped red onion
1 teaspoon cayenne pepper
½ teaspoon dried thyme
4 ribs celery, cut into ½" slices
Additional water, if needed
½ teaspoon black pepper
2 scallions, finely chopped
1 teaspoon granulated sugar

1. Rinse the shrimp and pat dry with paper towels. Cut the shrimp in half lengthwise. Place the shrimp in a large bowl and mix in 1 teaspoon salt, egg white, and cornstarch. Marinate for 10 minutes.

2. In a small bowl, combine ⅓ cup juice from the canned tomatoes with the tomato paste.

3. Heat a wok or skillet over medium-high heat until it is nearly smoking. Add 2 tablespoons oil. When the oil is hot, add the shrimp. Stir-fry until they turn pink and the ends have begun to curl, about 1 minute. Remove the shrimp from the pan and drain on paper towels.

4. Heat 1½ tablespoons oil in the same wok or skillet. When the oil is hot, add the ginger. Let the ginger brown for 2–3 minutes, then remove from the pan.

5. Add the chopped onion. Stir-fry until it begins to soften (about 2 minutes), sprinkling with the cayenne pepper and dried thyme.

6. Push to the sides and add the celery in the middle. Stir-fry for 2 minutes, sprinkling with up to ½ teaspoon salt and adding 1–2 tablespoons water if the celery begins to dry out.

7. Add the tomatoes, sprinkling with black pepper. Stir-fry for 1 minute, then add the tomato juice mixture. Bring to a boil.

8. Add the shrimp back into the pan. Stir in the scallions and the sugar. Stir-fry for 1 minute to heat through and blend all the ingredients. Serve hot over rice.

PER SERVING | Calories: 270 | Fat: 14g | Protein: 25g | Sodium: 1,264mg | Fiber: 1.8g | Carbohydrates: 11g | Sugar: 5g

Rock Shrimp Tacos

Seafood tacos are a beloved staple in Southern California.
A firm fish such as cod or mahi-mahi can be substituted in this recipe.

INGREDIENTS | SERVE 4

Spicy Avocado Crema

1½ cups ripe avocado, diced

½ cup Mexican crema or crème fraîche

¼ cup fresh cilantro, chopped

½ jalapeño pepper, finely diced and seeded

1 tablespoon lime juice

1 teaspoon kosher salt

½ teaspoon ground black pepper

Cabbage Slaw

½ cup olive oil

1 tablespoon agave syrup or honey

3 tablespoons red wine vinegar

½ teaspoon kosher salt

½ teaspoon ground black pepper

½ head red cabbage, finely sliced

Shrimp

1 pound rock shrimp, peeled and deveined

2 garlic cloves, finely minced

1 teaspoon lime zest

¼ teaspoon red pepper flakes

¼ teaspoon cayenne pepper

¼ teaspoon ground cumin

2 tablespoons vegetable oil

8 corn tortillas

½ cup Cotija cheese

Lime wedges

1. Prepare the avocado crema by combining the avocado, crema, ¼ cup cilantro, jalapeño pepper, and lime juice in a food processor. Purée until thoroughly combined. Season with salt and pepper and place in a bowl, cover with plastic wrap, and refrigerate for at least 1 hour.

2. Make the cabbage slaw: In a small bowl, whisk together the olive oil, agave syrup, and vinegar. Season with salt and pepper. Toss the cabbage with the vinegar mixture and refrigerate.

3. In a large bowl, place the rock shrimp, garlic, lime zest, red pepper flakes, cayenne pepper, and cumin. Allow to marinate for 10 minutes.

4. Heat a wok or large skillet over medium-high heat and add the vegetable oil. Once the oil is hot, add in the shrimp and stir-fry for 2–3 minutes until they are cooked through and pink. Remove and place on a platter.

5. Warm the tortillas in a cast-iron skillet. Divide the rock shrimp and cabbage among the tortillas. Top each taco with Cotija and crema and serve with lime wedges on the side.

PER SERVING | Calories: 566 | Fat: 45g | Protein: 28g | Sodium: 1,172mg | Fiber: 6g | Carbohydrates: 14g | Sugar: 4g

Basic Stir-Fried Scallops

If you are using large scallops, be sure to pull off the hard muscle on the side and cut the scallops in half after rinsing.

INGREDIENTS | SERVES 4

1 pound sea scallops

½ teaspoon kosher salt

1 tablespoon cornstarch

2 tablespoons vegetable or peanut oil

1 teaspoon minced ginger

2 teaspoons soy sauce

¼ teaspoon chili paste

½ teaspoon granulated sugar

3 green scallions, chopped

Classifying Scallops

Scallops can typically be classified into two categories—bay scallops or sea scallops. The ideal season for the smaller bay scallops is the fall whereas the larger sea scallops are best from fall to spring.

1. Rinse the scallops in cold running water and pat dry with paper towels. Place the scallops in a bowl and toss with the salt and the cornstarch.

2. Heat a wok or skillet over medium-high heat until it is nearly smoking. Add the oil. When the oil is hot, add the ginger. Stir-fry for 10 seconds.

3. Add the scallops and stir-fry for 1 minute, then splash with the soy sauce. Stir in the chili paste, sugar, and scallions. Continue stir-frying until the scallops are white but not too firm (total stir-frying time should be 2–3 minutes). Serve hot.

PER SERVING | Calories: 113 | Fat: 1g | Protein: 19g | Sodium: 631mg | Fiber: 0.2g | Carbohydrates: 6g | Sugar: 1g

Sea Scallops with Garlic and Red Pepper

*Although sea scallops have been specified for this dish,
the often sweeter bay scallops can be substituted.*

INGREDIENTS | SERVES 4

1 pound sea scallops

2 tablespoons vegetable or peanut oil

2 cloves garlic, chopped

½ teaspoon chili paste

½ cup chopped yellow onion

1 tablespoon Chinese rice wine or dry sherry

2 small red bell peppers, peeled and cut into bite-sized cubes

1. Rinse the scallops under cold running water and pat dry. Cut the scallops into quarters.

2. Heat a wok or skillet over medium-high heat until it is nearly smoking. Add the oil. When the oil is hot, add the garlic and the chili paste. Stir-fry for 10 seconds, mixing the chili paste in with the garlic.

3. Add the onion and stir-fry until it begins to soften (about 2 minutes).

4. Add the scallops. Stir-fry for about 2 minutes, until they begin to brown, splashing with the rice wine or dry sherry.

5. Add the bell pepper. Stir-fry for 1 minute or until the scallops are cooked through. Serve immediately.

PER SERVING | Calories: 132 | Fat: 1g | Protein: 19g | Sodium: 193mg | Fiber: 1.6g | Carbohydrates: 9g | Sugar: 3g

Scallops with Black Beans

If using frozen scallops, defrost them by leaving them in the refrigerator to thaw slowly or run them under cold water.

INGREDIENTS | SERVES 4

1 pound bay scallops

2 tablespoons fermented black beans

3 tablespoons vegetable or peanut oil, divided

1 teaspoon minced ginger

1 tablespoon rice wine or dry sherry

1 teaspoon chopped garlic

1 medium tomato, chopped

¼ cup chicken broth

1 tablespoon soy sauce

½ teaspoon brown sugar

2 scallions, chopped on the diagonal into 1" sections

1. Rinse the scallops under cold running water and pat dry with paper towels.

2. Rinse the black beans under cold running water for 10 minutes, drain, and chop. Place the black beans in a bowl and mash with a fork.

3. Heat a wok or skillet over medium-high heat until it is nearly smoking. Add 2 tablespoons oil. When the oil is hot, add the ginger. Stir-fry for 10 seconds.

4. Add the scallops. Stir-fry for 2–3 minutes, until the scallops are white but not too firm. Splash the scallops with the rice wine or sherry while stir-frying. Remove the scallops and drain in a colander or on paper towels.

5. Heat 1 tablespoon oil in the wok or skillet. When the oil is hot, add the garlic and the mashed black beans. Stir-fry for 30 seconds, mixing the garlic with the beans.

6. Add the tomato. Stir-fry for 1 minute, then add the chicken broth. Bring to a boil.

7. Add the scallops back into the pan. Stir in the soy sauce and brown sugar. Stir in the scallions. Stir-fry briefly for 30 seconds to blend the flavors, and serve hot.

PER SERVING | Calories: 130 | Fat: 1g | Protein: 20g | Sodium: 496mg | Fiber: 1g | Carbohydrates: 7g | Sugar: 2g

Scallops with Bok Choy

In this recipe the vegetables are stir-fried first and then returned to the pan to mix with the sauce in the final stages of cooking.

INGREDIENTS | SERVES 4

1 pound bay scallops

½ teaspoon ground white pepper

3 tablespoons chicken broth

1 tablespoon oyster sauce

1 teaspoon granulated sugar

3 tablespoons vegetable or peanut oil, divided

½ teaspoon minced garlic

½ pound bok choy or baby bok choy

1 large red bell pepper, peeled and cut into bite-sized chunks

½ teaspoon minced ginger

1. Rinse the scallops in cold running water and pat dry with paper towels. Place the scallops in a large bowl and toss with the white pepper.

2. In a small bowl, combine the chicken broth, oyster sauce, and sugar. Set aside.

3. Heat a wok or skillet over medium-high heat until it is nearly smoking. Add 2 tablespoons oil. When the oil is hot, add the garlic. Stir-fry for 10 seconds.

4. Add the bok choy. Stir-fry the bok choy for 1 minute, then add the red bell pepper. Stir-fry for 1–2 minutes or until the vegetables are tender but still crisp. Remove the vegetables and drain in a colander or on paper towels.

5. Heat 1 tablespoon oil in the wok or skillet. When the oil is hot, add the ginger. Stir-fry for 10 seconds.

6. Add the scallops. Stir-fry the scallops until they turn white and are just starting to firm up.

7. Add the broth mixture and bring to a boil. Add the vegetables back into the pan. Stir-fry for 1–2 more minutes to mix everything together. Serve hot.

PER SERVING | Calories: 131 | Fat: 1g | Protein: 20g | Sodium: 390mg | Fiber: 1.5g | Carbohydrates: 8.8g | Sugar: 3g

Marsala Scallops

Marsala is a fortified Italian wine. If you do not have Marsala, brandy or dry sherry can be substituted.

INGREDIENTS | SERVES 4

1 pound bay scallops
2 tablespoons olive oil
2 thin slices ginger
⅓ cup Marsala wine
⅓ cup chicken broth
2 shallots, chopped
½ pound shiitake mushrooms, thinly sliced
1 tablespoon butter
2 tablespoons chopped fresh parsley
1 tablespoon chopped fresh basil
½ teaspoon ground black pepper

1. Rinse the scallops under cold running water and pat dry.

   Heat a wok or skillet over medium-high heat until it is nearly smoking. Add the oil. When the oil is hot, add the ginger. Brown for 2–3 minutes, and then remove from the pan (this is to flavor the oil).

2. Add the scallops and stir-fry until they turn white. Remove the scallops from the pan and drain in a colander or on paper towels.

3. Add the wine to the pan and bring to a boil. Deglaze the pan by using a spatula to scrape off the browned bits from the stir-fried scallops.

4. Add the chicken broth and bring to a boil, then add the shallots and the mushrooms. Cook for 2–3 minutes, until the shallots have softened. Stir in the butter, parsley, basil, and black pepper. Add the scallops back into the wok and stir for 30 seconds. Serve immediately.

PER SERVING | Calories: 224 | Fat: 10g | Protein: 19g | Sodium: 271mg | Fiber: 0g | Carbohydrates: 6g | Sugar: 1.5g

Simple Stir-Fried Fish

As with meat and poultry, adding egg white to a seafood marinade helps protect the fish from the hot oil.

INGREDIENTS | SERVES 4

1 pound fish fillets, such as cod or pollock

½ teaspoon salt

¼ teaspoon ground black pepper

1 egg white

2 tablespoons Chinese rice wine or dry sherry, divided

2 teaspoons cornstarch

2 tablespoons vegetable or peanut oil

2 thin slices ginger

1 scallion, finely chopped

1 tablespoon soy sauce

1 teaspoon Asian sesame oil

1. Cut the fish fillets into 1½"–2" squares that are about ½" thick. Place the fish cubes in a large bowl and add the salt, black pepper, egg white, 1 tablespoon Chinese rice wine or sherry, and the cornstarch. Marinate the fish for 15 minutes.

2. Heat a wok or skillet over medium-high heat until it is nearly smoking. Add the oil. When the oil is hot, add the ginger and scallion. Stir-fry for 10 seconds.

3. Add the fish. Let the fish sit in the pan briefly, then gently stir-fry the fish cubes, moving them around the wok for 1–2 minutes or until they turn white and are firm.

4. Splash the fish cubes with the remaining 1 tablespoon rice wine or sherry and the soy sauce. Let the fish cook for another minute, remove it from the heat, and stir in the sesame oil. Serve hot.

PER SERVING | Calories: 123 | Fat: 2g | Protein: 21g | Sodium: 594mg | Fiber: 0g | Carbohydrates: 2g | Sugar: 0.2g

Storing Fresh Fish

While fresh fish should be eaten the same day you purchase it, it can be stored overnight. Always store fresh fish in the coldest part of the refrigerator—the temperature should not rise above 35°F (2°C). To store fresh fish, remove the packaging that it came in, rinse the fish under cold water, and wrap it loosely in plastic wrap.

Stir-Fried Cod

Other firm white fish will work well in this recipe, as they are able to hold their shape during stir-frying.

INGREDIENTS | SERVES 4

1 pound cod fillets

2 tablespoons light soy sauce

1 tablespoon Chinese rice wine or dry sherry

½ teaspoon sesame oil

3 teaspoons cornstarch, divided

⅓ cup chicken broth

1 tablespoon oyster sauce

1 teaspoon granulated sugar

4 teaspoons water

3 tablespoons vegetable or peanut oil, divided

2 teaspoons minced ginger, divided

2 ribs celery, cut on the diagonal into ½" pieces

¼ teaspoon salt

1 small red bell pepper, seeded and cut into bite-sized cubes

1–2 tablespoons additional water, optional

1. Cut the fish into cubes. Place the cubes in a large bowl, and add the light soy sauce, rice wine or sherry, Asian sesame oil, and 2 teaspoons cornstarch. Marinate the fish for 15 minutes.

2. In a small bowl, combine the chicken broth, oyster sauce, and sugar. Set aside.

3. In a separate small bowl, dissolve 1 teaspoon cornstarch into the water. Set aside.

4. Heat a wok or skillet over medium-high heat until it is nearly smoking and add 2 tablespoons oil. When the oil is hot, add half the ginger. Stir-fry for 10 seconds.

5. Add the fish cubes. Stir-fry the fish cubes for about 2 minutes or until they begin to brown. Remove the fish and drain in a colander or on paper towels.

6. Heat 1 tablespoon oil in the wok or skillet. When the oil is hot, add the remainder of the ginger. Stir-fry for 10 seconds, then add the celery. Stir-fry the celery for 1 minute, sprinkling with the salt. Add the red bell pepper, and stir-fry for 1 minute. Splash the vegetables with 1–2 tablespoons of water if they begin to dry out.

7. Push the vegetables to the sides of the pan. Add the chicken broth mixture and bring to a boil. Stir the cornstarch and water and add into the sauce, stirring quickly to thicken.

8. Once the sauce has thickened, add the fish back into the pan. Stir-fry for 1 minute to mix the ingredients. Serve hot.

PER SERVING | Calories: 140 | Fat: 1.8g | Protein: 21g | Sodium: 869mg | Fiber: 0.8g | Carbohydrates: 7g | Sugar: 2g

Fish with Oyster Sauce

If you are unsure about buying fresh fish, enlist the assistance of your local fishmonger.

INGREDIENTS | SERVES 4

1 pound white fish fillets, such as pollock or grouper

½ teaspoon salt

1 egg white

1 tablespoon Chinese rice wine or dry sherry

3 teaspoons cornstarch, divided

⅓ cup plus 4 teaspoons water, divided

4½ teaspoons oyster sauce

1 teaspoon dark soy sauce

3 tablespoons vegetable or peanut oil, divided

2 thin slices ginger

1 teaspoon minced ginger

½ teaspoon minced garlic

1 scallion, finely chopped

¼ pound fresh mushrooms, thinly sliced

¼ teaspoon black pepper

1. Cut the fish fillets into 1½"–2" squares that are about ½" thick. Place the fish cubes in a large bowl and add the salt, egg white, rice wine or sherry, and 2 teaspoons cornstarch. Marinate the fish for 15 minutes.

2. In a small bowl, combine ⅓ cup water, oyster sauce, and dark soy sauce. In a separate small bowl, dissolve 1 teaspoon cornstarch into 4 teaspoons water.

   Heat a wok or skillet over medium-high heat until it is nearly smoking. Add 2 tablespoons oil. When the oil is hot, add the sliced ginger. Let brown for 2–3 minutes, then remove from the pan. Add the minced ginger, stir-fry for 10 seconds.

3. Add the fish. Let the fish sit in the pan briefly, then gently stir-fry the fish cubes for 1–2 minutes or until they turn white and are firm. Remove the fish and drain in a colander or on paper towels.

4. Heat 1 tablespoon oil in the wok or skillet. When the oil is hot, add the garlic and the scallion. Stir-fry for 10 seconds, then add the mushrooms. Stir-fry the mushrooms for 2 minutes or until they begin to darken. Sprinkle black pepper over the mushrooms.

5. Push the mushrooms to the sides of the pan. Add the oyster sauce mixture in the middle of the pan and bring to a boil. Add the cornstarch and water mixture into the sauce, stirring quickly to thicken.

6. When the sauce has thickened, add the fish back into the pan. Stir-fry for 1 minute. Serve hot.

PER SERVING | Calories: 121 | Fat: 0 | Protein: 22g | Sodium: 631mg | Fiber: 0.4g | Carbohydrates: 4.5g | Sugar: 0.8g

Sweet-and-Sour Fish

Cod or sole would both be good choices for this recipe.
Garnish the fish with lemon wedges and fresh cilantro before serving.

INGREDIENTS | SERVES 4

1 pound white fish fillets

½ medium red bell pepper, seeded and cut into bite-sized pieces

½ medium green bell pepper, seeded and cut into bite-sized pieces

1 cup Sweet-and-Sour Sauce (see Chapter 2)

2 tablespoons vegetable or peanut oil

4 thin slices ginger

2 scallions, cut into thirds

1½ tablespoons soy sauce

½ teaspoon black pepper

1. Rinse the fish fillets, pat dry, and cut into bite-sized pieces.

2. Add the chopped bell peppers to the sweet and sour sauce. Warm the sauce and peppers in a small saucepan over low heat while cooking the fish.

3. Heat a wok or skillet over medium-high heat until it is almost smoking. Add the oil. When the oil is hot, add the ginger slices and the chopped scallions. Stir-fry for about 10 seconds.

4. Add the fish cubes. Stir-fry the fish cubes for 2–3 minutes or until they are opaque. Splash with soy sauce and continue cooking, stirring gently, until the fish cubes are cooked through. Season with black pepper.

5. Bring the Sweet-and-Sour Sauce to a boil, stirring. Pour over the stir-fried fish and serve.

PER SERVING | Calories: 171 | Fat: 0.8g | Protein: 20g | Sodium: 484mg | Fiber: 0.8g | Carbohydrates: 18g | Sugar: 15g

Teriyaki Salmon with Oyster Mushrooms

Arctic char or lake trout are great substitutes if salmon is not available. Serve with jasmine or brown rice.

INGREDIENTS | SERVES 2

1 pound salmon fillets
¼ cup Teriyaki Sauce (see Chapter 2)
¼ teaspoon red pepper flakes
1 teaspoon minced ginger
1 garlic clove, minced
2 tablespoons vegetable oil
1 pint oyster mushrooms, sliced
2 scallions, cut into 1" pieces
2 tablespoons furikake

Furikake

Furikake is a common Japanese condiment that contains ingredients like toasted sesame seeds, seaweed flakes, and dried fish. If furikake is not available, you can substitute with toasted sesame seeds.

1. Rinse the salmon, pat dry, and cut into bite-sized pieces.

2. In a large bowl, whisk together the Teriyaki Sauce, red pepper flakes, ginger, and garlic. Add in the salmon and allow to marinate in the refrigerator for 10 minutes.

3. Heat a wok or large skillet over medium-high heat and add the vegetable oil. Once the oil is hot, add in the mushrooms and stir-fry for 1 minute.

4. Add in the salmon and scallions and toss to cook for 1 minute.

5. Add in a few spoonfuls of the marinade and continue cooking for an additional 1–2 minutes or until the salmon is just cooked. Sprinkle the salmon with furikake.

PER SERVING | Calories: 578 | Fat: 32g | Protein: 51g | Sodium: 1,917mg | Fiber: 3.8 | Carbohydrates: 19g | Sugar: 8.8g

Black Bean Squid

Scoring the squid tubes makes the edges curl up nicely when they are stir-fried.
For extra color, add a sliced carrot to the stir-fry with the onion.

INGREDIENTS | SERVES 4

1 pound large squid tubes

2 tablespoons Chinese fermented black beans

2 cloves garlic, chopped

2 tablespoons water

¼ cup chicken broth

2 teaspoons dark soy sauce

1 tablespoon Chinese rice wine or dry sherry

4 tablespoons vegetable or peanut oil, divided

2 slices ginger, cut into thin strips

1 small yellow onion, thinly sliced

2 small red bell peppers, seeded and chopped into large chunks

2 scallions, cut into 1" sections

1. Cut the squid tubes in half lengthwise. Score the squid tubes in a crisscross pattern by holding the knife at a 45-degree angle and making a series of cuts, and then holding the knife at a 120-degree angle and making a second series of cuts. Cut the scored squid into 1" squares.

2. Rinse the black beans under cold running water for 10 minutes, drain, and chop. Place the black beans in a bowl with the garlic and mash with a fork. Stir in the water. In a separate bowl, combine the chicken broth, dark soy sauce, and rice wine or sherry.

3. Heat a wok or skillet over medium-high heat until it is nearly smoking. Add 2 tablespoons oil. When the oil is hot, add half of the black bean mixture. Stir-fry for 30 seconds.

4. Add the squid. Stir-fry the squid for about 1 minute or until it turns white and the edges begin to curl. Remove the squid and drain in a colander or on paper towels.

5. Heat 2 tablespoons oil in the wok or skillet. When the oil is hot, add the remaining black bean mixture and the ginger. Stir-fry for 30 seconds, then add the onion. Stir-fry the onion for 1–2 minutes or until it begins to soften, then add the bell pepper. Stir-fry for 1 minute.

6. Pour in the chicken broth mixture and bring to a boil. Add the squid back into the pan. Stir in the scallions. Stir-fry for 1 minute to blend the flavors. Serve hot.

PER SERVING | Calories: 155 | Fat: 2g | Protein: 19g | Sodium: 293mg | Fiber: 2g | Carbohydrates: 12g | Sugar: 4g

Korean Spicy Stir-Fry Squid

In lieu of squid, try using cuttlefish in this recipe.

INGREDIENTS | SERVES 4

1 pound large squid tubes
2 tablespoons gojuchang paste
2 tablespoons soy sauce
1 teaspoon sesame oil
½ tablespoon honey
½ tablespoon rice wine vinegar
2 tablespoons vegetable oil
1 teaspoon finely minced ginger
2 garlic cloves, minced
1 small green bell pepper, trimmed, ribs and seeds removed, cut into 1" pieces
1 small yellow onion, cut into 1" pieces
2 scallions, cut into 1" pieces
½ teaspoon ground black pepper

1. Cut the squid tubes in half lengthwise. Score the squid tubes in a crisscross pattern by holding the knife at a 45-degree angle and making a series of cuts, and then holding the knife at a 120-degree angle and making a second series of cuts. Cut the scored squid into 1" squares.

2. In a small bowl, whisk together the gojuchang, soy sauce, sesame oil, honey, and vinegar. Set aside.

3. Heat a wok or large skillet over medium-high heat and add the vegetable oil. Once the oil is hot, add the ginger and garlic and stir-fry for 30–45 seconds.

4. Add in the bell pepper and yellow onion and cook for an additional 2–3 minutes.

5. Add the squid, scallions, and several spoonfuls of the gojuchang sauce. Cook for an additional 1–2 minutes or until the squid is opaque. Season with black pepper and serve immediately.

PER SERVING | Calories: 213 | Fat: 9g | Protein: 18g | Sodium: 615mg | Fiber: 1.6g | Carbohydrates: 12g | Sugar: 5g

Clams with Ginger and Lemongrass

This quick dish is full of aromatic flavors and pairs well with jasmine rice.

INGREDIENTS | SERVES 2

2 tablespoons vegetable oil

2 large garlic cloves, finely minced

1 shallot, finely minced

2 fresh lemongrass stalks, tender inner white bulbs only, minced

1 tablespoon ginger, minced

1 chili pepper, seeded and minced

½ cup Chinese rice wine or dry white wine

½ tablespoon fish sauce

2 scallions, cut into 1" pieces

1½ pounds littleneck or Manila clams, scrubbed and cleaned

Fresh cilantro leaves

1. Heat a wok or large skillet over medium heat and add the oil.

2. Once the oil is hot, add the garlic, shallot, lemongrass, ginger, and chili, and stir-fry for 30 seconds.

3. Add in the rice wine, fish sauce, and scallions.

4. Add in the clams, stir the contents, and cover with a lid. Allow the clams to cook for 4–5 minutes or until the shells have opened. Plate the clams and garnish with the cilantro. Serve hot.

PER SERVING | Calories: 468 | Fat: 17g | Protein: 43g | Sodium: 194mg | Fiber: 0.8g | Carbohydrates: 16g | Sugar: 1.8g

Clams with White Wine and Tomatoes

Pair with crusty bread for a perfect light meal.

INGREDIENTS | SERVES 4

2 tablespoons olive oil

1 large shallot, thinly sliced

3 large garlic cloves, finely minced

½ small fennel bulb, thinly sliced

1 cup chardonnay or other dry white wine

½ teaspoon dried crushed red pepper

2½ pounds littleneck clams, scrubbed and cleaned

1 cup fresh basil, roughly chopped

3 Roma tomatoes, seeded and diced

1 teaspoon kosher salt

1. Heat a wok or large skillet over medium heat and add the olive oil.

2. Once the oil is hot, add in the shallot, garlic, and fennel. Stir-fry for 1 minute until golden. Add in the white wine and the red pepper.

3. When the liquids come to a boil, add in the clams, cover with a lid, and cook for 4–5 minutes or until the clams have opened.

4. Stir in the tomatoes, basil, and salt. Serve hot.

PER SERVING | Calories: 326 | Fat: 9g | Protein: 36g | Sodium: 752mg | Fiber: 0.7g | Carbohydrates: 10g | Sugar: 1.8g

Spicy Clams in Black Bean Sauce

If Thai chilies are not available, serranos or habaneros offer a great, spicy alternative.

INGREDIENTS | SERVES 2

½ cup clam juice or chicken broth

2 tablespoons Chinese black bean sauce

2 tablespoons vegetable oil

2 large garlic cloves, finely minced

1 shallot, finely minced

1 teaspoon ginger, minced

2 Thai chili peppers, seeded and minced

1½ pound littleneck or Manila clams, scrubbed and cleaned

2 scallions, cut into 1" pieces

Cleaning Clams

Clams and other types of mollusks can accumulate a good amount of grit. When cooking with them, it is important to thoroughly clean them to avoid a sandy dish. Clams should be scrubbed with a vegetable brush under cool running water. Continue rinsing until the clams are free of grit.

1. In a small bowl, whisk the clam juice and black bean sauce together. Set aside.

2. Heat a wok or large skillet over medium-high heat until it is nearly smoking and add the oil. Once the oil is hot, add the garlic, shallot, ginger, and chilies and stir-fry for 30–45 seconds.

3. Stir in the clams and stir-fry for 1–2 minutes.

4. Add in the clam juice mixture and cover with a lid. Allow the clams to cook for 3–4 minutes or until the shells have opened.

5. Leaving the liquids in the wok, transfer the clams to a serving platter. Turn the heat to high and reduce the liquids to a thickened sauce.

6. Stir in the scallions and pour the sauce over the clams. Serve hot.

PER SERVING | Calories: 431 | Fat: 18g | Protein: 45g | Sodium: 503mg | Fiber: 1.8g | Carbohydrates: 19g | Sugar: 3g

Portuguese-Style Clams

Portuguese chouriço provides a deep flavor from the combination of paprika and smoked red pepper.

INGREDIENTS | SERVES 6

2 tablespoons olive oil

2 shallots, minced

2 garlic cloves, minced

½ teaspoon red chili flakes

¾ pound sliced Portuguese chouriço or Spanish chorizo

½ cup dry white wine

1 cup clam juice

1 (32-ounce) can crushed San Marzano tomatoes

4 pounds littleneck clams, scrubbed and cleaned

5 or 6 sprigs fresh thyme

½ cup chopped Italian parsley, plus more for garnish

5 or 6 lemon slices, plus more for garnish

1½ teaspoons kosher salt

1 teaspoon ground black pepper

1. Heat a wok or large skillet over medium heat and add the olive oil. Once the oil is hot, add in the shallots, garlic, and chili flakes. Stir-fry for 30 seconds.

2. Add in the chouriço slices. Cook for 1 minute.

3. Deglaze the pan with the wine and use a wooden spoon to scrape up the brown bits. Allow 2–3 minutes to reduce the liquids by half.

4. Add in the clam juice and tomatoes with their juices. Once the liquids come to a slow boil, carefully add in the clams, thyme, parsley, and lemon slices. Cover and cook for 4–5 minutes until the clams have opened.

5. Remove the clams to a serving dish. Season with salt and pepper. Ladle the broth over the clams and garnish with additional parsley and lemon wedges. Serve immediately.

PER SERVING | Calories: 322 | Fat: 8g | Protein: 40g | Sodium: 1,031mg | Fiber: 2g | Carbohydrates: 17g | Sugar: 4g

Chouriço and Chorizo

Chorizo or chouriço can be found either as a smoked or fresh sausage. Portuguese chouriço are sausages that are filled with ground pork, paprika, garlic, spices, and red wine. The sausages are then smoked and cured.

Belgian-Beer Mussels

These mussels are often served with french fries or toasted sliced baguettes.

INGREDIENTS | SERVES 2

2 tablespoons olive oil

2 tablespoons unsalted butter, divided

½ cup diced yellow onion

½ cup diced leeks, white and light green parts, washed and rinsed thoroughly

2 large garlic cloves, finely minced

4 springs fresh thyme

½ teaspoon dried crushed red pepper

2 pounds black mussels, scrubbed and debearded

¼ cup fresh tarragon leaves, chopped

6 ounces Belgian wheat beer

1½ teaspoons kosher salt

1 teaspoon ground black pepper

½ cup chopped fresh parsley

Bearded Mussels

Like clams, mussels need to be scrubbed to remove any grit or sand that may have accumulated. However, most mussels will also have brown threads attached called "beards" that must be removed prior to cooking. To do so, pull the beard out and up toward the hinge of the shell and discard.

1. Heat a wok or large skillet over medium heat and add the olive oil and 1 tablespoon butter.

   Once the oil is hot and the butter has melted, add in the onion, leeks, garlic cloves, thyme, and red pepper. Stir-fry for 1–2 minutes.

2. Add in the mussels, tarragon leaves, and beer. Cover with a lid and cook for 5–7 minutes or until the mussels have opened.

3. Leaving the liquids in the wok, transfer the mussels using a slotted spoon to a serving platter.

4. Turn the heat to high and whisk in the remaining tablespoon of butter to finish the sauce. Season the sauce with salt and pepper before pouring over the mussels.

5. Sprinkle with fresh parsley and serve immediately.

PER SERVING | Calories: 682 | Fat: 35g | Protein: 55g | Sodium: 3,068mg | Fiber: 2g | Carbohydrates: 28g | Sugar: 2g

Green Curry Mussels

Kaffir limes are common in Southeast Asian and South Asian cuisine. The fruit is highly aromatic and the leaves can be found fresh, frozen, or dried in most Asian grocery stores.

INGREDIENTS | SERVES 2

2 tablespoons vegetable oil

2 large garlic cloves, finely minced

1 fresh lemongrass stalk, tender inner white bulbs only, minced

4 thin slices ginger or galangal

1 jalapeño pepper, seeded and minced

2 tablespoons green curry paste

½ tablespoon fish sauce

4 Kaffir lime leaves

1 cup clam juice

½ cup coconut milk

2 pounds black mussels, scrubbed and debearded

¼ cup chopped Thai basil leaves or cilantro

Lime wedges

Galangal versus Ginger

Galangal is closely related to the ginger root and is often used in Southeast Asian cuisine. The aromatic flavor is similar to ginger with additional peppery notes.

1. Heat a wok or large skillet over medium-high heat and add the oil. Once the oil is hot, add the garlic, lemongrass, ginger, and jalapeño pepper and stir-fry for 30–45 seconds.

2. Stir in the curry paste, fish sauce, and Kaffir lime leaves and cook for 1 minute.

3. Add in the clam juice and coconut milk and allow the liquids to come to a boil.

4. Add in the mussels, stir the contents, and cover with a lid. Cook for 5–7 minutes or until the shells have opened.

5. Transfer the mussels to a large serving dish and sprinkle the top with Thai basil and serve with lime wedges on the side.

PER SERVING | Calories: 663 | Fat: 37g | Protein: 57g | Sodium: 1,460mg | Fiber: 0.2g | Carbohydrates: 22g | Sugar: 2g

Mussels in Saffron Sauce

The floral broth from the saffron and mussels is best served alongside toasted bread to soak up the fragrant juices.

INGREDIENTS | SERVES 4

2 tablespoons olive oil

2 tablespoons unsalted butter

1 large shallot, thinly sliced

3 large garlic cloves, finely minced

1 cup dry white wine

½ cup clam juice or chicken stock

¼ teaspoon saffron threads

3 pounds black mussels, scrubbed and debearded

1½ teaspoons kosher salt

1 teaspoon ground black pepper

¼ cup flat-leaf parsley, chopped

Golden Spice

Saffron is one of the most expensive spices in the world. Deriving from the saffron crocus, dishes requiring this decadent spice only require a few threads to lend deep, floral flavors.

1. Heat a wok or large skillet over medium heat and add the olive oil and butter. Once the oil is hot and butter has melted, add in the shallots and garlic and stir-fry for 30 seconds.

2. Add in the wine, clam juice, and saffron threads. Once the liquids come to a boil, add in the mussels, cover with a lid, and cook for 5–7 minutes or until the mussels have opened.

3. Season with salt and pepper. Transfer contents to a large serving dish and sprinkle the top with the parsley. Serve immediately.

PER SERVING | Calories: 461 | Fat: 20g | Protein: 41g | Sodium: 1,894mg | Fiber: 15g | Carbohydrates: 15g | Sugar: 1g

CHAPTER 8

Vegetables, Tofu, and Eggs

Spring Vegetable Medley

You can create your own combination of spring vegetables to use in this simple stir-fry. Bell peppers, green beans (or French haricots verts), and zucchini are all good choices.

INGREDIENTS | SERVES 2

¼ cup chicken broth

1½ tablespoons red wine vinegar

2 teaspoons granulated sugar

½ cup cauliflower florets

2 tablespoons vegetable or peanut oil

½ teaspoon minced garlic

½ teaspoon minced ginger

1 cup shredded red cabbage

1 teaspoon salt

1 small carrot, julienned

1. In a small bowl, combine the chicken broth, red wine vinegar, and sugar. Set aside.

2. Fill a large saucepan with enough water to cover the cauliflower and bring to a boil. Blanch the cauliflower in the boiling water for 2 minutes. Remove the cauliflower, rinse under cold running water, and drain thoroughly.

3. Heat a wok or skillet over medium-high heat until it is nearly smoking. Add the oil. When the oil is hot, add the garlic and ginger. Stir-fry for 10 seconds.

4. Add the shredded cabbage. Stir-fry for 2 minutes, sprinkling with the salt. Add the carrot and stir-fry for 1 minute. Add the cauliflower and stir-fry for 1 minute.

5. Add the chicken broth mixture. Bring to a boil and continue cooking for 1–2 minutes or until the vegetables are tender but still crisp.

PER SERVING | Calories: 65 | Fat: 0.7g | Protein: 2g | Sodium: 1,352mg | Fiber: 2g | Carbohydrates: 13g | Sugar: 7g

Stir-Fried Bok Choy

If you like, thicken the sauce by stirring in 1 teaspoon cornstarch mixed with 2 teaspoons water at the end of cooking. Stir quickly until the sauce has thickened and serve immediately.

INGREDIENTS | SERVES 4

1 pound bok choy

1 tablespoon oyster sauce

3 tablespoons chicken broth

2 tablespoons vegetable or peanut oil

2 cloves garlic, crushed

½ teaspoon salt

Beautiful Bok Choy

The most popular vegetable in Chinese cooking, bok choy has white stalks and beautiful emerald leaves. Normally, bok choy stalks are separated from the leaves and stir-fried for a bit longer. However, if you're lucky enough to find baby bok choy, a smaller version of regular bok choy with a more delicate flavor, simply cut it in half lengthwise before stir-frying.

1. Separate the leaves of the bok choy from the stalks. Cut the stalks diagonally into 2" pieces. Cut the leaves crosswise into 2" pieces.

2. In a small bowl, stir the oyster sauce into the chicken broth. Set aside.

3. Heat a wok or skillet over medium-high heat until it is almost smoking. Add the oil. When the oil is hot, add the crushed garlic. Stir-fry for 10 seconds.

4. Add the bok choy stalks. Add the salt. Stir-fry for 1 minute, then add the leaves. Stir-fry for 1 more minute or until the bok choy turns bright green.

5. Add the chicken broth/oyster sauce mixture into the wok. Bring to a boil. Stir-fry for 1 minute and serve hot.

PER SERVING | Calories: 23 | Fat: 0.4g | Protein: 2g | Sodium: 539mg | Fiber: 1g | Carbohydrates: 4g | Sugar: 1g

Mixed-Vegetable Stir-Fry

The combination of baby corn, carrots, and bean sprouts provides an interesting contrast in color and texture. You can adapt this basic recipe to make chop suey or egg foo yung.

INGREDIENTS | SERVES 2

2 tablespoons vegetable or peanut oil

1 clove garlic, crushed

2 slices ginger

½ teaspoon salt

2 medium carrots, peeled and cut on the diagonal into 1½" slices

1 teaspoon granulated sugar

1 (8-ounce) can baby corn, drained

1 cup mung bean sprouts

1 tablespoon sesame oil

1. Heat a wok or skillet over medium-high heat until it is nearly smoking. Add the oil. When the oil is hot, add the garlic and ginger. Stir-fry for 10 seconds until aromatic.

2. Stir in the salt and the carrots. Stir-fry for 1 minute, then stir in the sugar and the baby corn. Stir-fry for 1 minute.

3. Add the bean sprouts. Stir-fry for 30–60 seconds, taking care not to overcook the bean sprouts. Add more salt or sugar if desired.

4. Remove from heat and stir in the sesame oil. Serve hot.

PER SERVING | Calories: 122 | Fat: 7g | Protein: 4.5g | Sodium: 637mg | Fiber: 1.7g | Carbohydrates: 12g | Sugar: 5g

Stir-Fried Zucchini

Zucchini is the perfect vegetable for quick stir-frying, as it is high in moisture and not too tough.

INGREDIENTS | SERVES 2

1 tablespoon vegetable oil

1 large zucchini, cut on the diagonal into 1" slices

¼ teaspoon salt

¼ teaspoon black pepper

1 tablespoon soy sauce

1. Heat a wok or skillet over medium-high heat until it is nearly smoking. Add the oil.

2. When the oil is hot, add the zucchini. Sprinkle the salt and pepper over the zucchini. Stir-fry for 1 minute, then stir in the soy sauce.

3. Stir-fry the zucchini until it turns dark green and is tender but still crisp (about 3 minutes). Serve hot.

PER SERVING | Calories: 92 | Fat: 7g | Protein: 2g | Sodium: 756mg | Fiber: 1.7g | Carbohydrates: 5g | Sugar: 4g

Lucky Three Vegetables

This dish can be served with rice or on top of Basic Stir-Fry Noodles (see Chapter 9).

INGREDIENTS | SERVES 2

1½ tablespoons vegetable or peanut oil

2 teaspoons minced ginger

1 large red bell pepper

4 Napa cabbage leaves

½ teaspoon salt

1 cup canned straw mushrooms

2 tablespoons chicken broth or water

1. Cut the bell pepper in half, remove the seeds, and cut into thin strips. Cut the cabbage leaves crosswise into thin strips. Cut the straw mushrooms in half.

2. Heat a wok or skillet on medium-high heat until it is nearly smoking. Add the oil. When the oil is hot, add the ginger. Stir-fry for 10 seconds, until aromatic.

3. Add the pepper and cabbage. Sprinkle with salt. Stir-fry for 1 minute, then add the mushrooms. Stir in the chicken broth or water. Stir-fry for 1 more minute, then remove from the pan. Serve hot.

PER SERVING | Calories: 50 | Fat: 0.7g | Protein: 2.5g | Sodium: 989mg | Fiber: 3g | Carbohydrates: 9.5g | Sugar: 4g

Stir-Fried Cabbage

Many people don't realize that Napa cabbage, which is named after the Napa Valley region of California where it is cultivated, is actually a type of Chinese cabbage, also called celery cabbage.

INGREDIENTS | SERVES 4

1½ tablespoons vegetable or peanut oil

3 cloves garlic, crushed

1 pound Napa cabbage, cored and cut crosswise into thin strips

½ teaspoon sugar

¼ cup chicken broth

1. Heat a wok or skillet over medium-high heat until it is nearly smoking. Add the oil. When the oil is hot, add the garlic and the cabbage. Sprinkle with the sugar.

2. Add the chicken broth. Stir-fry the cabbage for 3–4 minutes, until it is tender but still crisp. Remove the garlic before serving.

PER SERVING | Calories: 29 | Fat: 0g | Protein: 1.7g | Sodium: 75mg | Fiber: 1g | Carbohydrates: 5g | Sugar: 2g

Mushrooms and Bamboo Shoots

Don't want to use the soaking liquid from the mushrooms in the stir-fry?
Feel free to substitute an equal amount of chicken broth.

INGREDIENTS | SERVES 2

6–8 dried black mushrooms

2 tablespoons vegetable or peanut oil

3 slices ginger, minced

1 (8-ounce) can sliced bamboo shoots, rinsed and drained

1 teaspoon brown sugar

1 teaspoon sesame oil

Chinese Dried Black Mushrooms

Also known as flower mushrooms, Chinese dried black mushrooms lend a rich, savory flavor to stir-fries, soups, and other dishes. The mushrooms are soaked in hot water before using, both to soften and to remove any dirt or grit. Traditional Chinese medical practitioners believe eating black mushrooms helps lower blood pressure.

1. Soak the dried black mushrooms in hot water for 25–30 minutes, until they have softened. Reserve ¼ cup of the liquid used to soak the mushrooms (strain the liquid if it has any grit from the mushrooms in it). Cut the stems off the mushrooms and discard.

2. Heat a wok or skillet over medium-high heat until it is nearly smoking. Add the oil. When the oil is hot, add the ginger. Stir-fry for 10 seconds, until the ginger is aromatic.

3. Add the dried mushrooms and the bamboo shoots. Stir-fry for 1 minute.

4. Add the reserved mushroom broth. Stir in the brown sugar. Cook for 1 minute to heat through.

5. Remove from the heat and stir in the sesame oil. Serve immediately.

PER SERVING | Calories: 50 | Fat: 2g | Protein: 2g | Sodium: 8mg | Fiber: 1.5g | Carbohydrates: 5.8g | Sugar: 4g

Stir-Fried Cauliflower

This recipe works for any type of cauliflower, but Romanesco broccoli, a form of the common cauliflower, makes a colorful substitute. Romanesco broccoli has a striking appearance due to its bright green color and conical buds.

INGREDIENTS | SERVES 4

1 pound cauliflower
1½ tablespoons white wine vinegar
2½ tablespoons water
1½ teaspoons granulated sugar
2 tablespoons olive oil
2 teaspoons minced ginger

1. Remove the outer leaves and the stalk from the cauliflower. Cut off the florets, leaving part of the stem attached. Soak the florets in cold water for 15 minutes. Drain thoroughly.

2. Fill a large saucepan with enough water to cover the cauliflower, and bring to a boil. Blanch the cauliflower in the boiling water for 2 minutes. Remove the cauliflower, rinse under cold running water, and drain thoroughly.

3. In a small bowl, combine the white wine vinegar, water, and sugar in a bowl. Set aside.

4. Heat a wok or skillet over medium-high heat until it is nearly smoking. Add the oil. When the oil is hot, add the ginger. Stir-fry for 10 seconds.

5. Add the cauliflower florets. Stir-fry for 1 minute, then pour the white wine and vinegar mixture over the top. Stir-fry for another 2 minutes or until the cauliflower is tender but still crisp, stirring vigorously to keep the cauliflower from browning. Serve immediately.

PER SERVING | Calories: 97 | Fat: 7g | Protein: 2g | Sodium: 34mg | Fiber: 2g | Carbohydrates: 7g | Sugar: 3g

Bamboo Shoots

If you live near an Asian market, feel free to use a fresh bamboo shoot in this recipe. Boil the shoots for 15 minutes to soften, and then cut into ¼"-thick slices.

INGREDIENTS | SERVES 4

1 (8-ounce) can bamboo shoots, rinsed and drained
1½ tablespoons dark soy sauce
1½ tablespoons chicken broth
1 teaspoon granulated sugar
1½ tablespoons vegetable or peanut oil
2 slices ginger
½ teaspoon sesame oil

Preparing Canned Vegetables

Fresh is always best, but it's often easier to find canned versions of Chinese vegetables such as water chestnuts, bamboo shoots, and baby corn. To get rid of any taste of tin from the can, rinse the vegetables under running water or blanch them briefly in boiling water.

1. Slice the bamboo shoots and pat dry with paper towels.

2. In a small bowl, combine the dark soy sauce, chicken broth, and sugar. Set aside.

3. Heat a wok or skillet on medium-high heat. Add the oil, swirling it around the wok or skillet so that it covers the sides. When the oil is hot, add the ginger and stir-fry for 15 seconds.

4. Add the bamboo shoots. Stir-fry for 1 minute, then add the sauce. Stir for a few more seconds to mix the vegetables with the sauce; turn down the heat. Cover and simmer for 3 minutes or until the vegetables are tender.

5. Remove the wok or skillet from the heat. Stir in the sesame oil. Remove the ginger slices or leave in as desired. Serve immediately.

PER SERVING | Calories: 25 | Fat: 0.8g | Protein: 1g | Sodium: 512mg | Fiber: 0.8g | Carbohydrates: 3.5g | Sugar: 2g

Chinese Broccoli with Oyster Sauce

Can't find Chinese broccoli? Broccolini or green asparagus would be just as delicious.

INGREDIENTS | SERVES 4

2 tablespoons vegetable oil

1 teaspoon minced garlic

2 ginger slices

1 pound Chinese broccoli, washed and trimmed

½ cup vegetable stock

3 tablespoons oyster sauce

1. Heat wok over medium heat and add oil. Add the garlic and ginger and cook for 15 seconds.

2. Add in the broccoli. Toss broccoli in the wok and cook for 1 minute before pouring in the vegetable stock. Cover and let simmer for 5 minutes or until broccoli is tender.

3. Transfer the broccoli to a plate. Whisk 1 tablespoon of the liquids from the wok with the oyster sauce. Drizzle over the broccoli and serve immediately.

PER SERVING | Calories: 106 | Fat: 7g | Protein: 3g | Sodium: 406mg | Fiber: 3g | Carbohydrates: 9g | Sugar: 2g

Miso Eggplant

Japanese eggplants are slightly different from their Western counterparts—their skins are thinner and they do not contain as many seeds.

INGREDIENTS | SERVES 4

1 cup Chili Ponzu Marinade (see Chapter 2)

1 teaspoon minced yellow miso paste

1 pound Japanese eggplant, sliced at a diagonal

2 tablespoons vegetable oil

1 teaspoon minced garlic

2 tablespoons mirin

2 scallions, diced

1. In a bowl, whisk together the marinade and miso paste. Add the eggplants and allow to sit for 15 minutes.

2. Heat oil in a wok over medium heat. Add the garlic and cook for 20 seconds until fragrant.

3. Add in the eggplant. Stir-fry for 1 minute and then splash in the mirin. Continue cooking the eggplant for 2–3 minutes or until tender. Stir in the scallions and serve hot.

PER SERVING | Calories: 258 | Fat: 21g | Protein: 3g | Sodium: 1,834mg | Fiber: 3g | Carbohydrates: 16g | Sugar: 5.8g

Stir-Fried Shiitake and Scallions

*Although dried shiitake mushrooms are readily available,
it would be best to use fresh shiitake mushrooms in this dish.*

INGREDIENTS | SERVES 2

2 tablespoons mirin
1 tablespoon oyster sauce
2 tablespoons vegetable oil
1 teaspoon minced garlic
½ teaspoon minced ginger
1 small onion, thinly sliced
10 ounces shiitake mushrooms, sliced
4 scallions, cut into 1" pieces
¼ teaspoon black pepper

1. In a small bowl, whisk together mirin and oyster sauce.

2. Heat a wok over medium heat and add oil. Cook the garlic and ginger for 10 seconds.

3. Add in the onion. Stir-fry for 1 minute and then toss in the mushrooms. Stir-fry for 1 minute.

4. Pour in the mirin/oyster sauce mixture. Toss and cook for 2 minutes or until mushrooms become tender.

5. Stir in the scallions and black pepper; serve.

PER SERVING | Calories: 149 | Fat: 13g | Protein: 0.9g | Sodium: 251mg | Fiber: 1g | Carbohydrates: 6g | Sugar: 2g

Indian-Spiced Okra

In India this spicy vegetable dish would be cooked in a kadhai, the Indian version of the Chinese wok.

INGREDIENTS | SERVES 4

2 tablespoons peanut or vegetable oil
3 cloves garlic, minced
¼ teaspoon cumin
1 teaspoon red pepper flakes
1 shallot, chopped
1 pound okra, cut on the diagonal into slices ¼"–½" thick
1 large tomato, cut into 6 wedges, each wedge halved
1 teaspoon curry powder
1 teaspoon brown sugar

1. Heat a wok or skillet over medium-high heat until it is nearly smoking. Add the oil. When the oil is hot, add the garlic, cumin, red pepper flakes, and the shallot. Stir-fry for 30 seconds or until the shallot begins to soften.

2. Add the okra. Stir-fry for about 4 minutes or until is the okra just starts to turn golden brown.

3. Add the tomato, curry powder, and the brown sugar, and stir-fry for 1 minute. Serve hot or cold.

PER SERVING | Calories: 80 | Fat: 2g | Protein: 4g | Sodium: 13mg | Fiber: 4.8g | Carbohydrates: 12g | Sugar: 4g

Thai-Inspired Creamed Corn

Made from the fruit of the tropical palm tree, palm oil is the oil of choice for Thai stir-fry dishes. If unavailable, substitute peanut oil or a vegetable oil such as canola.

INGREDIENTS | SERVES 4

4 ears corn
1 teaspoon cornstarch
4 teaspoons water
2 tablespoons palm oil
3 cloves garlic, crushed
2 tablespoons fish sauce
½ cup coconut milk
2 Kaffir lime leaves
1 tablespoon palm sugar
1 teaspoon white pepper

Storing Canned Vegetables

If you have leftover straw mushrooms, water chestnuts, bamboo shoots, or baby corn, place the vegetables in a sealed container with enough water to cover, and store in the refrigerator. Stored in this manner, the canned vegetables will last for 3 or 4 days. For a fresher taste, change the water daily.

1. Remove the outer husk and the silky threads covering the corn kernels. Use a sharp knife to cut off the kernels. Rinse the corn kernels under warm running water. Drain thoroughly.

2. In a small bowl, dissolve the cornstarch into the water. Set aside.

3. Heat a wok or skillet over medium-high heat until it is almost smoking. Add the palm oil. When the oil is hot, add the crushed garlic and stir-fry for 10 seconds.

4. Add the corn. Stir-fry the corn for 1 minute, then add in the fish sauce and stir-fry for 1 minute. Add the coconut milk and Kaffir leaves. Stir in the palm sugar.

5. Bring the coconut milk mixture to a boil. Stir in the cornstarch and water mixture and keep stirring for 1–2 minutes or until thickened. Stir in the white pepper. Remove the crushed garlic before serving.

PER SERVING | Calories: 259 | Fat: 13g | Protein: 4.8g | Sodium: 11mg | Fiber: 3.7g | Carbohydrates: 35g | Sugar: 8g

Double Nutty Fiddlehead Greens with Sesame Seeds

*Toasting sesame seeds gives them a pleasant nutty flavor,
which nicely complements the natural nutty flavor of fiddlehead greens.*

INGREDIENTS | SERVES 2

1 pound fiddlehead greens, fresh or frozen

2 tablespoons olive oil

2 teaspoons minced ginger

1 teaspoon garlic salt

2 teaspoons sesame oil

2 tablespoons toasted sesame seeds

1. If using freshly picked fiddleheads, wash to remove any dirt and drain thoroughly.

2. Heat a wok or skillet over medium-high heat until it is nearly smoking. Add the olive oil. When the oil is hot, add the ginger and stir-fry for 10 seconds. Add the greens. Stir-fry for 1 minute, then stir in the salt.

3. Stir-fry for 1–2 more minutes, until the greens are tender but still firm. Remove from the heat and stir in the sesame oil. Garnish with sesame seeds.

PER SERVING | Calories: 293 | Fat: 23g | Protein: 11g | Sodium: 1,182mg | Fiber: 1g | Carbohydrates: 15g | Sugar: 0g

Glazed Carrots

*Glazed carrots make an excellent side dish for family dinners and special occasions.
They also add a bit of color to the spread.*

INGREDIENTS | SERVES 4

2 tablespoons olive oil

1 tablespoon minced garlic

2 teaspoons minced ginger

4 small carrots, peeled and thinly sliced on the diagonal into ½" slices

¼ teaspoon cayenne pepper

½ cup chicken broth

2 tablespoons brown sugar

1. Heat a wok or skillet over medium-high heat until it is nearly smoking. Add the oil. When the oil is hot, add the garlic and ginger and stir-fry for 10 seconds.

2. Add the carrots. Stir-fry for 1–2 minutes. Stir in the cayenne pepper. Add the chicken broth and the brown sugar. Bring to a boil. Cover and cook for 4 minutes.

3. Uncover and cook, stirring, until the carrots are tender but still crisp and nicely glazed with the broth and sugar mixture, which has been reduced (total cooking time is about 8 minutes). Serve hot.

PER SERVING | Calories: 134 | Fat: 7g | Protein: 1.5g | Sodium: 183mg | Fiber: 2g | Carbohydrates: 16g | Sugar: 10g

Burgundy Mushrooms

Stir-frying mushrooms releases their moisture, allowing them to soak up the burgundy and seasonings. If using reduced-sodium beef broth, you may want to add a bit of salt or salt substitute to the mushrooms in addition to the pepper.

INGREDIENTS | SERVES 2

¼ cup burgundy wine

½ cup beef broth

1½ tablespoons vegetable or peanut oil

1 teaspoon minced ginger

1 teaspoon minced garlic

2 shallots, chopped

½ teaspoon dried parsley

½ teaspoon dried basil

1 pound button mushrooms

¼ teaspoon black pepper

2 tablespoons unsalted butter

1. In a small bowl, combine the burgundy and beef broth. Set aside.

2. Heat a wok or skillet over medium-high heat until it is nearly smoking. Add the oil. When the oil is hot, add the minced ginger and garlic and stir-fry for 10 seconds.

3. Add the chopped shallots. Sprinkle the dried parsley and basil over the shallots and stir-fry for 1 minute, until the shallots begin to soften.

4. Add the mushrooms. Stir-fry for about 2 minutes, until they have browned. Stir in the black pepper. Add the burgundy mixture and lower the heat.

5. Simmer the mushrooms for 6–8 minutes. Remove from heat and stir in the butter. Serve immediately.

PER SERVING | Calories: 137 | Fat: 11g | Protein: 1g | Sodium: 199mg | Fiber: 0.3g | Carbohydrates: 2g | Sugar: 0.2g

Swiss Chard with Crispy Bacon

*If you prefer, you may leave out the bacon and add an additional
½ tablespoon of oil when cooking the shallots and garlic.*

INGREDIENTS | SERVES 2

½ tablespoon vegetable oil

3 slices smoked bacon, diced

1 tablespoon minced garlic

2 tablespoons minced shallots

½ teaspoon red pepper flakes

6 cups chopped Swiss chard

2 tablespoons red wine vinegar

¼ teaspoon kosher salt

¼ teaspoon black pepper

1. Heat the oil in a wok over medium heat. Add the bacon and cook until crispy, about 6–8 minutes. Use a slotted spoon to remove the bacon and drain on plates lined with paper towels. Chop bacon and set aside.

2. Leaving the bacon grease in the wok, add the garlic and shallots and cook for 1 minute. Add the pepper flakes and cook for 30 seconds, then stir in the chard. Stir-fry 3–4 minutes or until leaves are tender.

3. Remove from heat and stir in vinegar, salt, pepper, and crispy bacon bits. Serve immediately.

PER SERVING | Calories: 224 | Fat: 19g | Protein: 6g | Sodium: 811mg | Fiber: 2g | Carbohydrates: 7g | Sugar: 1g

Fried Plantains

*Cousin to the banana, plantains are typically lower in sugar and have
a higher level of starch. They are a great source of potassium and fiber.*

INGREDIENTS | SERVES 2

1 large plantain, peeled and sliced
  ½" thick

½ cup vegetable oil

½ teaspoon kosher salt

Plantain Chips

To make plantain chips, use a mandolin to slice thin strips of plantain and then deep-fry them for 3–4 minutes until crispy. Season the chips while they're hot with a little salt and cayenne pepper.

1. Heat oil in a wok to medium heat. Fry the plantain slices for 2 minutes on each side until they are golden brown and edges begin to caramelize.

2. Drain on plates lined with paper towels and season immediately with salt. Serve warm.

PER SERVING | Calories: 534 | Fat: 54g | Protein: 0.6g | Sodium: 589mg | Fiber: 1g | Carbohydrates: 13g | Sugar: 7g

Parmesan Brussels Sprouts

Brussels sprouts look like mini cabbages and grow on large stalks. They can be somewhat bitter. However, blanching the sprouts prior to cooking can remove some of that bitterness.

INGREDIENTS | SERVES 4

2 tablespoons olive oil

1 tablespoon unsalted butter

½ teaspoon red pepper flakes

4 fresh sage leaves

1 tablespoon minced shallots

1 tablespoon minced garlic

1 pound blanched Brussels sprouts, trimmed and quartered

¼ teaspoon kosher salt

¼ teaspoon black pepper

½ tablespoon lemon zest

¼ cup freshly grated Parmesan cheese

Blanching

Blanching is a cooking process that involves submerging a product into boiling water for a short time and then quickly transferring it into an ice bath to stop the cooking process. By shocking the product, it will retain its bright color as well as partially cook the item.

1. Heat oil in a wok over medium heat. Add the butter and swirl the wok around until it melts. Add in the red pepper flakes, sage, shallots, and garlic. Stir the ingredients around for 30 seconds.

2. Add in the Brussels sprouts and continue stir-frying for 3–4 minutes until the sprouts are browned and edges have begun to caramelize. Season with salt and pepper.

3. Pour the contents of the wok on a platter. Sprinkle with lemon zest and Parmesan cheese over the top. Serve hot.

PER SERVING | Calories: 139 | Fat: 10g | Protein: 4g | Sodium: 176mg | Fiber: 4g | Carbohydrates: 11g | Sugar: 2.5g

Vegetarian Fajitas

*You can load up this basic vegetarian filling with raw vegetables,
such as sliced tomato, avocado, or raw sweet red onion.*

INGREDIENTS | SERVES 4

¼ cup Fajita Marinade (see Chapter 2)

2 large portobello mushroom caps, sliced

2 tablespoons vegetable or peanut oil

½ tablespoon minced garlic

1 small white onion, sliced

1 large yellow bell pepper, seeded and sliced

1 large red bell pepper, seeded and sliced

¼ cup vegetable broth

2 scallions, cut on the diagonal into thirds

4 large tortillas

1 cup Fresh Pico de Gallo (see Chapter 2)

¼ cup chopped cilantro leaves

What Is a Diagonal Cut?

Recipes frequently call for vegetables to be cut on the diagonal prior to stir-frying. Diagonal cutting exposes more of the vegetable's surface area, allowing it to cook more quickly. To cut vegetables on the diagonal, hold the knife or cleaver at a 60-degree angle and cut the vegetable crosswise.

1. In a large bowl, combine the marinade with the mushrooms. Set aside for 15 minutes

2. Heat a wok with the oil over medium heat. Add the garlic and onion, and stir-fry for 15 seconds. Toss in the bell peppers and cook for 1 minute.

3. Add in the mushrooms and vegetable broth and cook for 2 minutes or until the mushrooms become tender and the broth has nearly evaporated. Stir in the scallions and remove from heat.

4. Warm the tortillas in a cast-iron skillet. Take 1 tortilla at a time and lay it on a flat surface. Spoon a portion of the stir-fried vegetable mixture onto the tortilla, making sure the filling isn't too close to the edges. Place a heaping spoonful of the pico de gallo on top of the mixture, then sprinkle on the cilantro. Fold in the left and right sides of the tortilla and tuck in the edges. Repeat with the remainder of the tortillas until the filling is used up.

PER SERVING | Calories: 103 | Fat: 4g | Protein: 2g | Sodium: 995mg | Fiber: 2.5g | Carbohydrates: 13g | Sugar: 5g

Saag Aloo (Indian Spinach and Potato Curry)

Garam masala is a fragrant mixture of cumin, coriander, cardamom, and other spices.

INGREDIENTS | SERVES 4

1 tablespoon minced ginger

½ tablespoon minced garlic

1 jalapeño pepper, seeded and diced

1 teaspoon garam masala, divided

¼ cup vegetable stock

½ cup vegetable oil

1 large Russet potato, peeled and cubed

½ cup diced white onions

1 (16-ounce) bag frozen spinach, thawed, drained, and chopped

1 tablespoon water

¼ teaspoon cayenne

½ teaspoon kosher salt

2 tablespoons plain low-fat yogurt

1. In a blender, purée the ginger, garlic, jalapeño, ½ teaspoon garam masala, and vegetable stock. Set aside.

2. Heat the oil in a wok over medium-high heat. Fry the potato cubes for 2 minutes or until golden brown. Remove to a paper-towel-lined plate.

3. Lower the heat to medium and carefully discard all but 1 tablespoon oil from the wok. Add the onions and cook for 2 minutes until browned. Stir in the remaining ½ teaspoon garam masala and allow the spice to toast for 30 seconds.

4. Add the spinach with water and allow 1–2 minutes for the leaves to wilt.

5. Stir in the puréed ginger-garlic mixture and reduce heat to medium low. Cook, stirring often, for about 5–6 minutes until the spinach has broken down and melded into the liquids.

6. Stir in the cayenne, salt, and yogurt. Add fried potatoes to the spinach and cover. Simmer for 2–3 minutes to allow the flavors to marry. Serve warm.

PER SERVING | Calories: 366 | Fat: 28g | Protein: 7g | Sodium: 389mg | Fiber: 5g | Carbohydrates: 25g | Sugar: 2.8g

Portobello Pesto Burgers

*The strong, "meaty" flavor of portobello mushrooms makes them a
popular substitute for meat, particularly ground beef, among vegetarians.*

INGREDIENTS | SERVES 6

6 large portobello mushrooms, stems removed

2 tablespoons olive oil

½ teaspoon kosher salt

¼ teaspoon black pepper

2 tablespoons vegetable oil

6 slices pepper jack cheese

1 cup Basil Pesto (see Chapter 2)

6 hamburger buns, toasted

2 Roma tomatoes, sliced

2 cups arugula leaves

1. Rub the mushrooms with olive oil and season with salt and pepper. Preheat oven broiler.

2. Heat a wok or skillet over medium heat and add the vegetable oil. When the oil is hot, add the mushrooms. If needed, stir-fry in batches for 2 minutes each until tender.

3. Transfer the mushrooms to a baking sheet and top each cap with a slice of cheese. Place the baking sheet underneath the broiler until the cheese melts and becomes bubbly. Remove and set aside.

4. Smear a few spoonfuls of pesto on both sides of each hamburger bun. Place the mushroom on one side and top with a tomato slice, arugula, and the top of the bun. Repeat with the remaining burgers and serve immediately.

PER SERVING | Calories: 330 | Fat: 32g | Protein: 9g | Sodium: 512mg | Fiber: 0.6g | Carbohydrates: 2g | Sugar: 1g

Vegetarian Jambalaya

Imitation ground beef crumbles are a good choice for this recipe.
Feel free to use white or brown rice as desired.

INGREDIENTS | SERVES 4

3 tablespoons olive oil, divided

2 cloves garlic, crushed

1 teaspoon cayenne pepper

1 medium white onion, chopped

2 okra, cut on the diagonal into thin slices

1¼ cups vegetable broth, or as needed

1 medium green bell pepper, seeded, cut into bite-sized chunks

2 medium tomatoes, halved and thinly sliced

1 teaspoon salt

1½ cups cooked rice

4 fresh thyme sprigs

¼ teaspoon dried oregano

1 cup vegetarian meat substitute

¼ teaspoon black pepper

1 bunch fresh parsley

1. Heat a wok or skillet over medium-high heat until it is nearly smoking. Add 2 tablespoons oil. When the oil is hot, add the garlic and the cayenne pepper and stir-fry for 10 seconds.

2. Add the onion. Stir-fry the onion for about 2 minutes, until it begins to soften.

3. Add the okra. Continue stir-frying for 2 minutes, splashing with a bit of vegetable broth if it begins to dry out.

4. Add the green bell pepper and tomatoes. Continue stir-frying until the green vegetables are tender but still crisp (about 2 minutes). Add more broth if needed while stir-frying and season the vegetables with salt. Remove the vegetables from the pan.

5. Heat 1 tablespoon oil in the wok or skillet. When the oil is hot, add the rice. Stir-fry for 1 minute until the grains turn a light brown. Stir in the thyme, oregano, and the meat substitute. Stir-fry for 1 minute.

6. Add 1 cup vegetable broth. Bring to a boil. Add the stir-fried vegetables. Stir in the black pepper.

7. Continue stir-frying for 2–3 minutes to mix all the ingredients together and until most of the liquid is absorbed. Garnish with fresh parsley and serve immediately.

PER SERVING | Calories: 325 | Fat: 16g | Protein: 12g | Sodium: 926mg | Fiber: 2g | Carbohydrates: 35g | Sugar: 3g

Vegetarian Chop Suey

*Instead of adding the cashews in the final stages of cooking, you can stir-fry
them separately. Stir-fry 1 minute, taking care not to burn the cashews,
and then remove from the pan. Add the cashews to the chop suey just before serving.*

INGREDIENTS | SERVES 4

½ cup vegetable broth

2 tablespoons soy sauce

1 teaspoon cornstarch

2 tablespoons vegetable or peanut oil

4 thin slices ginger, minced

1 medium onion, chopped

3 cups packaged fresh or frozen stir-fry
vegetable mix

1 cup mung bean sprouts

¼ teaspoon salt

½ cup cashews

1 teaspoon granulated sugar

¼ teaspoon black pepper

1. In a small bowl, combine the vegetable broth and soy sauce. Whisk in the cornstarch.

2. Heat a wok or skillet over medium-high heat until it is nearly smoking. Add the oil. When the oil is hot, add the sliced ginger and stir-fry for about 10 seconds.

3. Add the onion. Stir-fry the onion until it begins to soften (about 2 minutes).

4. Add the stir-fry vegetable mix. Stir-fry according to the package directions or until the vegetables are tender but still crisp.

5. Add the mung bean sprouts and the salt. Stir-fry for about 30 seconds.

6. Add the vegetable broth mixture. Bring to a boil, stirring continually. Stir in the cashews and the sugar. Add black pepper and serve hot.

PER SERVING | Calories: 103 | Fat: 2g | Protein: 5g |
Sodium: 767mg | Fiber: 0.6g | Carbohydrates: 16g | Sugar: 4g

Mushroom Risotto

Try an assortment of mushrooms—such as portobello, oyster, and shiitake—for a rich, earthy flavor.

INGREDIENTS | SERVES 6

½ cup hot water

½ ounce dried porcini mushrooms

3 tablespoons olive oil, divided

1½ tablespoons minced garlic, divided

1 pound sliced fresh mushrooms

½ teaspoon fresh thyme leaves

1 dried bay leaf

1 tablespoon unsalted butter

¼ teaspoon kosher salt

¼ teaspoon black pepper

4 cups mushroom or vegetable stock

¼ cup minced shallots

1 cup Arborio rice

½ cup dry white wine

½ cup grated Parmesan cheese

¼ teaspoon white pepper

2 tablespoons chopped Italian parsley

1. In a bowl, add the hot water to the dried porcinis. Allow to reconstitute for 20 minutes. Remove the porcinis and roughly chop. Strain and reserve the mushroom liquid.

2. Heat 1 tablespoon oil in a wok over medium heat. Add ½ tablespoon garlic, fresh mushrooms, thyme, bay leaf, and butter. Sauté for 3–5 minutes until lightly browned; season with salt and pepper. Add the dried porcini mushrooms and sauté for 1 minute, then transfer to a plate.

3. In a small pot, bring the mushroom or vegetable stock to a low simmer.

4. Heat remaining olive oil in a wok to medium heat, add the shallots and remaining garlic, and cook until softened, about 1–2 minutes. Add the rice and stir quickly until it is well-coated and opaque. Lower the heat to medium low. Stir in wine and porcini-soaking liquid. Cook, stirring frequently, until the liquid is nearly all evaporated.

5. Ladle 1 cup of the broth into the rice. Simmer and slowly stir until the rice has absorbed the liquid. Add the remaining broth, 1 cup at a time. Continue to simmer and stir, allowing the rice to absorb each addition of broth before adding more. Cooking should take approximately 20 minutes in total.

6. Transfer the mushrooms (reserving about 2–3 tablespoons) to the rice mixture. Stir in Parmesan cheese and white pepper, and cook briefly until melted. Spoon risotto into dishes and top with a few of the reserved mushrooms and chopped parsley before serving.

PER SERVING | Calories: 285 | Fat: 11g | Protein: 9.5g | Sodium: 235mg | Fiber: 2.5g | Carbohydrates: 33g | Sugar: 2g

Eggplant Parmesan

Like mushrooms, eggplants are somewhat "meaty" and offer a wonderful vegetarian option to dishes. Serve with pasta or roasted potatoes.

INGREDIENTS | SERVES 4

1 large eggplant, cut into ½" pieces
1 tablespoon Italian seasoning
½ teaspoon black pepper
1 tablespoon kosher salt
½ cup grated Parmesan cheese
¾ cup all-purpose flour
3 large eggs, beaten
1 cup Italian bread crumbs
4 tablespoons vegetable oil
2 cups Marinara Sauce (see Chapter 2)
8 slices mozzarella cheese
¼ cup chopped fresh Italian parsley

1. Season the eggplant with Italian seasoning, pepper, and salt.

2. In a shallow dish, mix together the Parmesan cheese and flour. In a separate dish, place the beaten eggs. In a third dish place the Italian bread crumbs.

3. Working with 1 piece of eggplant at a time, dredge the eggplant into the flour mixture, then in the beaten eggs, and finally the bread crumbs. Use fingers to gently adhere the bread crumbs to the eggplant and place on a baking sheet. Repeat with the remaining eggplant slices.

4. Heat wok over medium heat and add 2 tablespoons vegetable oil. In batches, fry the eggplant, for 1–2 minutes on each side until golden. Transfer the fried eggplant to a plate and tent with aluminum foil. Repeat with the remaining eggplant, adding more oil as needed.

5. Preheat oven broiler. Place the eggplant in a baking dish. Cover the tops with the Marinara Sauce and place 1 slice cheese on top of each eggplant slice. Broil until the cheese has bubbled and browned. Top the eggplant with parsley.

PER SERVING | Calories: 648 | Fat: 38g | Protein: 29g | Sodium: 3,023mg | Fiber: 3.6g | Carbohydrates: 45g | Sugar: 5g

Fried Tofu with Tomato Sauce

If you are unable to find prefried tofu, simply take firm tofu cubes and blot dry with paper towels to remove excess moisture. Heat vegetable oil to 375°F and deep-fry until golden brown (about 4–5 minutes).

INGREDIENTS | SERVES 4

1 tablespoon vegetable oil

1 tablespoon minced garlic

¼ cup diced shallots

4 Roma tomatoes, seeded and roughly diced

2 scallions, thinly sliced

1 red jalapeño, thinly sliced

¼ cup ketchup

1 tablespoon fish sauce

4 cups fried tofu, cubed

½ teaspoon black pepper

¼ cup cups chopped cilantro

2 cups steamed white rice

1. In a wok, heat oil over medium heat and add the garlic and shallots. Cook for about 2 minutes.

2. Add tomatoes, scallions, and jalapeño and cook for an additional 2–3 minutes until softened.

3. Stir in ketchup and fish sauce. Lower the heat and simmer for about 5 minutes.

4. Toss in fried tofu and coat evenly. Season with black pepper and garnish with fresh cilantro. Serve with rice.

PER SERVING | Calories: 431 | Fat: 4g | Protein: 8g | Sodium: 176mg | Fiber: 3g | Carbohydrates: 89g | Sugar: 7g

Tofu and Eggplant Stir-Fry

Can't find Thai basil? Substitute with sweet basil and a few pinches of coriander powder. This dish pairs well with jasmine rice.

INGREDIENTS | SERVES 4

1 (12.3-ounce) block firm tofu, cut into 1" cubes

4 tablespoons vegetable oil, divided

1 small eggplant, cubed

1 small red bell pepper, seeded and diced

2 red chilies, minced

1 tablespoon minced garlic

2 tablespoons minced shallots

2 scallions, chopped

1 tablespoon fish sauce

½ cup chopped Thai basil

1. Dry the tofu with paper towels to remove excess moisture.

2. Heat 2 tablespoons oil in a wok over medium heat. Add the tofu and stir-fry for 2–3 minutes until golden brown. Transfer to a plate.

3. Add 1 tablespoon oil to wok and swirl it around the pan. Stir-fry the eggplant and bell peppers for 2 minutes, tossing the wok every so often. Remove from wok and add to the tofu.

4. Heat the remaining 1 tablespoon oil and add the chilies, garlic, shallots, and scallions. Stir and cook for 1 minute.

5. Return the tofu, eggplant, and bell peppers to the wok and add the fish sauce.

6. Remove from heat and stir in the basil.

PER SERVING | Calories: 201 | Fat: 16g | Protein: 7g | Sodium: 36mg | Fiber: 1g | Carbohydrates: 7g | Sugar: 3g

Mapo Tofu

While ground pork is traditionally used to make mapo tofu, ground beef can be used as well. If Szechuan peppercorn is unavailable, you may substitute ground coriander.

INGREDIENTS | SERVES 4

½ pound ground pork

1 tablespoon soy sauce

1 teaspoon granulated sugar

¼ teaspoon black pepper

3 teaspoons cornstarch, divided

4 teaspoons water plus 2 tablespoons, divided

1 tablespoon Chinese fermented black beans

2 cloves garlic, minced

2 tablespoons vegetable or peanut oil

2 thin slices ginger, minced

½ tablespoon chili paste

1 small green bell pepper, chopped into bite-sized chunks

½ cup chicken broth

¾ pound firm tofu, drained and cut into ½" cubes

1 teaspoon freshly ground Szechuan peppercorn

1. In a large bowl, combine the ground pork with the soy sauce, sugar, black pepper, and 1 teaspoon cornstarch. Marinate the pork for 15 minutes.

2. In a small bowl, dissolve 2 teaspoons cornstarch into 4 teaspoons water. Set aside.

3. Rinse the black beans under cold running water for 10 minutes, drain, and chop. Place the black beans in a bowl with the garlic and mash with a fork. Stir in 2 tablespoons water.

4. Heat a wok or skillet over medium-high heat until it is nearly smoking. Add the oil. When the oil is hot, add the minced ginger. Stir-fry for 10 seconds.

5. Add the ground pork. Stir-fry the pork for 2–3 minutes or until it is no longer pink and is nearly cooked through.

6. Add the chili paste and the mashed black beans and garlic. Stir-fry for about 30 seconds, then add the bell pepper. Stir-fry for 1 minute, stirring to mix the bell pepper and pork in with the seasonings. Add 1 tablespoon of the chicken broth if the green pepper begins to dry out.

7. Add the chicken broth. Bring to a boil, then add the tofu cubes. Stir-fry for 1 minute, stirring gently. Stir in the ground Szechuan peppercorn.

8. Stir the cornstarch and water mixture, then add into the pan, stirring to thicken. Serve hot.

PER SERVING | Calories: 238 | Fat: 24g | Protein: 16g | Sodium: 371mg | Fiber: 1g | Carbohydrates: 9g | Sugar: 3g

Mu Shu Tofu

Sweet and spicy hoisin sauce adds extra flavor to the tofu in this vegetarian take on a classic northern Chinese recipe.

INGREDIENTS | SERVES 2

½ pound firm tofu, drained and cut into ½" cubes

1 tablespoon dark soy sauce

1 tablespoon hoisin sauce

3 large eggs

½ teaspoon salt

¼ teaspoon black pepper

3 tablespoons vegetable or peanut oil, divided

2 thin slices ginger, chopped

1 clove garlic, chopped

¼ pound fresh mushrooms, thinly sliced

½ cup canned sliced bamboo shoots, drained

1 tablespoon plus ¼ cup water, divided

1 teaspoon granulated sugar

2 scallions, cut diagonally into 1" slices

1. In a medium bowl, combine the tofu cubes with the dark soy sauce and hoisin sauce.

2. In a separate bowl, lightly beat the eggs, stirring in the salt and pepper.

3. Heat a wok or skillet over medium-high heat until it is nearly smoking. Add 1½ tablespoons oil. When the oil is hot, add the lightly beaten eggs. Scramble the eggs until they are cooked and remove from the pan. Clean out the pan.

4. Heat 1½ tablespoons oil in the wok or skillet. When the oil is hot, add the ginger and garlic and stir-fry for 10 seconds.

5. Add the mushrooms. Stir-fry for about 2 minutes or until they have browned.

6. Add the canned bamboo shoots. Stir-fry for 1 minute, adding 1 tablespoon water if the vegetables begin to dry out.

7. Add the tofu. Stir-fry for 1 minute, then add ¼ cup water. Stir in the sugar and the scallions. Add the scrambled eggs. Stir-fry for 1 minute to mix everything together. Serve hot.

PER SERVING | Calories: 231 | Fat: 11g | Protein: 20g | Sodium: 1,321mg | Fiber: 1g | Carbohydrates: 13g | Sugar: 8g

Tofu Curry

Serve this dish with Coconut-Scented Rice (see Chapter 10).

INGREDIENTS | SERVES 4

1 (12⅓-ounce) block firm tofu, cut into 1" cubes

¾ cup Curry Sauce (see Chapter 2)

3 tablespoons vegetable oil, divided

½ teaspoon minced garlic

½ teaspoon minced ginger

1 red chili, minced

1 medium red bell pepper, seeded and diced

1 cup sugar snap peas

½ cup coconut milk

½ teaspoon ground black pepper

1. In a large bowl, add the tofu cubes and the Curry Sauce and mix to coat well. Refrigerate for 1 hour.

2. Remove tofu from marinade, reserving the marinade. Heat 2 tablespoons oil in a wok over medium heat. Add drained tofu and stir-fry for 2–3 minutes until golden brown. Transfer to a plate.

3. Add remaining 1 tablespoon oil and cook the garlic, ginger, chili, bell pepper, and peas for 1 minute.

4. Whisk the coconut milk into the reserved marinade.

5. Add the tofu back into the wok and pour in the marinade mixture. Bring to a soft boil and reduce heat to medium low. Simmer for 15–20 minutes. Serve hot.

PER SERVING | Calories: 260 | Fat: 19g | Protein: 9g | Sodium: 396mg | Fiber: 3g | Carbohydrates: 14g | Sugar: 6g

Tofu and Soba Noodles

If you prefer not to stir-fry your tofu, feel free to add the cubes directly into the noodles after they have marinated in the ponzu.

INGREDIENTS | SERVES 4

1 cup Chili Ponzu Marinade (see Chapter 2)

10 ounces firm tofu, cut into 1" cubes

½ cup Ponzu Sauce (see Chapter 2)

1 tablespoon miso paste

½ tablespoon honey

1 teaspoon sesame oil

3 tablespoons canola oil, divided

¼ teaspoon cayenne pepper

½ cup blanched edamame beans

½ cup thinly sliced cucumbers

¼ cup diced red bell peppers

10 ounces cooked soba noodles, cooled

2 scallions, minced

1 teaspoon toasted sesame seeds

Soba Noodles

Soba is a Japanese noodle made from buckwheat flour. It can be served in both hot and cold dishes.

1. In a shallow dish, combine the marinade with tofu cubes. Cover and refrigerate for 20 minutes, flipping the cubes halfway through.

2. In a large bowl, whisk together Ponzu Sauce, miso paste, honey, sesame oil, 2 tablespoons canola oil, and cayenne pepper. Add in the edamame beans, cucumbers, bell peppers, and cooked soba noodles. Toss well to evenly coat the ingredients. Cover the bowl and refrigerate for 20 minutes.

3. Remove the tofu from the refrigerator and blot dry with paper towels. Heat the remaining 1 tablespoon oil in a wok over medium-high heat. Toss in the tofu and stir-fry for 1–2 minutes until the cubes become lightly golden.

4. Remove tofu from wok. Toss with the chilled soba, and then toss in the scallions. Transfer to plates and sprinkle with the sesame seeds.

PER SERVING | Calories: 758 | Fat: 52g | Protein: 19g | Sodium: 3,233mg | Fiber: 5g | Carbohydrates: 58g | Sugar: 7g

Tofu Salad with Ginger Miso Dressing

If you prefer not to further cook the tofu cubes, feel free to add them into the salad directly after they have marinated.

INGREDIENTS | SERVES 4

1 (12⅓-ounce) block firm tofu

2 tablespoons low-sodium soy sauce

1 tablespoon honey

1 teaspoon sesame oil

2 scallions, diced

2 garlic cloves, minced

4 tablespoons vegetable oil, divided

8 cups mixed greens

1 cup sliced cucumbers

½ cup shredded carrots

3 Roma tomatoes, seeded and quartered

½ small red onion, thinly sliced

½ cup Ginger Miso Dressing (see Chapter 2)

1 teaspoon toasted sesame seeds

1. Dry the tofu with paper towels to remove excess moisture. Cut the tofu into 1" cubes. In a bowl, whisk together the soy sauce, honey, sesame oil, scallions, garlic, and 2 tablespoons vegetable oil. Add the tofu cubes to the bowl and toss to coat. Refrigerate for 1 hour.

2. Divide the mixed green among 4 bowls. Top each bowl with cucumbers, carrots, tomatoes, and onion.

3. Heat the remaining vegetable oil in a wok over medium heat. Add in the tofu and stir-fry for 2–3 minutes until the cubes have become golden brown. Divide the tofu cubes among the four bowls.

4. Drizzle the Ginger Miso Dressing over the salads and sprinkle with toasted sesame seeds.

PER SERVING | Calories: 243 | Fat: 17g | Protein: 8g | Sodium: 512mg | Fiber: 2g | Carbohydrates: 14g | Sugar: 9g

Spicy Tofu Tacos

In lieu of tofu, use hearty vegetables such as eggplant or portobello mushrooms for another satisfying vegetarian option.

INGREDIENTS | SERVES 4

1 cup Korean-Inspired Marinade (see Chapter 2)

3 tablespoons gojuchang paste

½ teaspoon red pepper flakes

1 (12⅓-ounce) block firm tofu, cut into ½" cubes

2 tablespoons vegetable oil

¼ cup chopped scallions

½ small white onion, sliced

12 corn tortillas

2 cups kimchee, chopped

1 teaspoon toasted sesame seeds

1 cup seasoned and toasted seaweed, cut into thin strips

1. In a shallow dish, whisk together the marinade, gojuchang paste, and red pepper flakes. Add the tofu and refrigerate for at least 1 hour.

2. Heat wok over medium-high heat and add the vegetable oil. Once the oil is hot, stir-fry the scallions and onions for 30 seconds.

3. Add in the tofu and stir-fry for 2 minutes until browned. Transfer to a plate.

4. Warm the tortillas in a cast-iron skillet. Divide the tofu and kimchee among the tortillas. Top each taco with toasted sesame seeds and seaweed strips. Serve warm.

PER SERVING | Calories: 326 | Fat: 17g | Protein: 8g | Sodium: 1,153mg | Fiber: 3g | Carbohydrates: 34g | Sugar: 24g

Egg Foo Yung

For extra flavor, add 1 or 2 teaspoons oyster sauce to the egg mixture with the other seasonings. Vegetarians can use a vegetarian version of oyster sauce made with mushrooms.

INGREDIENTS | SERVES 4

2 tablespoons vegetable or peanut oil, divided

½ medium onion, chopped

¼ pound button mushrooms, thinly sliced

1 medium carrot, shredded

1 medium red bell pepper, seeded and diced

1 cup mung bean sprouts

6 large eggs

¼ teaspoon salt

¼ teaspoon white pepper

1 teaspoon sesame oil

Vegetable Stir-Fry Times

Softer vegetables like zucchini and bell peppers need to be stir-fried for only a couple of minutes, while thicker, harder vegetables like broccoli and carrots take longer. If you're planning to combine several types of vegetables in a stir-fry and aren't sure about cooking times, simply stir-fry them all separately and combine them in the wok in the final stages of cooking.

1. Heat a wok or skillet over medium-high heat until it is nearly smoking. Add 1 tablespoon oil. When the oil is hot, add the onion and the mushrooms. Stir-fry for about 2 minutes or until the onion begins to soften.

2. Stir in the shredded carrot and red bell pepper. Stir-fry for 1 minute, then add the bean sprouts. Cook for an additional minute. Remove the vegetables from the pan.

3. In a large bowl, beat the eggs lightly, stirring in the salt, pepper, and sesame oil. Stir in the cooked vegetables.

4. Heat 1 tablespoon oil in the wok or skillet. When the oil is hot, add the egg mixture. Cook for 1 minute on each side or until golden brown. Serve hot.

PER SERVING | Calories: 152 | Fat: 9g | Protein: 11g | Sodium: 267mg | Fiber: 1g | Carbohydrates: 7g | Sugar: 3g

Parmesan Eggs over Asparagus

This delightful dish can be served as an appetizer or for breakfast with toasted sourdough bread. The runny egg yolks serve as an unctuous "sauce" for the dish. If you prefer, try it with poached eggs instead.

INGREDIENTS | SERVES 2

1 pound asparagus, trimmed

3 tablespoons olive oil, divided

1 teaspoon garlic salt

½ teaspoon dried thyme leaves

¼ teaspoon red pepper flakes

2 extra-large eggs

¼ teaspoon kosher salt

¼ teaspoon freshly cracked black pepper

¼ cup freshly shaved Parmesan cheese

1. Cut the asparagus spears in half. In a bowl, toss the spears with 1 tablespoon olive oil, garlic salt, thyme leaves, and red pepper flakes.

2. Heat a wok over medium heat. Add 1 tablespoon olive oil and swirl it around the wok. Toss in the asparagus and stir-fry for 2–3 minutes. Divide the asparagus between two dishes.

3. Add the remaining 1 tablespoon oil to the wok. Carefully crack the eggs in one at a time, side by side. Do not disturb the eggs, and allow them to set until the edges begin to slightly curl up and the whites become opaque. Allow the eggs to fry for a total of 1–2 minutes for sunny-side up with runny yolks.

4. Place 1 egg on top of each asparagus plate. Season with kosher salt and freshly cracked pepper. Sprinkle the top with the shaved Parmesan and serve immediately.

PER SERVING | Calories: 308 | Fat: 26g | Protein: 12g | Sodium: 1,560mg | Fiber: 5g | Carbohydrates: 9g | Sugar: 4g

Green Eggs and Ham

It is important not to overcook eggs or they will become quite rubbery. A good rule of thumb is to remove them from the pan right before they appear done as the carryover heat will allow them to continue cooking.

INGREDIENTS | SERVES 2

5 large eggs

2 tablespoons milk

¼ teaspoon kosher salt

¼ teaspoon black pepper

1 tablespoon olive oil

1 tablespoon unsalted butter

¼ cup Chimichurri Sauce (see Chapter 2)

2 slices Serrano ham, torn or chopped into small pieces

Serrano Ham

Serrano ham is a dry-cured Spanish ham. It is typically sliced thin similar to prosciutto.

1. In a large bowl, whisk together the eggs and milk. Season with salt and pepper.

2. Heat oil in a wok over medium heat. Add the butter and swirl the wok around until it melts. Pour the egg mixture into the wok. Once the edges are set, use a rubber spatula and fold the eggs over themselves. Once all the liquids have disappeared, remove from heat.

3. Quickly stir in the Chimichurri Sauce and divide the eggs between two plates. Top with the pieces of Serrano ham and serve immediately with toast.

PER SERVING | Calories: 433 | Fat: 39g | Protein: 16g | Sodium: 925mg | Fiber: 0.5g | Carbohydrates: 5.5g | Sugar: 4g

Spinach, Mushroom, and Goat Cheese Omelette

When using frozen spinach, be sure to drain all the liquids out before adding it into your dish. You can use a dishtowel to help ring out the excess liquids.

INGREDIENTS | SERVES 1

1½ tablespoons vegetable oil, divided

1 cup crimini mushrooms

½ teaspoon fresh thyme leaves

¼ teaspoon garlic salt

¼ cup frozen spinach, thawed and drained

2 large eggs, beaten

2 tablespoons goat cheese

½ teaspoon chopped chives

1. Heat 1 tablespoon oil in a wok over medium heat. Add the mushrooms and stir-fry for 2 minutes or until tender. Toss in the thyme leaves, garlic salt, and spinach. Cook for 1 minute and then transfer to a bowl.

2. Use paper towels to wipe the wok clean. Add the remaining ½ tablespoon oil and swirl the wok around to coat the pan. Pour the beaten eggs into the center of the wok. Once the eggs begin setting, use a rubber spatula and push the edges toward the center and tilt the wok so that the uncooked eggs fill in any of the gaps.

3. Cover half of the omelet with the mushroom mixture. Crumble pieces of the goat cheese over the filling. Using the rubber spatula, carefully fold over the omelet to cover the filling. Allow to set for an additional 30 seconds, then carefully slide the omelet onto a plate.

4. Garnish with chives and serve immediately.

PER SERVING | Calories: 339 | Fat: 30g | Protein: 14g | Sodium: 732mg | Fiber: 0.7g | Carbohydrates: 3g | Sugar: 2g

Southwestern Omelet

Serve this omelet with Roasted Tomato Salsa (see Chapter 2).

INGREDIENTS | SERVES 1

2 large eggs, beaten

¼ teaspoon cumin powder

¼ teaspoon garlic salt

1 pinch cayenne pepper

1 tablespoon vegetable oil

¼ cup diced tomatoes

1 tablespoon pickled jalapeño peppers, diced

2 tablespoons chopped cilantro, divided

½ small avocado, sliced

¼ cup shredded pepper jack cheese

1. In a small bowl, whisk together the eggs, cumin, garlic salt, and cayenne pepper.

2. Heat the oil in a wok over medium heat. Pour the beaten eggs into the center of the wok. Once the eggs begin setting, use a rubber spatula and push the edges toward the center and tilt the wok so that the uncooked eggs fill in any of the gaps.

3. Cover half of the omelet with tomatoes, jalapeños, 1½ tablespoons cilantro, avocado slices, and cheese. Using the rubber spatula, carefully fold over the omelet to cover the filling. Allow to set for an additional 30 seconds, then carefully slide the omelet onto a plate.

4. Garnish with the remaining cilantro and serve immediately.

PER SERVING | Calories: 381 | Fat: 32g | Protein: 20g | Sodium: 1,027mg | Fiber: 0.8g | Carbohydrates: 3g | Sugar: 2g

Roast Pork Omelet

Roast pork and Chinese oyster sauce lend a savory flavor to this quick and easy omelet.

INGREDIENTS | SERVES 2

6 large eggs

2 tablespoons milk

¼ teaspoon salt

¼ teaspoon black pepper

2 tablespoons oyster sauce

4 tablespoons vegetable or peanut oil, divided

2 thin slices ginger

¼ cup finely chopped onion

¾ cup diced roast pork

1 scallion, chopped

1. In a medium bowl, lightly beat the eggs and milk. Stir in the salt, black pepper, and oyster sauce.

2. Heat a wok or skillet over medium-high heat until it is nearly smoking, then add 2 tablespoons oil. When the oil is hot, add the ginger. Brown the ginger for 2–3 minutes, then remove it from the pan. (This is to flavor the oil.)

3. Add the onion and stir-fry until it begins to soften (about 2 minutes). Add the roast pork and scallion and stir-fry briefly (less than 1 minute). Remove from the pan and drain on a plate lined with paper towels.

4. Add the stir-fried pork and onion to the egg mixture.

5. Heat 2 tablespoons oil in the wok or skillet. Pour in half of the egg mixture. Cook until the edges begin to firm, tilting the pan so that the egg mixture is evenly distributed throughout the pan. Turn down the heat to medium if the bottom is cooking too quickly.

6. When the omelet is evenly cooked, carefully use a spatula to fold it over. Slide the omelet out of the pan and onto a plate. Cook the second omelet, cleaning out the pan and adding more oil as needed.

PER SERVING | Calories: 243 | Fat: 15g | Protein: 19g | Sodium: 1,005mg | Fiber: 0.5g | Carbohydrates: 6g | Sugar: 3g

CHAPTER 9

Noodles and Pasta

Basic Stir-Fry Noodles

Fresh noodles should be cooked until they are tender but still firm and a bit chewy in the middle—what the Italians call al dente, or "to the teeth."

INGREDIENTS | SERVES 4

2 quarts water

1 teaspoon salt

½ pound linguine or Chinese egg noodles

2 teaspoons vegetable, peanut, or sesame oil

Perfect Pasta Cooking Tips

Always cook pasta in plenty of water. Wait for the water to come to a full rolling boil before adding the noodles. Stir the pasta to separate the strands. Finally, calculate the cooking time for the pasta from the moment the water returns to a rolling boil.

1. In a large pot, bring the water to a boil with the salt. Add the noodles and cook for 8–10 minutes or until they are firm but tender.

2. Drain the noodles thoroughly. Stir in the oil.

3. Use the noodles as called for in a stir-fry recipe. Adding noodles to the stir-fry allows them to soak up the sauce.

PER SERVING | Calories: 207 | Fat: 0.8g | Protein: 7g | Sodium: 607mg | Fiber: 1g | Carbohydrates: 41g | Sugar: 1.5g

Garlic Noodles

These buttery garlic noodles are the perfect accompaniment to seafood.

INGREDIENTS | SERVES 6

1 pound fresh thick chow mein noodles

4 tablespoons unsalted butter

2 tablespoons olive oil

2 tablespoons minced garlic

½ tablespoon light brown sugar

1½ tablespoons Maggi Seasoning

⅓ cup grated Parmesan cheese

1. Fill a large pot with water and bring to a boil. Add the noodles and cook for 2–3 minutes. Drain the noodles in a colander and reserve ¼ cup of the starchy water.

2. In a wok, melt the butter and olive oil. Add the garlic and stir-fry for 30 seconds. Add the sugar and Maggi. Stir until the sugar is dissolved.

3. Remove the pan from the heat and quickly toss the noodles into the mixture. Add the Parmesan and toss the noodles until thoroughly covered. Add the starchy liquid 1 tablespoon at a time to thin the sauce.

PER SERVING | Calories: 533 | Fat: 36g | Protein: 8g | Sodium: 414mg | Fiber: 3g | Carbohydrates: 45g | Sugar: 1g

Ginger Peanut Noodles

These noodles are perfect alone or as an accompaniment to stir-fried chicken or shrimp.

INGREDIENTS | SERVES 6

¾ cup smooth peanut butter

1 tablespoon honey

⅓ cup low-sodium soy sauce

¼ cup rice wine vinegar

1½ tablespoons toasted sesame oil

1½ tablespoons sambal chili paste

2 tablespoons minced fresh ginger

1 tablespoon minced garlic

1 teaspoon lime zest

½ tablespoon fresh lime juice

¼ cup water

1 pound Shanghai noodles

2 tablespoons vegetable oil

2 tablespoons minced shallots

½ teaspoon red pepper flakes

2 scallions, cut into 1" strips

¼ cup crushed roasted peanuts

1 teaspoon toasted sesame seeds

1. In a blender, combine the peanut butter, honey, soy sauce, vinegar, sesame oil, sambal, ginger, garlic, lime zest, and lime juice. Blend until smooth. Add the water if the sauce is too thick. Set aside.

2. Fill a large pot with water and bring to a boil. Add the noodles and cook for 1–2 minutes. Drain the noodles in a colander and reserve ¼ cup of the starchy water.

3. In a wok, heat the vegetable oil to medium and toss in the shallots. Stir fry the shallots for 30 seconds before adding in the red pepper flakes and cooked noodles. Stir fry the items for an additional 30 seconds.

4. Ladle in 2–3 spoonfuls of the peanut sauce at a time until the noodles have been thoroughly coated. Add 1–2 tablespoons of the starchy water to loosen the sauce. Toss in the scallions and stir-fry until for an additional 30 seconds. Plate the noodles and top with the peanuts and sesame seeds.

PER SERVING | Calories: 643 | Fat: 42g | Protein: 15g | Sodium: 1,333mg | Fiber: 5g | Carbohydrates: 55g | Sugar: 7g

Homemade Chow Mein Noodles

This recipe is also called noodle pancake or twice-browned noodles, but whatever the name, these fried noodles go well with a chow mein recipe such as Tomato Beef Chow Mein (see recipe in this chapter). Just pour the stir-fried meat and vegetables over the noodles.

INGREDIENTS | SERVES 2

½ pound dried egg noodles

1 tablespoon sesame oil

¼ teaspoon salt

1 teaspoon granulated sugar

¼ cup vegetable or peanut oil

The Perfect Noodle Pancake

Draining the noodles in a large colander for about an hour before cooking will cause them to naturally form into a pancake shape. Use a spatula to slide the noodles from the colander into the pan. To brown the bottom side of a noodle pancake, slide the noodle pancake out of the pan onto a large plate, invert it onto another plate, and slide it back into the pan.

1. In a large pot, bring 2 quarts water to a boil. Add the noodles and cook for 1–2 minutes or until they are firm but tender. Drain the noodles and stir in the sesame oil, salt, and sugar. Allow the noodles to dry in a colander for 1 hour.

2. Heat a large flat skillet over medium-high heat until it is nearly smoking. Add ¼ cup vegetable oil. When the oil is hot, carefully slide the dried noodles into the pan, spreading them out so that they cover the entire pan. Cook for 6–8 minutes, until the noodles are browned on the bottom. Turn the heat down to medium if the pan starts smoking.

3. Turn the noodle pancake over and brown on the other side (it should take less time to brown the bottom side). Slide the noodle pancake out of the pan. Use a knife to cut the noodle pancake into the number of serving portions needed.

PER SERVING | Calories: 658 | Fat: 41g | Protein: 9g | Sodium: 786mg | Fiber: 4g | Carbohydrates: 66g | Sugar: 2g

Chicken Lo Mein

For extra flavor, marinate the chicken strips in a bowl with 2 tablespoons oyster sauce, black or white pepper to taste, and 1 teaspoon cornstarch for 15 minutes before stir-frying. Cook the noodles and prepare the other ingredients while the chicken is marinating.

INGREDIENTS | SERVES 4

1½ teaspoons salt, divided

½ pound fresh egg noodles or linguine

1 cup chicken broth

2 tablespoons soy sauce

1 tablespoon cornstarch

3 tablespoons vegetable or peanut oil, divided

2 cloves garlic, crushed

½ pound boneless, skinless chicken breast, cut in thin strips

¼ pound mushrooms, thinly sliced

6 ounces snow peas, trimmed

1 medium red bell pepper, thinly sliced

¼ teaspoon black pepper

1. In a large pot, bring 2 quarts water to a boil with 1 teaspoon salt. Add the egg noodles and cook for 2–3 minutes until they are firm but tender. If using linguine, cook for 8–10 minutes. Drain the cooked pasta.

2. In a large bowl, combine the chicken broth and the soy sauce, then whisk in the cornstarch.

3. Heat a wok or skillet over medium-high heat until it is nearly smoking. Add 2 tablespoons oil. When the oil is hot, add the crushed garlic and stir-fry for 10 seconds.

4. Add the chicken. Let it sit briefly, then stir-fry the chicken for 2 minutes or until it turns white and is nearly cooked. Remove the chicken from the pan and drain in a colander or on paper towels.

5. Heat 1 tablespoon oil in the wok or skillet. Add the mushrooms and snow peas, sprinkling ½ teaspoon salt on the vegetables if desired. Stir-fry for 1 minute, then add the red bell pepper. Stir-fry for 1 more minute or until the vegetables are tender but still crisp.

6. Add the broth/soy sauce mixture into the pan and bring to a boil.

7. Add the noodles. Stir-fry for 1 minute to mix the noodles with the other ingredients.

8. Return the chicken to the pan. Stir-fry for 2 more minutes or until everything is heated through. Season with the black pepper and remaining salt. Serve hot.

PER SERVING | Calories: 343 | Fat: 3g | Protein: 23g | Sodium: 1,668mg | Fiber: 4g | Carbohydrates: 53g | Sugar: 5g

Curried Rice Noodles with Beef

Thin rice vermicelli noodles soak up the curry flavor in this easy stir-fry recipe that makes a complete one-dish meal.

INGREDIENTS | SERVES 4

1 pound flank steak, cut across the grain into ½" x 2" long strips

1½ tablespoons light soy sauce

1 tablespoon Chinese rice wine or dry sherry

¼ teaspoon black pepper

2 teaspoons cornstarch

5 ounces rice vermicelli noodles

1 large tomato

3 tablespoons chicken broth

1 tablespoon dark soy sauce

¾ teaspoon granulated sugar

¼ teaspoon salt

¼ teaspoon chili paste

4 tablespoons vegetable or peanut oil, divided

2 cloves garlic, minced

2 thin slices ginger, minced

3 tablespoons curry powder

1 small yellow onion, chopped

1 cup mung bean sprouts

1. Place steak in a bowl with the light soy sauce, rice wine, pepper, and cornstarch. Marinate for 15 minutes.

2. Soak the rice noodles in hot water for 15–20 minutes until they are softened. Drain thoroughly and cut the noodles crosswise into thirds. Cut the tomato into thin slices and cut each slice in half.

3. In a small bowl, combine the chicken broth, dark soy sauce, granulated sugar, salt, and chili paste.

4. Heat a wok or skillet over medium-high heat and add 2 tablespoons oil. When the oil is hot, add half the minced garlic and ginger and stir-fry for 10 seconds.

5. Add half the beef. Let the meat sear for about 30 seconds before stir-frying for 1–2 minutes or until it loses any pinkness and is nearly cooked through. Remove and drain on a plate lined with paper towels. Repeat with the remainder of the beef.

6. Heat 2 tablespoons oil in the wok or skillet. When the oil is hot, add the remainder of the minced garlic and ginger and the curry powder. Stir-fry for 10 seconds.

7. Add the chopped onion. Stir-fry the onion for 2 minutes. Add the tomato and stir-fry for 1 minute. Stir in the mung bean sprouts and stir-fry for about 1 minute.

8. Add the beef and the noodles. Pour in the chicken broth mixture. Stir-fry for 1 minute or until the noodles have absorbed the chicken broth mixture. Serve hot.

PER SERVING | Calories: 368 | Fat: 9g | Protein: 28g | Sodium: 894mg | Fiber: 3g | Carbohydrates: 40g | Sugar: 2g

Singapore Noodles

Additional curry powder can be added for a more prominent flavor.

INGREDIENTS | SERVES 4

½ pound flat rice stick noodles

1 pound small shrimp, shelled and deveined

½ cup chicken broth

2 tablespoons oyster sauce

1 tablespoon granulated sugar

3 tablespoons vegetable or peanut oil

2 cloves garlic, chopped

1 teaspoon minced ginger

1 tablespoon Madras curry powder

6 ounces snow peas, trimmed

2 cups mung bean sprouts, rinsed and drained

½ teaspoon black pepper

1 scallion, chopped

What Are Rice Stick Noodles?

Made with rice flour and water, rice stick noodles are flat white noodles that come in varying widths. Like many other types of noodles, rice noodles should be softened in hot water before cooking.

1. Soak the rice noodles in warm water for 15 minutes or until they have softened. Drain the noodles.

2. Rinse the shrimp under cold running water and pat dry.

3. In a small bowl, combine the chicken broth, oyster sauce, and sugar. Set aside.

4. Heat a wok or skillet over medium-high heat and add the oil. When the oil is hot, add the garlic, ginger, and curry powder. Stir-fry for 10 seconds, then add the snow peas. Stir-fry for about 2 minutes, until they are tender but still crisp.

5. Push the snow peas to the sides of the pan and add the shrimp in the middle. Stir-fry the shrimp until they turn pink, then add the oyster sauce mixture. Bring to a boil, then add the noodles. Stir-fry for 1 minute, then stir in the mung bean sprouts.

6. Stir in the black pepper. Stir-fry for 1 minute to heat everything through. Sprinkle with the chopped scallion. Serve hot.

PER SERVING | Calories: 404 | Fat: 3g | Protein: 30g | Sodium: 565mg | Fiber: 2g | Carbohydrates: 61g | Sugar: 5.5g

Vermicelli Beef with Vegetables

Need a little help with julienning the vegetables? Try using a mandoline to cut the work in half.

INGREDIENTS | SERVES 2

1 (6-ounce) package rice vermicelli
½ pound flank steak
2 tablespoons vegetable or peanut oil
2 cloves garlic, chopped
2 ribs celery, julienned
½ medium red bell pepper, sliced
1 small carrot, peeled and julienned
½ teaspoon salt
½ cup water or chicken broth
2 teaspoons dark soy sauce
½ teaspoon granulated sugar

1. Soak the rice noodles in a bowl filled with hot water until they are softened (15–20 minutes). Drain the noodles, lay them out horizontally on a cutting board, and cut crosswise into thirds.

2. Cut the flank steak across the grain into thin strips 1½" long.

3. Heat a wok or skillet over medium-high heat until it is nearly smoking and add the oil. When the oil is hot, add the garlic and stir-fry for 10 seconds.

4. Add the beef. Let sear briefly, then stir-fry the beef until it is no longer pink and is nearly cooked (about 2 minutes).

5. Add the celery, bell pepper, carrots, and stir-fry for 1 minute. Season the mixture with salt.

6. Add the water or chicken broth and bring to a boil. Stir in the dark soy sauce and sugar. Reduce the heat to medium, cover, and cook for about 2 minutes, until the vegetables are tender but still crisp.

7. Uncover and stir in the noodles. Stir-fry for another 2 minutes. Serve hot.

PER SERVING | Calories: 516 | Fat: 8g | Protein: 27g | Sodium: 1,155mg | Fiber: 3g | Carbohydrates: 77g | Sugar: 4g

Gingered Pork with Udon Noodles

Used in Japanese cooking, udon noodles are made with wheat flour, water, and salt.

INGREDIENTS | SERVES 2

½ pound lean pork
1 tablespoon soy sauce
1 tablespoon Chinese rice wine or dry sherry
1 teaspoon cornstarch
½ pound Japanese udon noodles
2 tablespoons vegetable or peanut oil
1 tablespoon chopped ginger
¼ cup finely chopped scallions
½ cup chicken broth
½ teaspoon salt
1 tablespoon sesame oil

1. Cut the pork into thin strips about 1½" long, ¼" wide, and ⅛" thick. Place the pork strips in a bowl and add the soy sauce, rice wine or sherry, and cornstarch. Marinate the pork for 15 minutes.

2. Cook the udon noodles according to the package directions and drain.

3. Heat a wok or skillet over medium-high heat until it is nearly smoking. Add the oil. When the oil is hot, add the ginger and scallions. Stir-fry for 10 seconds.

4. Add the pork. Stir-fry the pork for 2–3 minutes or until it is no longer pink and is nearly cooked.

5. Add the chicken broth and bring to a boil. Add the noodles. Stir-fry for 2 more minutes to blend all the ingredients. Stir in the salt and sesame oil and serve hot.

PER SERVING | Calories: 255 | Fat: 11g | Protein: 27g | Sodium: 1,182mg | Fiber: 0.6g | Carbohydrates: 7g | Sugar: 1g

Roast Pork Chow Fun

Chinese barbecued roast pork can be found readily in Chinese supermarkets. However, grilled pork that has been marinated in a mixture of soy sauce, ginger, and honey can be substituted.

INGREDIENTS | SERVES 4

1 pound fresh chow fun noodles

3 tablespoons vegetable or peanut oil, divided

1 clove garlic, crushed

1 medium yellow onion, cut into rings

½ pound barbecued roast pork, thinly sliced

½ medium green bell pepper, seeded and cut into chunks

½ medium red bell pepper, seeded and cut into chunks

2 cups mung bean sprouts

½ teaspoon salt

1 tablespoon soy sauce

1 tablespoon oyster sauce

2 scallions, quartered

1. Separate the chow fun noodles to keep them from sticking together.

2. Heat a wok or skillet over medium-high heat until it is nearly smoking and add 2 tablespoons oil. When the oil is hot, add the chow fun noodles. Stir-fry the noodles until they are soft and translucent (about 4 minutes), adding a bit of water, soy sauce, or chicken broth if they begin to dry out. Remove the noodles from the pan.

3. Heat 1 tablespoon oil in the same wok or skillet. When the oil is hot, add the garlic. Stir-fry for 10 seconds, then add the onion. Stir-fry the onion for 1 minute or until it begins to soften.

4. Add the roast pork and stir-fry for 1 minute. Add the bell peppers. Stir-fry for 1 minute, and then add the mung bean sprouts. Sprinkle with the salt. Stir-fry the entire mixture briefly (about 30 seconds).

5. Add the noodles back into the pan. Stir in the soy sauce, oyster sauce, and scallions. Stir-fry briefly to heat everything through and serve hot.

PER SERVING | Calories: 713 | Fat: 36g | Protein: 26g | Sodium: 1,170mg | Fiber: 5g | Carbohydrates: 73g | Sugar: 2g

Sesame Pork with Noodles

Thin Chinese noodles (sometimes called lo mein noodles), spaghetti, and linguine would all work well in this recipe. Remember to allow more time for the noodles to cook if you are using dried noodles.

INGREDIENTS | SERVES 2

1½ teaspoons salt, divided

½ pound thin noodles, fresh or dried

½ pound lean pork

2 teaspoons dark soy sauce

2 teaspoons Chinese rice wine or dry sherry

1 teaspoon cornstarch

2 tablespoons vegetable or peanut oil, divided

½ teaspoon minced garlic

½ teaspoon minced ginger

1 cup shredded carrot

1 cup shredded celery

¾ cup Sesame Sauce (see Chapter 2)

1 scallion, finely chopped

1. In a large pot, bring 2 quarts water to a boil with 1 teaspoon salt. Add the noodles and cook for 2–3 minutes until they are firm but tender. If using linguine or spaghetti, cook for 8–10 minutes until they are firm but tender. Drain the noodles.

2. Cut the pork into thin strips about 1½" long. Place the pork in a bowl and add the dark soy sauce, rice wine or dry sherry, and cornstarch. Marinate the pork for 15 minutes.

3. Heat a wok or skillet over medium-high heat until it is nearly smoking. Add 1 tablespoon oil. When the oil is hot, add the garlic. Stir-fry for 10 seconds.

4. Add the pork. Stir-fry the pork for 2–3 minutes or until it is no longer pink and is nearly cooked through.

5. Push the pork to the sides of the pan and heat 1 tablespoon oil in the middle. Add the ginger and stir-fry for 10 seconds. Add the carrot and the celery. Stir-fry for 1 minute, sprinkling ½ teaspoon salt over the vegetables. Stir to combine the vegetables with the pork.

6. Stir in the cooked noodles. Add the Sesame Sauce and bring to a boil. Stir-fry for 1–2 more minutes to mix all the ingredients together. Sprinkle the top with the chopped scallions. Serve hot.

PER SERVING | Calories: 880 | Fat: 30g | Protein: 45g | Sodium: 3,794mg | Fiber: 6g | Carbohydrates: 103g | Sugar: 11g

Pork Lo Mein

Using barbecued pork from an Asian market adds extra flavor to this simple stir-fry.

INGREDIENTS | SERVES 2

1 teaspoon salt

½ pound fresh lo mein noodles

¾ cup chicken broth

2 tablespoons oyster sauce

1 tablespoon dark soy sauce

1 teaspoon granulated sugar

2 tablespoons vegetable or peanut oil

2 cloves garlic, chopped

2 thin slices ginger, chopped

1 cup chopped carrots

1 cup chopped red bell pepper

½ pound barbecued pork, sliced

1 tablespoon light soy sauce

2 scallions, quartered

1 teaspoon sesame oil

Noodle Cooking Times

The amount of time needed to cook the noodles in the boiling water will vary depending on whether you are using fresh or dried noodles. Fresh noodles usually require about 3 minutes to reach al dente stage, while dried noodles need several minutes longer.

1. In a large pot, bring 2 quarts water to a boil with the salt. Add the noodles and cook for 2–3 minutes until they are firm but tender. Drain the noodles.

2. In a small bowl, combine the chicken broth, oyster sauce, dark soy sauce, and sugar. Set aside.

3. Heat a wok or skillet over medium-high heat until it is nearly smoking and add the oil. When the oil is hot, add the chopped garlic and ginger. Stir-fry for 10 seconds. Add the chopped carrots and stir-fry for 1 minute, then add the chopped bell pepper. Stir-fry for 1 minute or until the vegetables are tender but still crisp.

4. Add the barbecued pork. Stir-fry for 1 minute, splashing with the soy sauce. Add the noodles. Stir-fry briefly to mix the noodles with the vegetables, then add the sauce. Stir in the scallions. Stir-fry for 1 minute to heat through. Remove from the heat and stir in the sesame oil. Serve hot.

PER SERVING | Calories: 868 | Fat: 42g | Protein: 39g | Sodium: 3,551mg | Fiber: 8g | Carbohydrates: 85g | Sugar: 9g

Vegetable Chow Mein

Cashews take the place of meat or tofu in this healthy recipe.
Instead of noodles, you could also substitute ¾ cup cooked brown rice.

INGREDIENTS | SERVES 2

1 teaspoon salt

½ pound fresh wheat noodles

1 cup unsalted cashews

2 tablespoons vegetable or peanut oil

1 teaspoon chopped fresh ginger

½ cup chopped yellow onion

1 small carrot, julienned

1 cup sliced mushrooms

1 cup snow peas

1 tablespoon soy sauce

⅓ cup Simple Stir-Fry Sauce (see Chapter 2)

¾ teaspoon granulated sugar

1. In a large pot, bring 2 quarts water to a boil with the salt. Add the noodles and cook for 1–2 minutes until they are firm but tender. Drain the noodles.

2. Roast the cashews in a heavy frying pan over medium heat, shaking the pan continuously so that the nuts do not burn. Roast until the cashews are browned (about 5 minutes). Remove the cashews from the pan to cool.

3. Heat a wok or skillet over medium-high heat until it is nearly smoking. Add the oil. When the oil is hot, add the ginger and stir-fry for 10 seconds. Add the onion and stir-fry for 2 minutes or until the onion begins to soften. Add the carrot. Stir-fry for 1 minute, then add the mushrooms. Stir-fry for 1 minute, then add the snow peas. Splash the vegetables with 1 tablespoon soy sauce and stir-fry for an additional minute.

4. Add the noodles. Stir in the Simple Stir-Fry Sauce and bring to a boil.

5. Stir in the roasted cashews and the sugar. Stir-fry for 1 minute to heat everything through, and serve hot.

PER SERVING | Calories: 676 | Fat: 34g | Protein: 13g | Sodium: 3,998mg | Fiber: 7g | Carbohydrates: 82g | Sugar: 10g

Spicy Shredded Beef with Rice Noodles

*Strips of beef are cooked in a spicy sauce with stir-fried noodles
in this tasty stir-fry that is great for busy weeknights.*

INGREDIENTS | SERVES 2

5 ounces rice vermicelli noodles

2 tablespoons vegetable or peanut oil

2 cloves garlic, chopped

2 teaspoons chopped red chilies

2 scallions, chopped into 1" pieces

½ pound flank steak, shredded

¼ cup Hot and Sour Sauce (see Chapter 2)

½ teaspoon granulated sugar

Handling Rice Vermicelli

These thin rice noodles can pose a challenge the first time you add them to a stir-fry. Once softened, rice vermicelli noodles are like sponges, drawing up the liquid around them. You can end up with globs of liquid-soaked noodles. Cut rice vermicelli crosswise into sections to make handling easier, and go sparingly on the sauce the first few times you use them in cooking.

1. Soak the rice noodles in a bowl filled with hot water until they are softened (15–20 minutes). Drain the noodles thoroughly, lay them out horizontally on a cutting board, and cut crosswise into thirds.

2. Heat a wok or skillet over medium-high heat until it is almost smoking. Add the oil. When the oil is hot, add the garlic, red chilies, and scallions. Stir-fry for 10 seconds.

3. Add the shredded beef. Stir-fry for about 2 minutes, until it is no longer pink and is nearly cooked through.

4. Add the noodles. Stir-fry for a few seconds, and add the Hot and Sour Sauce. Stir-fry for 2 minutes or until everything is heated through. Stir in the sugar. Serve hot.

PER SERVING | Calories: 474 | Fat: 8g | Protein: 26g | Sodium: 233mg | Fiber: 1g | Carbohydrates: 69g | Sugar: 8g

Tomato Beef Chow Mein

If you're pressed for time and in too much of a hurry to prepare the noodles for this recipe, use packaged dried chow mein noodles, which are available in most supermarkets.

INGREDIENTS | SERVES 4

½ pound flank steak

2 teaspoons oyster sauce

2 teaspoons plus 1 tablespoon rice vinegar, divided

½ teaspoon plus 1 tablespoon cornstarch, divided

¼ cup chicken broth

1 tablespoon tomato paste or ketchup

1 tablespoon dark soy sauce

1 tablespoon sugar

4 tablespoons water

2 tablespoons vegetable oil

2 slices ginger

2 small tomatoes, thinly sliced, each slice cut in half

2 ribs celery, cut on the diagonal into ½" slices

Homemade Chow Mein Noodles (see recipe in this chapter)

1. Cut the beef across the grain into thin strips that are approximately 2" long. Place the strips of beef in a bowl and add the oyster sauce, 2 teaspoons rice vinegar, and ½ teaspoon cornstarch. Marinate the beef for 15 minutes.

2. In a small bowl, combine the chicken broth, tomato paste, 1 tablespoon rice vinegar, dark soy sauce, and sugar.

3. In a separate small bowl, dissolve 1 tablespoon cornstarch in the water. Set aside.

4. Heat a wok or skillet on medium-high heat until it is nearly smoking. Add the oil. When the oil is hot, add the ginger. As soon as the ginger sizzles, add the beef, laying it flat in the pan. Let sear (brown) briefly, then stir-fry the meat, stirring and tossing for 1–2 minutes or until it is nearly cooked through.

5. Push the beef to the sides of the pan. Add the tomato and celery in the middle. Stir-fry for 1 minute, or until the celery turns a darker green.

6. Add the sauce in the middle and bring to a boil. Add the cornstarch and water mixture into the sauce, stirring continually. When the sauce thickens, stir-fry for 1–2 more minutes to mix it with the beef and vegetables. Pour the beef and vegetable stir-fry over the noodles.

PER SERVING | Calories: 520 | Fat: 31g | Protein: 17g | Sodium: 831mg | Fiber: 3g | Carbohydrates: 42g | Sugar: 6g

Hoisin-Flavored Cellophane Noodles

When cooking with chicken broth, try to use low-sodium broth so that you can control the salt level.

INGREDIENTS | SERVES 2

1 bundle (3½ ounces) cellophane noodles

½ cup chicken broth

2 tablespoons hoisin sauce

¼–½ teaspoon chili paste

2 tablespoons vegetable or peanut oil

1 teaspoon minced garlic

½ teaspoon minced ginger

2 scallions, cut into 1" pieces

6 ounces fresh portobello mushrooms, cubed

1 small red bell pepper, seeded and cubed

⅛ teaspoon freshly ground white pepper

Cellophane Noodles

Made from mung bean flour, cellophane noodles are also called bean thread noodles and slippery noodles, due to their transparent appearance and slippery texture. Like rice vermicelli, mung bean noodles are very absorbent. Always soften the noodles in hot water for 15–20 minutes before cooking; otherwise, the noodles will quickly absorb most of the liquid in the dish.

1. Soak the noodles in a bowl filled with hot water until they are softened (15–20 minutes). Drain the noodles thoroughly, lay them out horizontally on a cutting board, and cut crosswise into thirds.

2. In a small bowl, combine the chicken broth, hoisin sauce, and chili paste. Set aside.

3. Heat a wok or skillet over medium-high heat until it is nearly smoking. Add the oil. When the oil is hot, add the garlic, ginger, and scallions. Stir-fry for 10 seconds, then add the mushrooms. Stir-fry for 1 minute, then add the red bell pepper. Stir-fry for 1 minute or until the mushrooms have darkened and the red bell pepper is tender but still crisp.

4. Add the noodles into the wok or skillet. Stir-fry briefly, then add the hoisin sauce mixture. Bring to a boil and stir-fry for another 1–2 minutes, until everything is heated through. Stir in the freshly ground white pepper. Serve hot.

PER SERVING | Calories: 283 | Fat: 2g | Protein: 6g | Sodium: 640mg | Fiber: 4g | Carbohydrates: 59g | Sugar: 9g

Oyster Sauce–Flavored Pork with Noodles

*Bok choy and red bell pepper add extra color to this tasty dish,
and the sauce flavors the egg noodles wonderfully.*

INGREDIENTS | SERVES 2

1½ teaspoons salt, divided
½ pound fresh Chinese egg noodles
½ pound lean pork
1½ tablespoons light soy sauce
2½ tablespoons vegetable or peanut oil, divided
¼ teaspoon black pepper
½ cup chicken broth
¼ cup oyster sauce
2 tablespoons dark soy sauce
2 tablespoons rice wine or dry sherry
1 teaspoon granulated sugar
2 cloves garlic, chopped
2 thin slices ginger, chopped
2 cups chopped bok choy
1 small red bell pepper, cubed
1 cup mung bean sprouts

1. In a large pot, bring 2 quarts water to a boil with 1 teaspoon salt. Add the noodles and cook for 2–3 minutes or until they are firm but tender. Drain the noodles.

2. Cut the pork into cubes. Place the pork in a medium bowl and add the light soy sauce, 1½ teaspoons vegetable oil, and pepper. Marinate the pork for 20 minutes.

3. In a small bowl, combine the chicken broth, oyster sauce, dark soy sauce, rice wine or sherry, and the sugar. Set aside.

4. Heat a wok or skillet over medium-high heat until it is nearly smoking. Add 2 tablespoons oil. When the oil is hot, add the garlic and ginger and stir-fry for 10 seconds.

5. Add the pork. Stir-fry for 2 minutes or until the pork is no longer pink and is nearly cooked.

6. Push the pork to the sides of the wok or skillet and add the bok choy in the middle. Stir-fry the bok choy for 1 minute, sprinkling ½ teaspoon salt over the top. Add the red bell pepper and the mung bean sprouts. Stir-fry for 1 minute or until the bok choy turns bright green. Splash the vegetables with water if they begin to dry out during stir-frying.

7. Add the noodles. Stir-fry briefly, then add the sauce. Stir-fry for 1–2 more minutes to heat everything through. Serve hot.

PER SERVING | Calories: 877 | Fat: 40g | Protein: 43g | Sodium: 5,187mg | Fiber: 6g | Carbohydrates: 86g | Sugar: 6g

Shrimp Chow Mein

If you don't have leftover cooked ham, substitute 4 ounces lean pork, cut into thin strips, and stir-fry it separately. Don't increase the amount of shrimp, as its strong flavor can overpower the other ingredients.

INGREDIENTS | SERVES 2

1¼ teaspoons salt, divided

½ pound fresh egg noodles

¼ pound shelled, deveined large shrimp

¼ cup water

2 teaspoons oyster sauce

2 teaspoons Chinese rice wine or dry sherry

1 teaspoon light soy sauce

3 tablespoons vegetable or peanut oil

2 thin slices ginger, minced

4 ounces sliced mushrooms

1 rib celery, cut on the diagonal into ½" slices

1 small red bell pepper, cubed

1 additional tablespoon soy sauce, if needed

¼ teaspoon black pepper

1. In a large pot, bring 2 quarts water to a boil with 1 teaspoon salt. Add the noodles and cook for 2–3 minutes or until they are firm but tender. Drain the noodles.

2. Rinse the shrimp under cold running water and toss with ¼ teaspoon salt.

3. In a small bowl, combine the water, oyster sauce, rice wine or sherry, and light soy sauce.

4. Heat a wok or skillet over medium-high heat until it is nearly smoking. Add the oil. When the oil is hot, add the ginger and stir-fry for 10 seconds.

5. Add the shrimp. Stir-fry the shrimp until they turn pink.

6. Push the shrimp to the sides of the wok or skillet. Add the mushrooms. Stir-fry for 1 minute, then add the celery and the red bell pepper. Stir-fry for 1 minute, until the mushrooms have darkened and the celery has turned a bright green. Splash the vegetables with 1 tablespoon soy sauce if they begin to dry out.

7. Add the noodles. Stir in the sauce and bring to a boil. Stir-fry for 1–2 more minutes to mix everything together. Add black pepper and serve hot.

PER SERVING | Calories: 692 | Fat: 35g | Protein: 23g | Sodium: 2,368mg | Fiber: 6g | Carbohydrates: 71g | Sugar: 4g

Chinese-Style Steak over Noodles

Rice vermicelli noodles puff up nicely when deep-fried. However, if you don't have any on hand, you can serve the steak and vegetables with tortilla or taco chips.

INGREDIENTS | SERVES 2

½ pound flank steak

1½ tablespoons tomato paste

1½ tablespoons Worcestershire sauce

1 tablespoon soy sauce

1½ tablespoons water

1½ teaspoons brown sugar

3 tablespoons vegetable or peanut oil, divided

1 teaspoon minced garlic

2 shallots, peeled and chopped

½ small green bell pepper, cut into thin strips

½ pound fresh mushrooms, thinly sliced

½ small red bell pepper, cut into thin strips

4 ounces deep-fried rice vermicelli (see sidebar)

How to Deep-Fry Rice Vermicelli

To fry rice noodles, pour 2 inches of oil into a wok or deep-sided heavy skillet and heat to 375°F. When the oil is hot, remove the noodles from the package and use tongs to lower them into the hot oil. Cook briefly (for 1 second), turn over, and cook for 1 second more. Remove the noodles and drain in a colander or on paper towels.

1. Cut the steak across the grain into thin strips, 1½"–2" long, ⅛" wide, and ⅛" thick.

2. In a small bowl, combine the tomato paste, Worcestershire sauce, soy sauce, water, and brown sugar. Set aside.

3. Heat a wok or skillet over medium-high heat until it is nearly smoking. Add 1½ tablespoons oil. When the oil is hot, add half the garlic and stir-fry for 10 seconds.

4. Add the flank steak. Let it sear briefly, then stir-fry the beef for 2–3 minutes or until it is no longer pink and is nearly cooked. Remove the beef and drain on a plate lined with paper towels.

5. Heat 1½ tablespoons oil in the wok or skillet. Add the remaining garlic and stir-fry for 10 seconds. Add the shallots and stir-fry for 1 minute or briefly, until they begin to soften. Add the green bell pepper and the mushrooms. Stir-fry for 1 minute, then add the red bell pepper. Continue cooking for 2 minutes and splash the vegetables with 1 tablespoon water or dry sherry if they begin to dry out during stir-frying.

6. Add the tomato/soy sauce mixture and bring to a boil. Add the beef back into the pan. Stir-fry for 2–3 more minutes to blend the flavors. Serve hot over the deep-fried rice vermicelli.

PER SERVING | Calories: 493 | Fat: 35g | Protein: 28g | Sodium: 742mg | Fiber: 2.8g | Carbohydrates: 16g | Sugar: 10g

Zha Jiang Mian

Zha Jian Mian is sometimes referred to as a Chinese Bolognese due to the thick, meaty sauce that is served on top of the noodles.

INGREDIENTS | SERVES 4

½ pound fresh Shanghai noodles
¼ cup black bean sauce
2 tablespoons yellow soybean paste
¼ cup chicken broth
¼ cup rice wine
1 chicken bouillon cube
1 tablespoon vegetable oil
2 garlic cloves, minced
2 tablespoons minced shallots
1 pound pork loin, coarsely ground
2 scallions, diced
1 cup julienned cucumbers

1. Fill a large pot with water and bring to a boil. Add the noodles and cook for 2 minutes. Drain the noodles in a colander and then divide the portions into 4 bowls.

2. In a bowl, whisk together the black bean sauce, soybean paste, chicken broth, rice wine, and bouillon.

3. In a wok, heat oil over medium heat. Add in garlic and shallots and cook for 1 minute.

4. Toss in the pork and stir-fry for 3–4 minutes. Use a wooden spoon to crumble up the meat while it cooks.

5. Stir in the black bean mixture and allow the mixture to come to a boil. Continue to cook the sauce for 3–4 minutes, then stir in the scallions. Spoon the sauce over the noodles and top with the cucumbers. Serve immediately.

PER SERVING | Calories: 705 | Fat: 47g | Protein: 24g | Sodium: 958mg | Fiber: 3g | Carbohydrates: 41g | Sugar: 1.8g

Pork Chow Mein

*Quick-cooking snow peas and packaged chow mein noodles
make this recipe a great choice for busy weeknights.*

INGREDIENTS | SERVES 2

½ pound lean pork

2 teaspoons Chinese rice wine or dry sherry

2 teaspoons dark soy sauce

2½ teaspoons cornstarch, divided

¼ cup water

1 tablespoon oyster sauce

1 teaspoon light soy sauce

½ teaspoon granulated sugar

¼ teaspoon black pepper

4 tablespoons vegetable or peanut oil, divided

1 clove garlic, chopped

2 thin slices ginger, minced

1 medium shallot, chopped

1 cup snow peas, trimmed

1 cup mung bean sprouts

¼ teaspoon salt

10 ounces packaged chow mein noodles

1. Julienne the pork. Place the strips of pork in a bowl and add the rice wine or sherry, dark soy sauce, and 1 teaspoon cornstarch. Marinate the pork for 20 minutes.

2. In a small bowl, combine the water, oyster sauce, light soy sauce, sugar, and black pepper for the gravy. Whisk in 1½ teaspoons cornstarch.

3. Heat a wok or skillet over medium-high heat until it is nearly smoking. Add 2 tablespoons oil. When the oil is hot, add half the garlic and ginger and stir-fry for 10 seconds.

4. Add the pork. Let it sit briefly, then stir-fry, stirring and moving the pork around the pan, for 1–2 minutes or until it turns white and is nearly cooked through. Remove from the pan and drain in a colander or on paper towels.

5. Heat 2 tablespoons oil in the wok. When the oil is hot, add the shallot and the remainder of the garlic and ginger. Stir-fry until the shallot begins to soften (about 1 minute). Add the snow peas and stir-fry until they turn dark green and are tender but still crisp (about 2 minutes). Stir in the mung bean sprouts, sprinkling with ¼ teaspoon salt if desired.

6. Push the vegetables to the sides of the wok or skillet. Add the sauce in the middle, stirring quickly to thicken. Add the pork back into the pan. Stir-fry for 1–2 more minutes to mix all the ingredients together. Pour over the chow mein noodles.

PER SERVING | Calories: 952 | Fat: 47g | Protein: 42g | Sodium: 1,667mg | Fiber: 6g | Carbohydrates: 92g | Sugar: 2g

Sesame-Flavored Fusilli

For added protein, toss in cooked shredded chicken to the dish.

INGREDIENTS | SERVES 4

1¾ teaspoons salt, divided
1 pound fusilli pasta
¼ cup water
1 tablespoon dark soy sauce
1 tablespoon rice vinegar
1 teaspoon sesame oil
2 tablespoons vegetable or peanut oil
1 teaspoon minced garlic
2 scallions, quartered
¼ teaspoon black pepper

1. In a large pot, bring 3 quarts water to a boil with 1½ teaspoons salt. Add the noodles and cook for 8–9 minutes or until they are firm but tender. Drain the noodles.

2. In a small bowl, combine the water, dark soy sauce, rice vinegar, and sesame oil. Set aside.

3. Heat a wok or skillet over medium-high heat until it is nearly smoking. Add the oil. When the oil is hot, add the garlic and scallions and stir-fry for 10 seconds.

4. Add the noodles. Stir-fry briefly, then add the sauce. Stir in remaining salt and the black pepper. Stir-fry for 1–2 more minutes to heat everything through. Serve hot or cold.

PER SERVING | Calories: 430 | Fat: 2.8g | Protein: 14g | Sodium: 1,264mg | Fiber: 3g | Carbohydrates: 84g | Sugar: 3g

Shrimp Pad Thai

*If you would like to create a vegetarian version, substitute the shrimp
with cooked tofu and use a watered down soy sauce in lieu of fish sauce.*

INGREDIENTS | SERVES 4

10 ounces flat rice stick noodles

⅓ cup tamarind liquid

4 teaspoons lime juice

2 tablespoons tamari

4 teaspoons tomato paste

4 teaspoons granulated sugar

2 tablespoons vegetable or peanut oil

2 shallots, chopped

1 small carrot, julienned

1 tablespoon fish sauce

2 eggs

½ pound shrimp, shelled and deveined

1 cup mung bean sprouts, rinsed

3 scallions, cut into 1" pieces

1 tablespoon ground red chilies

½ cup roasted peanuts, crushed

4 lime wedges

1. Soak the rice noodles in warm water for 15 minutes or until they have softened.

2. In a small bowl, combine the tamarind liquid, lime juice, tamari, tomato paste, and sugar. Set aside.

3. Heat a wok or skillet over medium-high heat until it is nearly smoking. Add the oil. When the oil is hot, add the chopped shallots and stir-fry for 30 seconds or until they begin to soften. Add the carrots. Stir-fry for an additional minute or until they are tender but still crisp and then add in the fish sauce.

4. Push the carrot mixture up the sides of the wok. Add the shrimp and cook for 1 minute or until they have turned pink and push them toward the sides along with the carrots. Add the eggs in the middle of the wok and stir until they begin to set, and then mix with the carrots and shrimp. Remove the items to a plate. Pour in the liquid mixture into the wok and allow it to come to a boil.

5. Add the noodles, stirring continually. After a minute, stir in the mung bean sprouts, scallions, and the ground chilies. Stir-fry for 1 more minute and then add the egg and shrimp. Toss the items in the wok to mix everything through. Garnish with the crushed peanuts and serve with lime wedges.

PER SERVING | Calories: 430 | Fat: 4g | Protein: 19g | Sodium: 305mg | Fiber: 3g | Carbohydrates: 78g | Sugar: 14g

Korean Chap Chae Noodles

*Chap Chae, also seen as Jap Chae, is a beloved Korean dish
that can be served hot or at room temperature.*

INGREDIENTS | SERVES 6

1 pound sweet potato noodles

½ cup low-sodium soy sauce

1 tablespoon sugar

2 tablespoons vegetable oil

½ pound boneless, skinless chicken breast, thinly sliced

2 small shallots, sliced

1 small carrot, julienned

1 small red bell pepper, julienned

1 cup shitake mushrooms, sliced

1 cup inoke mushrooms, cut into 2" pieces

1 tablespoon minced garlic

2 scallions, cut into 1" pieces

2 cups spinach leaves, washed well and drained

¼ cup mirin

½ tablespoon sesame oil

1 tablespoon toasted sesame seeds

1. Fill a large pot with water and bring to a boil. Add the noodles and cook until firm, about 5–6 minutes. Strain the noodles and rinse with cold water. Using kitchen shears, cut the noodles about 4–6 inches in length.

2. In a small bowl, stir the sugar into the soy sauce until dissolved. Set aside.

3. Heat vegetable oil in a large wok over medium-high heat. Add in the chicken and stir-fry for 2–3 minutes, tossing the wok to cook the chicken evenly.

4. Add in shallots, carrots, bell peppers, and mushrooms and stir-fry for 1–2 minutes or until tender. Add in garlic, scallions, and spinach and cook for 1 minute.

5. Use the mirin to deglaze the pan and then season with black pepper. Quickly toss in the noodles and half of the soy sauce mixture. Stir-fry for an additional 1–2 minutes.

6. Remove from heat and drizzle in the sesame oil. Sprinkle the sesame seeds over the top.

PER SERVING | Calories: 531 | Fat: 30g | Protein: 16g | Sodium: 1,585mg | Fiber: 4g | Carbohydrates: 50g | Sugar: 4g

Shrimp and Pork Pancit

A beloved dish of the Philippines, pancit can be made with a variety of meat or seafood or can be prepared vegetarian.

INGREDIENTS | SERVES 4

1 (8-ounce) package rice noodles
½ pound pork loin, thinly sliced
½ pound shrimp, shelled and deveined
¼ teaspoon kosher salt
¼ teaspoon black pepper
4 tablespoons vegetable oil, divided
1 tablespoon minced garlic
1 small yellow onion, diced
1 small carrot, julienned
½ cabbage, sliced thinly
¼ cup chicken broth
2 scallions, cut into 1" pieces
1½ tablespoons fish sauce
Lemon or kalamansi wedges

Puckering Up with Kalamansi

Kalamansi, also spelled calamansi, is a citrus fruit indigenous to the Philippines. The flavor is similar to lemon juice with light notes of oranges.

1. Soak the rice noodles in a large bowl filled with hot water for 15 minutes. Drain and cut into 4" pieces.

2. In a bowl, season the pork and shrimp with the salt and pepper. Allow to sit for 10 minutes.

3. Heat 2 tablespoons oil in a wok over medium-high heat. Toss in the pork and shrimp and stir-fry for 3–4 minutes until cooked through. Remove to a bowl.

4. Add the remaining oil to the wok and cook the garlic and onions for 30 seconds. Toss in the carrots and cabbage and stir-fry for 2–3 minutes until the vegetables have softened.

5. Pour in the chicken broth and bring to a boil. Add in the noodles, meat mixture, and scallions. Toss the items together and then add in the fish sauce. Allow the pancit to cook for an additional 1 minute, then serve with lemon wedges or kalamansi.

PER SERVING | Calories: 590 | Fat: 28g | Protein: 24g | Sodium: 474mg | Fiber: 4.5g | Carbohydrates: 58g | Sugar: 5g

Fried Saimin

Saimin is popular in local Hawaiian cuisine. The noodles are similar to ramen noodles, and the latter can be substituted if saimin cannot be found.

INGREDIENTS | SERVES 4

1 (9-ounce) package fresh saimin noodles or ramen noodles

3 tablespoons vegetable oil, divided

6 ounces Spam, cut into matchsticks

1 cup kamaboko, cut into matchsticks (optional)

½ small yellow onion, finely diced

2 cups shredded cabbage

2 tablespoons oyster sauce

1 tablespoon low-sodium soy sauce

2 scallions, diced

2 teaspoons sesame oil

½ cup toasted seaweed, julienned

1 teaspoon toasted sesame seeds

What Is Kamaboko?

Kamaboko is a Japanese fish cake that is typically made of white fish, eggs, sake, and soy sauce. It is a versatile ingredient that can be thrown in dishes such as noodles, porridge, fried rice, sushi, and even omelets. If you cannot find kamaboko at your local Japanese or Asian grocery store, try substituting with imitation crab meat.

1. Fill a large pot with water and bring to a boil. Add the noodles and cook for 2 minutes. Drain the noodles and reserve ¼ cup of the starchy water.

2. Heat 1 tablespoon oil in a wok over medium-high heat. Add the Spam and kamaboko and stir-fry for 2 minutes until they turn lightly golden. Remove to a plate lined with paper towels.

3. Add the remaining oil to the wok and cook the onion and cabbage for 3–4 minutes.

4. Stir in the oyster sauce, soy sauce, and the reserved starchy water and allow the liquids to boil. Add the Spam mixture, saimin, scallions, and sesame oil to the wok. Toss well to combine.

5. Sprinkle with seaweed and toasted sesame seeds. Serve immediately.

PER SERVING | Calories: 416 | Fat: 22g | Protein: 8g | Sodium: 1,321mg | Fiber: 3g | Carbohydrates: 46g | Sugar: 3g

Chicken and Miso Soba

Edamame, or soybeans, have a vast number of health benefits.
They are a form of low-calorie protein that is high in fiber and helps to lower cholesterol.

INGREDIENTS | SERVES 4

10 ounces soba (buckwheat noodles)
1 boneless, skinless chicken breast
¼ teaspoon black pepper
½ teaspoon kosher salt
1 tablespoon vegetable oil
½ tablespoon minced garlic
1 teaspoon minced ginger
½ cup diced red bell peppers
2½ tablespoons miso paste
½ cup shelled edamame
1 teaspoon sesame oil
½ tablespoon toasted sesame seeds

1. Bring a large pot of water to a boil. Cook the soba for 4–6 minutes. Drain the noodles, reserving ¼ cup of the starchy water.

2. Slice the chicken into thin strips. In a bowl, mix the chicken, pepper, and salt. Set aside for 10 minutes.

3. Heat oil in a wok over medium heat. Add the garlic and ginger and cook for 30 seconds.

4. Add in the chicken and bell peppers and stir-fry for 3–4 minutes.

5. In a small bowl, whisk together the starchy water with the miso paste.

6. Once the chicken has thoroughly cooked, add the miso mixture to the wok and toss in the soba, edamame, and sesame oil. Sprinkle the sesame seeds over the top. Serve immediately.

PER SERVING | Calories: 560 | Fat: 31g | Protein: 24g | Sodium: 1,076mg | Fiber: 5g | Carbohydrates: 48g | Sugar: 1g

Uni (Sea Urchin Roe) Pasta

Fresh uni can be found in trays in the refrigerated section of most Japanese markets.

INGREDIENTS | SERVES 2

2½ teaspoons kosher salt, divided

¼ pound linguine, or pasta of your choice

1 tablespoon olive oil

1 tablespoon unsalted butter

1 garlic clove, finely minced

¼ teaspoon red chili flakes

¼ cup heavy cream

5 ounces fresh uni

½ teaspoon white pepper

1 tablespoon fresh chives, finely diced

1 teaspoon toasted sesame seeds

¼ cup seasoned nori (seaweed), chiffonade

Sea Urchins' Menacing Armor

At first glance, sea urchins appear quite intimidating, as their exterior is made entirely of foreboding spikes. But with the assistance of gloves and sharp kitchen scissors, you can make your way to extract the tasty lobes and enjoy the briny, unctuous delicacy.

1. Bring a large pot of water to boil and add 2 teaspoons salt. Add the linguine and cook the pasta for 8–10 minutes or until al dente.

2. In a wok over medium heat, melt the olive oil and butter together. Add garlic and sauté for 1–2 minutes.

3. Add the chili flakes and heavy cream. Bring to a slight slimmer and add all but 4 pieces of the uni.

4. Remove from heat and whisk items together until the uni has broken down into the sauce. Toss in the cooked pasta until the noodles have been evenly coated. Season with remaining salt and white pepper.

5. Transfer pasta to a plate and place the remaining whole uni segments on top. Sprinkle the tops with chives, sesame seeds, and nori. Serve immediately.

PER SERVING | Calories: 490 | Fat: 25g | Protein: 17g | Sodium: 3,007mg | Fiber: 2g | Carbohydrates: 46g | Sugar: 1g

Hunter's Chicken and Pasta

If you don't have linguine on hand, spaghetti or other types of thin pastas can also be used in this recipe.

INGREDIENTS | SERVES 6

2½ teaspoons salt, divided

¾ pound linguine

1½ pounds boneless, skinless chicken thighs

9 tablespoons dry white wine, divided

½ teaspoon black pepper

1 tablespoon cornstarch

6 tablespoons chicken broth

5 tablespoons olive oil, divided

2 shallots, chopped

½ pound fresh mushrooms, thinly sliced

¼ cup tomato sauce

¼ cup fresh basil leaves, roughly torn

1 tablespoon chopped fresh thyme

1. In a large pot, bring 3 quarts water to a boil with 1½ teaspoons salt. Add the noodles and cook for 4–5 minutes, until they are firm but still tender. Drain the cooked pasta.

2. Cut the chicken into thin strips approximately 1½"–2" long. Place the chicken strips in a bowl and add 3 tablespoons dry white wine, 1 teaspoon salt, black pepper, and cornstarch. Marinate the chicken for 20 minutes. Combine the chicken broth and 6 tablespoons white wine in a bowl. Set aside.

3. Heat a wok or skillet over medium-high heat until it is almost smoking. Add 3 tablespoons oil. When the oil is hot, add the chicken strips. Let them brown briefly, then stir-fry, stirring and tossing the chicken for 4–5 minutes until it has changed color and is nearly cooked. Remove the chicken from the pan.

4. Heat 2 tablespoons oil in the pan. When the oil is hot, add the shallots. Stir-fry for 1 minute or until they begin to soften, then add the sliced mushrooms and stir-fry for about 1 minute.

5. Add the chicken broth mixture. Stir in the tomato sauce and bring to a boil.

6. Add the chicken back into the pan. Stir in the fresh basil and thyme. Stir-fry for 2 more minutes to blend all the ingredients and make sure the chicken is cooked.

7. Serve the chicken over the noodles. Garnish with extra thyme and basil leaves if desired.

PER SERVING | Calories: 481 | Fat: 16g | Protein: 31g | Sodium: 1,204mg | Fiber: 2g | Carbohydrates: 46g | Sugar: 2.8g

Creamy Pesto Rigatoni

Using store-bought pesto can make this dish even easier for a quick yet delicious meal.

INGREDIENTS | SERVES 6

1 pound boneless, skinless chicken breasts

1½ teaspoons kosher salt

¼ teaspoon black pepper

1 pound rigatoni pasta

2 tablespoons olive oil, divided

1 tablespoon minced garlic

1 cup grape tomatoes, halved

¼ teaspoon red chili flakes

1 cup Basil Pesto (see Chapter 2)

½ cup heavy cream

¼ cup grated Parmesan cheese

Going Nuts for Pesto

Traditional pesto uses lightly toasted pignoli (pine nuts) and fresh basil. However, by using different nuts such as almond or walnuts and other greens such as cilantro or arugula, old recipes can get a quick and easy makeover.

1. Slice the chicken breasts into strips and season with ½ teaspoon salt and pepper. Set aside.

2. Fill a large pot of water and bring it to a boil. Add the remaining 1 teaspoon salt and cook pasta for 8–10 minutes until al dente. Drain the cooked pasta.

3. In a wok, add 1 tablespoon olive oil and heat over medium heat. Brown the chicken breasts and stir-fry for 5–6 minutes. Remove the chicken from the wok.

4. Add remaining olive oil and cook garlic over medium heat for 1–2 minutes before tossing in the tomatoes and red chili flakes. Cook mixture for about 2 minutes.

5. Stir in the pesto. Heat the pesto and then stir in the heavy cream. Once incorporated, toss in the pasta, chicken, and Parmesan cheese and coat well. Serve warm.

PER SERVING | Calories: 636 | Fat: 30g | Protein: 29g | Sodium: 916mg | Fiber: 3g | Carbohydrates: 58g | Sugar: 2g

Linguine alla Carbonara

Traditional carbonara uses guanciale, an aged and unsmoked Italian bacon made from pork jowls.

INGREDIENTS | SERVES 2

2 large eggs, room temperature

⅓ cup grated Parmesan cheese

3 tablespoons chopped Italian parsley, divided

4 strips thick cut bacon, diced

2 teaspoons salt

⅓ pound linguine

3 tablespoons finely chopped shallots

2 garlic cloves, diced finely

¼ teaspoon red chili flakes

1. In a large bowl, whisk together the eggs and Parmesan cheese. Once combined, mix in 2 tablespoons parsley. Set bowl aside.

2. Add bacon to a wok and turn burner to medium heat. Slowly sauté the bacon until it becomes crispy and the fat has rendered down—about 5 minutes.

3. While the bacon is browning, fill a large pot with water and 2 teaspoons salt. Bring to a boil. Cook the pasta for 8–10 minutes or until al dente.

4. Once the bacon is crispy, use a slotted spoon and transfer it to a plate covered with paper towels. Chop bacon and set aside. Reserve 1 tablespoon of bacon drippings in the wok and discard the rest.

5. Sauté the shallots in the bacon drippings for 30 seconds or until translucent. Add garlic and cook for an additional 2 minutes. Add chili flakes and cook for 1 minute. Transfer the mixture to a bowl and cool.

6. Once cooked, drain the hot pasta and quickly toss it in the egg/cheese mixture until the sauce has thickened. Add all but 2 tablespoons of the chopped bacon and the shallot mixture. Continue to mix until all items have been thoroughly incorporated.

7. Remove the pasta to a platter and sprinkle with remaining bacon and parsley. Serve immediately.

PER SERVING | Calories: 437 | Fat: 10g | Protein: 23g | Sodium: 2,692mg | Fiber: 2g | Carbohydrates: 60g | Sugar: 2g

Shrimp Scampi

Adding caper berries into the dish at the end gives another level of flavor and brightness.

INGREDIENTS | SERVES 2

½ pound linguine noodles

1½ tablespoons kosher salt

¼ teaspoon black pepper

½ pound large shrimp, cleaned and peeled

2 tablespoons unsalted butter

1 tablespoon olive oil

2 tablespoons fresh garlic, minced finely

½ teaspoon red pepper flakes

Zest of 1 lemon

¼ cup fresh lemon juice

½ cup dry white wine

¼ cup chopped Italian parsley

2 tablespoons grated Parmesan cheese

1. Fill a large pot of water and bring to boil. Stir in 1 tablespoon kosher salt and cook linguine for 8–10 minutes or until al dente. Drain the linguine while reserving ¼ cup of the starchy water the pasta was cooked in.

2. Season shrimp with remaining salt and pepper.

3. In a wok, melt butter and olive oil over medium heat. Add garlic and red pepper flakes and stir-fry for 30 seconds.

4. Add the shrimp and lemon zest. Cook shrimp on both sides until they turn pink—approximately 1–2 minutes on each side. Remove the shrimp to a plate.

5. Add the lemon juice and white wine and bring to a boil. Allow the liquids to reduce for 3–4 minutes.

6. Toss in the shrimp, cooked linguine, pasta water, parsley, and Parmesan cheese. Serve immediately.

PER SERVING | Calories: 803 | Fat: 24g | Protein: 41g | Sodium: 5,590mg | Fiber: 5g | Carbohydrates: 94g | Sugar: 5g

CHAPTER 10

Rice

Basic Cooked Rice

When cooking long-grain rice such as jasmine rice, rinse the grains with cool water to remove any grit and to avoid clumping while it cooks.

INGREDIENTS | YIELDS 3 CUPS; SERVING SIZE: ¾ CUP

1½ cups water
1 cup long-grain rice

1. Bring the water and rice to a boil in a saucepan over medium heat.

2. When the water is boiling, partially cover and lower the heat to medium low.

3. Cook for approximately 20 minutes until most of the liquid is absorbed.

4. Cover and cook on low heat for about 3–5 minutes. Remove from the heat and let sit, covered, for 5 minutes. Use a fork to fluff the rice before serving.

PER SERVING | Calories: 168 | Fat: 0.3g | Protein: 3g | Sodium: 5mg | Fiber: 0.6g | Carbohydrates: 36g | Sugar: 0g

Chicken Adobo Fried Rice

Many Filipino rice dishes are served with a side of vinegar that contains either chilies or black pepper.

INGREDIENTS | SERVES 6

2 tablespoons vegetable oil
1 small onion, sliced thinly
1½ cups Chicken Adobo, cut into 1" pieces (see Chapter 5)
3 cups Garlic Rice (see recipe in this chapter)
1 tablespoon soy sauce
1 teaspoon sesame oil

1. Heat oil in a wok over medium heat. Add onion and cook for 30 seconds.

2. Add in the chicken pieces and stir-fry for an additional minute.

3. Add in the rice. Continue stir-frying the rice for an additional 2 minutes. Add soy sauce and sesame oil, tossing well to combine. Serve hot.

PER SERVING | Calories: 854 | Fat: 34g | Protein: 95g | Sodium: 4,137mg | Fiber: 1.5g | Carbohydrates: 34g | Sugar: 2g

Coconut-Scented Rice

Replacing the water with other liquids such as chicken stock or coconut milk provides an easy and flavorful alternative to your dish.

INGREDIENTS | YIELDS 3 CUPS; SERVING SIZE: ¾ CUP

¾ cup coconut milk

¾ cup water

1 cup long-grain rice

¼ teaspoon salt

1. Bring the coconut milk, water, salt, and rice to a boil in a saucepan over medium heat. When the water is boiling, partially cover and lower the heat to medium low. Cook for approximately 15 minutes or until most of the liquid is absorbed.

2. Cover and continue cooking on low heat for 3–5 minutes or until the liquid is fully absorbed. Remove the rice from the heat and let sit, covered, for 5 minutes. Use a fork to fluff the rice before serving.

PER SERVING | Calories: 168 | Fat: 0.3g | Protein: 3g | Sodium: 5mg | Fiber: 0.6g | Carbohydrates: 36g | Sugar: 0g

Basic Fried Rice

Fried rice is a quick and delicious way to utilize leftovers.

INGREDIENTS | SERVES 4

2 large eggs

¼ teaspoon salt

¼ teaspoon black pepper

3 tablespoons vegetable or peanut oil, divided

2 cloves garlic, minced

3½ cups cooked rice

1 tablespoon soy sauce

½ cup frozen peas

2 scallions, finely chopped

1 teaspoon sesame oil

1. In a small bowl, beat the eggs with the salt and pepper.

2. Heat 2 tablespoons oil in a wok or skillet over medium-high heat. Add the eggs. Stir the eggs until they are lightly scrambled. Remove the eggs and clean out the pan.

3. Heat 1 tablespoon oil. Add the garlic and cook for 30 seconds or until fragrant. Add in the rice and stir-fry for 2 minutes. Stir in the soy sauce.

4. Stir in the peas. Stir-fry for 30 seconds, then add the eggs, scallions, and sesame oil. Serve hot.

PER SERVING | Calories: 278 | Fat: 4g | Protein: 8g | Sodium: 409mg | Fiber: 1g | Carbohydrates: 50g | Sugar: 1g

Fried Rice with Shrimp

This recipe calls for a relatively small amount of shrimp to keep the shrimp flavor from overpowering the other ingredients. If you want more protein, add 2 thinly sliced Chinese sausages.

INGREDIENTS | SERVES 4

4 ounces large shrimp, shelled and deveined

¼ teaspoon salt

2 tablespoons chicken broth

1 tablespoon oyster sauce

1 tablespoon soy sauce

2 large eggs

⅛ teaspoon black pepper

3 tablespoons vegetable or peanut oil, divided

2 thin slices ginger

2 scallions, finely chopped

½ small onion, chopped

1 cup frozen peas

3 cups cooked rice

1 small tomato, sliced

½ small cucumber, sliced

Fried Rice Origins

While the Chinese were the first to come up with the idea of adding stir-fried vegetables to leftover cooked rice, the precise origins of this popular restaurant dish have been lost to history. However, fried rice was probably invented in the eastern province of Yangzhou, during the Sui dynasty (A.D. 581–617).

1. Rinse the shrimp under cold running water and pat dry with paper towels. Toss with the salt.

2. In a small bowl, combine the chicken broth, oyster sauce, and soy sauce. Set aside. Lightly beat the eggs, stirring in the black pepper.

3. Heat a wok or skillet over medium-high heat until it is nearly smoking. Add 2 tablespoons oil. When the oil is hot, add the sliced ginger and scallions. Stir-fry for 10 seconds, then add the shrimp. Stir-fry the shrimp briefly until it turns bright pink.

4. Push the shrimp to the sides and add the onion in the middle of the wok or skillet. Stir-fry for 2 minutes or until it begins to soften. Add the peas. Stir-fry for 1 minute or until it is tender but still crisp. Remove the shrimp and vegetables from the pan.

5. Heat 1 tablespoon oil in the wok or skillet. When the oil is hot, add the rice. Stir-fry the rice for 1 minute or until it begins to turn golden. Add the lightly beaten eggs and scramble, mixing them in with the rice. Add the chicken broth mixture. Add the shrimp and vegetables back into the pan. Stir-fry for 1–2 minutes to mix everything together. Garnish with the slices of tomato and cucumbers. Serve hot.

PER SERVING | Calories: 268 | Fat: 3.5g | Protein: 13g | Sodium: 606mg | Fiber: 1g | Carbohydrates: 44g | Sugar: 2g

Kimchee Fried Rice

The longer your kimchee is aged, the more its prominent flavors will come through.

INGREDIENTS | SERVES 2

1½ tablespoons vegetable oil

1 tablespoon minced garlic

1 cup diced white onions

1 cup kimchee, drained and roughly chopped (reserve ¼ cup liquid)

2 cups cooked white rice

½ tablespoon low-sodium soy sauce

1 scallion, diced

½ tablespoon garlic powder

¼ teaspoon black pepper

1 teaspoon sesame oil

1 tablespoon furikake

1. Heat a wok over medium heat with the vegetable oil. Add the garlic and onions and cook until aromatic, about 30 seconds.

2. Stir in the kimchee and cook for 1 minute before adding in the rice. Stir-fry for 2 minutes, then add kimchee liquid and soy sauce. Toss to cook for 2–3 minutes or until the liquids have absorbed.

3. Add in the scallion, garlic powder, black pepper, and sesame oil. Stir-fry for 1 minute and divide between two dishes.

4. Sprinkle each dish of rice with furikake. Serve immediately.

PER SERVING | Calories: 993 | Fat: 25g | Protein: 21g | Sodium: 302mg | Fiber: 4g | Carbohydrates: 166g | Sugar: 4g

Spam Fried Rice

Not into Spam? Feel free to substitute smoked ham.

INGREDIENTS | SERVES 6

3½ tablespoons vegetable oil, divided

6 ounces Spam, cubed

3 eggs, slightly beaten

3 cups jasmine rice, cooked and
refrigerated overnight

2 scallions, minced

½ cup frozen peas

½ cup frozen diced carrots

1½ tablespoons Maggi Seasoning

1 teaspoon sesame oil

½ teaspoon ground black pepper

Demystifying Spam

Spam is a precooked pork product by the Hormel Foods Corporation that was introduced in the 1930s. The humbled canned good has made its way to become a staple in local Hawaiian cuisine. In fact, more Spam is consumed in the islands of Hawaii per year than the rest of the United States.

1. Add 1 tablespoon oil to a wok and heat over medium heat. Add the Spam and cook for approximately 2 minutes or until golden brown. Remove the Spam to a plate lined with paper towels.

2. Add ½ tablespoon oil to the wok and pour in the eggs. Scramble and cook the eggs for 1 minute and remove to a plate.

3. Add the remaining oil to the wok. Add the cooked rice and stir-fry for 3–4 minutes, tossing the wok periodically.

4. Stir in the cooked eggs, Spam, scallions, peas, carrots, Maggi, and sesame oil. Stir-fry for an additional 1–2 minutes. Season with the black pepper and serve immediately.

PER SERVING | Calories: 465 | Fat: 11g | Protein: 10g | Sodium: 47mg | Fiber: 2g | Carbohydrates: 77g | Sugar: 1g

Garlic Rice

This garlic rice is a common staple in Filipino cuisine and can be found alongside dishes such as fried milk fish, chicken adobo, and tocino.

INGREDIENTS | YIELDS 3 CUPS; SERVING SIZE: ¾ CUP

2 tablespoons vegetable oil, divided
3 tablespoons minced garlic, divided
1 cup long-grain rice
1½ cups water
2 scallions, diced

1. Heat 1 tablespoon oil in a heavy-bottomed pot and cook 1 tablespoon garlic until fragrant. Add in the rice and stir until the grains are coated. Add the water and bring to a boil. When the water is boiling, partially cover and lower the heat to medium low. Cook for approximately 10 minutes or until most of the liquid is absorbed.

2. Cover and continue cooking the rice on low heat for approximately 5 additional minutes or until the water is fully absorbed. Remove the rice from the heat and let sit, covered, for 5 minutes. Use a fork to fluff the rice and cool for several hours.

3. Heat the remaining oil in a wok over medium-high heat. Add the remaining garlic and stir for 20–30 seconds before adding in the cooled rice and scallions. Stir-fry the rice with the scallions for 2–3 minutes and serve immediately.

PER SERVING | Calories: 240 | Fat: 7g | Protein: 3g | Sodium: 6mg | Fiber: 0.8g | Carbohydrates: 39g | Sugar: 0.4g

Chimichurri Rice

Although shrimp is used in this recipe, any meat would work well with this dish.

INGREDIENTS | SERVES 4

½ pound large shrimp, peeled and deveined, cut in half

1 teaspoon garlic salt

½ teaspoon red pepper flakes

1 teaspoon lemon zest

1 tablespoon olive oil

2 tablespoons vegetable oil

½ tablespoon minced garlic

2 tablespoons minced shallots

½ cup frozen peas

3 cups cooked long-grain rice

½ cup Chimichurri Sauce (see Chapter 2)

1. In a large bowl, combine the shrimp, garlic salt, red pepper flakes, zest, and olive oil. Refrigerate for 20 minutes.

2. Heat vegetable oil in a wok over medium heat. Add garlic and shallots and cook for 30 seconds.

3. Toss in the shrimp and stir-fry for 1 minute. Add the peas and cook for an additional minute.

4. Add in the rice. Stir and move the items around the wok and cook for 2–3 minutes.

5. Remove from heat and add Chimichurri Sauce. Toss the rice to ensure the ingredients have fully incorporated. Serve hot.

PER SERVING | Calories: 458 | Fat: 25g | Protein: 16g | Sodium: 1,123mg | Fiber: 2g | Carbohydrates: 41g | Sugar: 3g

Mushroom Fried Rice

For a deeper level of mushroom flavor, try an assortment of wild mushrooms such as shiitake, oyster, and trumpet.

INGREDIENTS | SERVES 4

2 large eggs

⅛ teaspoon salt

⅛ teaspoon black pepper

1 tablespoon hoisin sauce

2 teaspoons water

3 tablespoons vegetable or peanut oil, divided

3 cups cooked wild rice

1 tablespoon soy sauce

1 cup sliced portobello mushrooms

½ cup frozen peas, thawed

2 scallions, finely chopped

1 teaspoon sesame oil

1. In a small bowl, lightly beat the eggs, stirring in the salt and pepper.

2. In a separate small bowl, combine the hoisin sauce with the water.

3. Heat a wok or skillet over medium-high heat until it is nearly smoking. Add 2 tablespoons oil. When the oil is hot, add the eggs. Stir the eggs until they are lightly scrambled. Remove the scrambled eggs and clean out the pan.

4. Heat 1 tablespoon oil. When the oil is hot, add the rice. Stir-fry for 2 minutes, stirring and tossing the rice. Stir in the soy sauce.

5. Stir in the mushrooms. Stir-fry for 1 minute, then add the peas. Stir to mix the rice and the vegetables.

6. Stir in the scrambled eggs, the hoisin sauce mixture, and the scallions. Cook for 1 minute to blend the flavors. Remove from the heat and stir in the sesame oil. Serve hot.

PER SERVING | Calories: 202 | Fat: 4g | Protein: 10g | Sodium: 405mg | Fiber: 3g | Carbohydrates: 32g | Sugar: 4g

Pineapple Fried Rice

Want a show-stopping way to present this dish?
Hollow out halved pineapples and fill them with this delectable fried rice.

INGREDIENTS | SERVES 4

¼ pound large shrimp, shelled and deveined

2 eggs

1 teaspoon salt

¼ teaspoon black pepper

4 tablespoons vegetable or peanut oil, divided

1 teaspoon chopped garlic

½ cup chopped onion

1 small red bell pepper, seeded and cut into bite-sized chunks

1 tablespoon Chinese light soy sauce or fish sauce

1 cup pineapple chunks

3 cups Coconut-Scented Rice (see recipe in this chapter), refrigerated overnight

2 scallions, cut into 1" pieces

1 tablespoon oyster sauce

Rice—The Staff of Life

Rice is the primary source of energy for over half of the world's population, largely because it is an excellent source of energy and has a high calorie count, and is relatively inexpensive to grow. Also, rice can be directly consumed after harvesting, without any further processing (unlike cereal crops such as wheat, which need to be processed into cereal, flour, or another food before being consumed).

1. Rinse the shrimp under cold running water and pat dry with paper towels.

2. In a small bowl, lightly beat the eggs, stirring in the salt and pepper.

3. Heat a wok or skillet over medium-high heat and add 1 tablespoon oil. When the oil is hot, reduce the heat to medium and add the egg mixture. Lightly scramble the eggs for 1 minute. Remove them from the pan and clean out the pan.

4. Heat 2 tablespoons oil in the wok or skillet. When the oil is hot, add the garlic and stir-fry for 10 seconds.

5. Add the onion and the shrimp. Stir-fry for about 2 minutes, until the shrimp turns pink and the onion begins to soften.

6. Add the red bell pepper. Stir-fry for 1 minute, stirring in the soy sauce while stir-frying. Stir in the pineapple.

7. Push the vegetables to the sides or remove from the wok (whether you need to do this will depend on the size of your wok) and heat 1 tablespoon oil. Add the cooked rice to the hot oil and stir-fry briefly.

8. Add the vegetables back into the pan and stir to mix. Stir in the scrambled eggs and the scallions. Stir in the oyster sauce. Stir-fry briefly to heat through, and serve hot.

PER SERVING | Calories: 362 | Fat: 12g | Protein: 14g | Sodium: 1,173mg | Fiber: 2g | Carbohydrates: 49g | Sugar: 6g

Indonesian Fried Rice (Nasi Goreng)

*Made from fermented shrimp, shrimp paste is available in Asian grocery stores.
You can adjust this recipe to use only chicken or shrimp or to use uncooked chicken and shrimp if desired
(just stir-fry the ingredients first and then use as called for in the recipe).*

INGREDIENTS | SERVES 3

2 large eggs

1 teaspoon salt

¼ teaspoon black pepper

3 tablespoons vegetable or peanut oil, divided

2 cloves garlic, crushed

1 small onion, chopped

1 teaspoon chili powder

1 tablespoon shrimp paste

3 cups cooked long-grain white rice

½ pound cooked chicken breast, shredded

6–8 cooked medium shrimp

2 tablespoons kecap manis or dark soy sauce

1. In a small bowl, lightly beat the eggs, stirring in the salt and pepper.

2. Heat a wok or skillet over medium-high heat and add 1 tablespoon oil. When the oil is hot, reduce the heat to medium and pour in the beaten eggs. Cook for 1 minute or until the eggs are firm, turning over once. Remove the cooked eggs and cut into thin strips. Clean out the pan.

3. Heat 2 tablespoons oil in the wok or skillet over medium-high heat. When the oil is hot, add the garlic and onion. Sprinkle the chili powder over the mixture and stir-fry for about 2 minutes, until the onion begins to soften. Add the shrimp paste and continue stir-frying for 1 minute or until the onion has softened.

4. Add the rice and stir-fry for 1–2 minutes, until it begins to turn golden.

5. Stir in the cooked chicken and shrimp. Add in the kecap manis or dark soy sauce and stir-fry for 1–2 more minutes, to blend the ingredients.

6. To serve, divide the fried rice among 3 plates, then lay the strips of egg on top of each serving.

PER SERVING | Calories: 883 | Fat: 7g | Protein: 44g | Sodium: 931mg | Fiber: 3g | Carbohydrates: 152g | Sugar: 2g

Spanish Rice

This easy and colorful side dish pairs well with tacos and fajitas.

Rice Around the World

Spain is the birthplace of paella Valencia—an elaborate dish with shellfish, meat, and rice that is flavored with saffron and a tomato-based sauce. Jambalaya is a Cajun/Creole adaptation of paella Valencia made with ingredients readily available in the southern United States. Japan's signature dish, sushi, is often served with a bowl of sushi rice—a sticky rice seasoned with rice vinegar and sugar.

1. Bring the chicken broth, bouillon cubes, and rice to a boil in a saucepan over medium heat.

2. When the broth is boiling, partially cover and lower the heat to medium low. After 8–10 minutes or when the broth is nearly absorbed, cover the rice and cook for approximately 5 more minutes over low heat until the broth is completely absorbed.

3. Purée the tomatoes in a food processor or blender.

4. Heat a wok or skillet over medium heat until it is nearly smoking. Add the olive oil. Add the rice and stir-fry, stirring it in the oil until it turns golden brown.

5. Add the onion and garlic. Sprinkle the chili powder over the mixture. Stir in the puréed tomato and the chopped cilantro. Continue stir-frying for about 2 minutes or until the onion is softened. Serve hot.

PER SERVING | Calories: 284 | Fat: 8g | Protein: 5g | Sodium: 405mg | Fiber: 1g | Carbohydrates: 45g | Sugar: 2g

Stir-Fried Coconut Basmati

Coconut soda, such as Coco Rico or Goya's Coconut Soda, can be used instead of chicken broth in this side dish for an added boost of coconut flavor.

INGREDIENTS | SERVES 4

1 cup basmati rice, uncooked
¾ cup chicken broth
¾ cup coconut milk
2 tablespoons olive oil
3 tablespoons raisins
2 shallots, chopped
2 cloves garlic, chopped
3 tablespoons tomato paste
1 tablespoon fish sauce
1 tablespoon brown sugar
½ teaspoon ground white pepper

Scented Rice

Also called fragrant rice, scented rice refers to several varieties of rice that have a pleasant aroma. Basmati and jasmine are the two most well-known types of scented rice. Originally grown in the Himalayan foothills, basmati rice is famous for its pleasant nutty flavor and fine texture. While not as flavorful, jasmine rice also has a nutty flavor and is much cheaper than basmati.

1. Bring the rice, chicken broth, and coconut milk to a boil in an uncovered saucepan on medium heat.

2. When the liquid is boiling, partially cover and lower the heat to medium low. Cook for 8–10 minutes or until most of the liquid is absorbed.

3. When the broth is nearly absorbed, completely cover and cook for an additional 5 minutes over low heat until the broth is completely absorbed.

4. Heat a wok or skillet over medium heat until it is nearly smoking. Add the olive oil. When the oil is hot, add the rice, stirring it in the oil until it turns golden brown. Stir in the raisins.

5. Stir the shallots and garlic into the rice. Continue stir-frying for about 3 minutes or until the shallots are softened.

6. Stir in the tomato paste, fish sauce, and the brown sugar. Mix in white pepper and serve hot.

PER SERVING | Calories: 377 | Fat: 16g | Protein: 5g | Sodium: 303mg | Fiber: 1g | Carbohydrates: 52g | Sugar: 9g

Ground Beef with Broccoli and Rice

Enjoy the flavor of Chinese beef with broccoli during the week with this easy one-pot dish.

INGREDIENTS | SERVES 4

2 teaspoons salt, divided

¼ teaspoon black pepper

1½ teaspoons cornstarch

¾ pound ground beef

2 teaspoons plus 3 tablespoons vegetable or peanut oil, divided

1 teaspoon minced garlic

2 teaspoons minced ginger

2 cups chopped broccoli

½ cup water

1 cup cooked white rice

1⅓ cup Basic Chinese Brown Sauce (see Chapter 2)

1 teaspoon granulated sugar

Fried Rice Fundamentals

When making fried rice, use previously cooked rice if possible. Day-old rice is ideal, which is one of the reasons why fried rice is perfect to use up leftovers with. Sprinkle a few drops of water on the rice, and use your fingers or a spatula to break up the clumps.

1. In a bowl, mix 1 teaspoon salt, pepper, and cornstarch in with the ground beef. Let the ground beef stand for 20 minutes.

2. Heat wok or skillet over medium-high heat until it is nearly smoking. Add 2 teaspoons oil. When the oil is hot, add the ground beef. Stir-fry, stirring and tossing it in the pan until there is no trace of pink and the ground beef is nearly cooked through, about 8–10 minutes. Remove the ground beef and drain in a colander or on paper towels.

3. Clean out the wok or skillet and add 2 tablespoons oil. When the oil is hot, add the garlic and ginger and stir-fry for 10 seconds.

4. Add the broccoli and stir-fry for 2 minutes, sprinkling with 1 teaspoon salt. Add ½ cup water, cover, and cook the broccoli for 4–5 minutes, until it is tender but still crisp. Remove the broccoli and drain on a plate lined with paper towels.

5. Heat 1 tablespoon oil in the wok or skillet. When the oil is hot, add the rice. Stir-fry the rice in the oil for about 1 minute or until it begins to brown.

6. Add the ground beef and broccoli back into the pan. Add the brown sauce, stirring quickly to thicken. Stir in the sugar. Stir-fry for 1–2 more minutes. Serve hot.

PER SERVING | Calories: 297 | Fat: 11g | Protein: 20g | Sodium: 2,142mg | Fiber: 1g | Carbohydrates: 25g | Sugar: 4g

Beef in Rice

To add extra flavor to this dish, try cooking the rice in chicken broth or beef broth instead of water.

INGREDIENTS | SERVES 4

½ teaspoon salt

¼ teaspoon black pepper

1½ teaspoons cornstarch

¾ pound ground beef

2 teaspoons plus 3 tablespoons olive oil, divided

2 cloves garlic, minced

2 thin slices ginger, minced

1 small onion, chopped

1 tablespoon paprika

1½ cups cooked white rice

1 cup frozen corn

1 cup beef broth

1 tablespoon Worcestershire sauce

1 tablespoon brown sugar

1. In a large bowl, mix the salt, pepper, and cornstarch in with the ground beef. Let stand for 20 minutes.

2. Heat wok or skillet over medium-high heat until it is nearly smoking. Add 2 teaspoons olive oil. When the oil is hot, add the ground beef. Stir-fry, stirring and tossing it in the pan, until there is no trace of pink and the ground beef is nearly cooked through, about 8–10 minutes. Remove the ground beef and drain in a colander or on paper towels.

3. Clean out the wok or skillet and add 2 tablespoons olive oil. When the oil is hot, add the garlic and ginger and stir-fry for 10 seconds.

4. Add the onion. Stir-fry the onion until it begins to soften (about 2 minutes), sprinkling the paprika over the onion while you are stir-frying.

5. Add 1 tablespoon oil in the middle of the pan. Add the rice and stir-fry, stirring it in the oil for 1 minute until it begins to turn golden brown. Add the frozen corn and stir-fry for 1 minute, mixing the corn with the onion and seasonings.

6. Add the beef broth and bring to a boil. Stir in the cooked ground beef. Stir in the Worcestershire sauce and brown sugar. Continue stir-frying for 2–3 minutes to mix all the ingredients together and until most of the liquid is absorbed. Serve hot.

PER SERVING | Calories: 426 | Fat: 21g | Protein: 21g | Sodium: 592mg | Fiber: 2g | Carbohydrates: 37g | Sugar: 5g

Curried Beef Fried Rice

As always, feel free to adjust the amount of seasoning according to your own tastes, adding more or less curry powder as desired.

INGREDIENTS | SERVES 4

1 pound sirloin steak, cut into thin strips

2 tablespoons light soy sauce

1 tablespoon Chinese rice wine or dry sherry

1 teaspoon sesame oil

2 teaspoons cornstarch

½ cup chicken broth

1½ tablespoons dark soy sauce

5 tablespoons vegetable or peanut oil, divided

2 cloves garlic, chopped

2 thin slices ginger, chopped

1 tablespoon rice wine or sherry, optional

1 small onion, chopped

3 tablespoons curry powder

1 cup frozen peas

1½ cups cold cooked rice

½ teaspoon salt

1 teaspoon granulated sugar

¼ teaspoon black pepper

1. Place the beef in a bowl, and add the light soy sauce, rice wine or sherry, sesame oil, and cornstarch. Marinate for 15 minutes. In a small bowl, combine the chicken broth and dark soy sauce. Set aside.

2. Heat a wok or skillet over medium heat until it is nearly smoking. Add 2 tablespoons oil. When the oil is hot, add half the garlic and ginger and stir-fry for 10 seconds.

3. Add half the beef, laying it flat in the pan. Let sear briefly, then stir-fry the meat for 1–2 minutes, until it is nearly cooked. Remove the meat and drain on paper towels. Repeat with the other half of the beef. If the beef begins to dry out, splash with 1 tablespoon of rice wine instead of adding more oil.

4. Add 2 tablespoons oil to the wok. When the oil is hot, add the remainder of the garlic and ginger. Stir-fry for 10 seconds, then add the onion. Stir-fry the onion for about 2 minutes, until it starts to soften, sprinkling the curry powder over the top. Add the frozen peas and stir-fry for 1 minute.

5. Push the vegetables to the side and add 1 tablespoon oil in the middle. Add the rice and stir-fry in the oil for 1 minute until the rice begins to turn golden. Sprinkle the salt over the rice.

6. Add the chicken broth mixture. Stir in the sugar and black pepper. Return the beef to the pan. Stir-fry for another 1–2 minutes and serve hot.

PER SERVING | Calories: 339 | Fat: 8g | Protein: 29g | Sodium: 987mg | Fiber: 4g | Carbohydrates: 35g | Sugar: 4g

Pork in Rice

To add extra flavor to this dish, you can try cooking the rice in beef broth instead of water.

INGREDIENTS | SERVES 3

½ teaspoon salt

¼ teaspoon black pepper

1½ teaspoons cornstarch

¾ pound ground pork

2 teaspoons plus 3 tablespoons olive oil, divided

2 cloves garlic, minced

2 thin slices ginger, minced

1 small onion, chopped

1 tablespoon paprika

1½ cups cooked white rice

1 cup chopped red bell pepper

1 tablespoon light soy sauce

1 tablespoon tomato paste

1 cup chicken broth

1 tablespoon brown sugar

Healthy Rice

While low-carb dieters may shun it, rice provides a high degree of nutritional bang for the caloric buck. Besides being low in fat and cholesterol, rice contains no sodium and is a good source of iron and the B vitamins thiamin, riboflavin, and niacin. Rice also contains pantothenic acid, believed to help ward off signs of aging, such as gray hair and wrinkles!

1. In a large bowl, mix the salt, pepper, and cornstarch in with the ground pork. Let stand for 20 minutes.

2. Heat wok or skillet over medium-high heat until it is nearly smoking. Add 2 teaspoons olive oil. When the oil is hot, add the pork. Stir-fry until there is no trace of pink and the pork is nearly cooked through, about 8–10 minutes. Remove the pork and drain on paper towels.

3. Clean out the wok or skillet and add 2 tablespoons olive oil. When the oil is hot, add the garlic and ginger. Stir-fry for 10 seconds and add the onion. Stir-fry the onion until it begins to soften (about 2 minutes), sprinkling the paprika over the onion.

4. Push the onion mixture to the sides of the wok and add 1 tablespoon oil in the center of the wok. Add the rice and stir-fry, stirring it in the oil for 1 minute until it begins to turn golden brown.

5. Add the bell pepper and stir-fry for 1 minute, mixing with the onion and seasonings. Stir in the soy sauce.

6. In a small bowl, add the tomato paste and chicken broth and stir to combine. Add into the pan and bring to a boil.

7. Stir in the cooked ground pork and brown sugar. Continue stir-frying for 2–3 minutes to mix all the ingredients together, until most of the liquid is absorbed. Serve hot.

PER SERVING | Calories: 661 | Fat: 42g | Protein: 24g | Sodium: 854mg | Fiber: 3g | Carbohydrates: 45g | Sugar: 9g

One-Dish Chicken and Rice Stir-Fry

Hoisin sauce adds a sweet-and-spicy flavor to this simple chicken and rice stir-fry that is a great cold-weather dish.

INGREDIENTS | SERVES 3

¾ pound boneless, skinless chicken breast

1½ tablespoons light soy sauce

2 teaspoons plus 2 tablespoons Chinese rice wine or dry sherry, divided

¼ teaspoon black pepper

4 tablespoons hoisin sauce

4 tablespoons chicken broth

4 tablespoons dark soy sauce

1 teaspoon granulated sugar

4 tablespoons vegetable or peanut oil, divided

2 thin slices ginger, minced

2 cloves garlic, minced

1 scallion, finely chopped

1 small onion, chopped

1½ cups cooked white rice

1 cup canned baby corn, drained

½ teaspoon salt

1. Cut the chicken into thin strips. Place the chicken in a bowl and add the light soy sauce, 2 teaspoons rice wine or sherry, and the black pepper. Marinate the chicken for 20 minutes.

2. In a small bowl, combine the hoisin sauce, chicken broth, dark soy sauce, 2 tablespoons rice wine or sherry, and the sugar. Set aside.

3. Heat a wok or skillet over medium-high heat until it is nearly smoking and add 2 tablespoons oil. When the oil is hot, add half the ginger and garlic and stir-fry for 10 seconds.

4. Add the chicken. Let sit briefly, then stir-fry the chicken for 2–3 minutes or until it turns white and is nearly cooked through. Remove the chicken and drain in a colander or on paper towels.

5. Heat 2 tablespoons oil in the wok or skillet. Add the scallions and the remaining ginger and garlic. Stir-fry for 10 seconds, then add the onion. Stir-fry the onion for about 2 minutes or until it begins to soften.

6. Add the rice and stir-fry for 1 minute, until it begins to turn golden brown. Add the baby corn and stir-fry for 1 minute, sprinkling with the salt.

7. Add the hoisin sauce mixture and bring to a boil. Stir in the cooked chicken. Continue stir-frying for 2–3 minutes to mix all the ingredients together and until most of the liquid is absorbed. Serve hot.

PER SERVING | Calories: 361 | Fat: 4g | Protein: 29g | Sodium: 2,604mg | Fiber: 1g | Carbohydrates: 45g | Sugar: 9g

Arroz con Pollo

A classic of Spain and Latin America, arroz con pollo often uses saffron threads to add a floral flavoring as well as give a striking color to the dish.

INGREDIENTS | SERVES 4

1 pound boneless, skinless chicken thighs

1 teaspoon salt

½ teaspoon black pepper

5 tablespoons olive oil, divided

2 cloves garlic, chopped

2 teaspoons chopped red chili peppers

1 small onion, chopped

1 tablespoon paprika

1½ cups cooked rice

½ small red bell pepper, seeded and cubed

½ small orange bell pepper, seeded and cubed

¼ cup chicken broth

6 saffron threads (optional)

¼ cup tomato sauce

Sticky Glutinous Rice

Glutinous rice is famous for its texture, earning it the nickname "sticky rice." The unusually sticky texture of glutinous rice comes from a starch called amylopectin. Amylopectin comprises over 80 percent of the starch in glutinous rice, compared to only 70 percent in regular long-grain white rice.

1. Cut the chicken thighs into thin strips about 1½" long and ⅛" wide. Place the chicken strips in a bowl and stir in the salt and black pepper.

2. Heat a wok or skillet over medium-high heat until it is nearly smoking and add 2 tablespoons oil. When the oil is hot, add the chicken. Let the chicken brown briefly, then stir-fry until it turns white and is nearly cooked through, about 5–7 minutes. Remove and drain on a plate lined with paper towels.

3. Heat 2 tablespoons oil in the wok or skillet and add the garlic and red chili peppers. Stir-fry for 10 seconds and add the onion. Stir-fry the onion until it begins to soften (about 2 minutes), sprinkling the paprika over the onion while you are stir-frying.

4. Add 1 tablespoon oil in the middle of the pan. Add the rice and stir-fry, stirring it in the oil for 1 minute until it begins to turn golden brown.

5. Add the bell peppers and stir-fry for 1 minute or until the peppers are tender but still crisp, adding 1 or 2 tablespoons chicken broth if the vegetables begin to dry out.

6. Add the chicken broth and saffron threads and bring to a boil. Stir in the tomato sauce. Return the chicken to the pan. Continue stir-frying for 2–3 minutes to mix all the ingredients together. Serve hot.

PER SERVING | Calories: 420 | Fat: 22g | Protein: 25g | Sodium: 965mg | Fiber: 2g | Carbohydrates: 28g | Sugar: 3g

Shrimp Risotto

Risotto refers to a cooking method that involves frequent stirring with the slow addition of hot liquids.

INGREDIENTS | SERVES 4

4 tablespoons olive oil, divided

1 pound large shrimp, shelled and deveined

1 teaspoon grated lemon zest

1 teaspoon fresh thyme leaves

¼ teaspoon red pepper flakes

4 cups shrimp stock

½ cup diced white onions

2 tablespoons minced garlic

1 cup Arborio rice

½ cup dry white wine

¼ cup grated Parmesan cheese

¼ teaspoon kosher salt

¼ teaspoon white pepper

2 tablespoons chopped Italian parsley

Garlic Health Benefits

Garlic adds more than a powerful aroma to stir-fry dishes. Modern research shows that the same chemical reaction that gives garlic its characteristic odor is also responsible for the numerous health benefits that are derived from eating it, including lower blood pressure and inhibition of the free radical cells that can cause cancer.

1. In a large bowl, mix together 1 tablespoon olive oil, shrimp, lemon zest, thyme leaves, and pepper flakes. Set aside for 10 minutes.

2. In a small saucepan, bring the shrimp stock to a low simmer.

3. Heat 1 tablespoon olive oil in a wok over medium heat. Cook the shrimp for 2–3 minutes until they turn pink. Remove to a plate and set aside.

4. Add the remaining olive oil and cook the onions and garlic until softened but not browned, about 1–2 minutes.

5. Add the rice and stir quickly until it is well-coated and opaque. Lower the heat to medium low and stir in the white wine. Cook for 2–3 minutes or until the liquid is nearly all evaporated.

6. Ladle in 1 cup of the broth into the rice. Simmer and slowly stir until the rice has absorbed the liquid. Add the remaining broth, 1 cup at a time. Continue to simmer and stir, allowing the rice to absorb each addition of broth before adding more—approximately 20 minutes in total cooking time. The risotto should be slightly firm and creamy.

7. Gently fold the cooked shrimp into the risotto. Stir in Parmesan cheese and cook briefly until the cheese has melted. Add the salt and pepper. Spoon risotto into dishes and top with chopped parsley before serving.

PER SERVING | Calories: 570 | Fat: 20g | Protein: 35g | Sodium: 756mg | Fiber: 2g | Carbohydrates: 53g | Sugar: 5g

Simple Beans and Rice

This simple dish is a great way to use up leftover cooked rice. To add extra flavor, use crushed tomatoes that have been flavored with herbs and seasonings.

INGREDIENTS | SERVES 3

3 tablespoons vegetable or peanut oil, divided

2 cloves garlic, minced

1 small onion, chopped

1 tablespoon paprika

1 small green bell pepper, cut into bite-sized chunks

1 tablespoon soy sauce or water, optional

1½ cups cooked rice

1 (14-ounce) can kidney beans, drained

½ cup chicken broth

1½ cups crushed tomatoes

¼ teaspoon kosher salt

¼ teaspoon black pepper

Healthy Beans

Beans are high in protein and dietary fiber. Scientists recommend a diet rich in kidney, pinto, garbanzo, and other types of beans for people trying to lower their cholesterol levels. Their high fiber content also makes beans a good choice for people with diabetes, as it helps prevent blood-sugar levels from rising too rapidly after a meal has been consumed.

1. Heat a wok or skillet over medium-high heat and add 2 tablespoons oil. When the oil is hot, add the garlic. Stir-fry for 10 seconds, then add the onion. Stir-fry until the onion has softened (about 2 minutes), stirring in the paprika while you are stir-frying.

2. Add the pepper and stir-fry about 5 minutes until it is tender but still crisp. Add 1 tablespoon soy sauce or water if the bell pepper begins to dry out during stir-frying.

3. Push the vegetables to the sides of the wok or skillet. Heat 1 tablespoon oil in the middle. Add the rice and stir-fry until it begins to turn golden brown.

4. Add the beans. Stir-fry for 1 minute, then add the chicken broth and crushed tomatoes. Bring to a boil. Season with the salt and pepper. Cook for another 1–2 minutes to blend all the flavors. Serve hot.

PER SERVING | Calories: 621 | Fat: 2g | Protein: 35g | Sodium: 410mg | Fiber: 36g | Carbohydrates: 117g | Sugar: 8g

Hoppin' John

There are numerous versions of this popular Southern dish, but they all contain black-eyed peas and rice. While Hoppin' John is traditionally made with bacon or ham hock, chicken can be used as well.

INGREDIENTS | SERVES 4

1 pound boneless, skinless chicken breasts

1 tablespoon soy sauce

1 tablespoon dry white wine or dry sherry

¼ teaspoon black pepper

2 teaspoons cornstarch

3 tablespoons olive oil, divided

1 teaspoon minced garlic

1 teaspoon minced ginger

1 cup chopped Vidalia onion

1 tablespoon paprika

2 ribs celery, thinly sliced

1 cup black-eyed peas

1 cup diced tomatoes, undrained

½ teaspoon ground cumin

½ teaspoon kosher salt

3 cups Basic Cooked Rice (see recipe in this chapter)

1. Cut the chicken into thin strips. Place the chicken strips in a bowl and add the soy sauce, white wine or sherry, black pepper, and cornstarch. Marinate the chicken for 20 minutes.

2. Heat a wok or skillet over medium-high heat until it is nearly smoking. Add 2 tablespoons olive oil. When the oil is hot, add half the garlic and ginger and stir-fry for 10 seconds.

3. Add the chicken. Let it brown briefly, then stir-fry the chicken for 2–3 minutes or until it turns white and is nearly cooked through. Remove and drain in a colander or on paper towels.

4. Heat 1 tablespoon oil in the wok or skillet. When the oil is hot, add the remainder of the garlic and ginger. Stir-fry for 10 seconds, then add the onion. Sprinkle the paprika over the mixture, and stir-fry until the onion begins to soften (about 2 minutes).

5. Add the celery and stir-fry for 1 minute, until the celery turns a darker green, mixing it with the onion and seasonings.

6. Stir in the black-eyed peas and diced tomatoes with juice. Bring to a boil. Return the chicken to the pan. Stir in the ground cumin and salt. Continue stir-frying for 2–3 minutes to mix all the ingredients together. Serve hot over the cooked rice.

PER SERVING | Calories: 569 | Fat: 14g | Protein: 38g | Sodium: 371mg | Fiber: 7g | Carbohydrates: 70g | Sugar: 6g

Glossary of Basic Cooking Terms Used in Stir-Frying

al dente
An Italian term literally meaning "to the teeth." Al dente is used to describe the state to which pasta should be cooked. Pasta that is cooked al dente has no taste of flour remaining, but there is still a slight resistance when bitten and it is still slightly chewy. Like Italian pasta, Chinese egg noodles should be cooked al dente.

aromatics
In stir-frying, garlic and ginger are frequently added to the hot oil before the other ingredients, in order to flavor the oil.

blanch
A means of cooking food by immersing it in boiling water. In Chinese cooking, thicker, denser vegetables such as broccoli are often briefly blanched prior to being added to a stir-fry. This helps ensure that all the vegetables in the stir-fry finish cooking at the same time. After blanching, the cooked food is immediately placed in cold water to stop the cooking process. Always drain blanched foods thoroughly before adding to a stir-fry.

chop
Cutting food into small pieces. While chopped food doesn't need to be perfectly uniform, the pieces should be roughly the same size.

deep-fry
A means of cooking food by immersing it briefly in hot oil. Along with stir-frying and steaming, deep-frying is one of the three main Chinese cooking techniques. In Chinese cuisine, some recipes call for food to be deep-fried first before it is added to the other ingredients in a stir-fry.

deglaze
Using a liquid to clean out the browned bits of drippings left over from cooking meat in a pan. Adding liquid (usually broth or alcohol) to the pan makes it easier to lift up the browned bits with a spatula. The flavored liquid is then used in a sauce or gravy. While deglazing the pan isn't a standard Chinese technique, it can be used in stir-fry recipes such as Steak Diane (see Chapter 4) and Marsala Scallops (see Chapter 7).

dice
Cutting food into small cubes, usually ¼" in size or less. Unlike chopping, the food should be cut into even-sized pieces.

drain
Drawing off the liquid from a food. In stir-frying, washed vegetables are drained thoroughly before stir-frying so that excess water is not added to the pan, while meat is drained after stir-frying to remove any excess oil. Either a colander (a perforated bowl made of metal or plastic) or paper towels can be used to drain food.

dredge
Coating food with a dry ingredient such as flour, bread crumbs, or potato starch before frying. Spices are frequently added to the coating for extra flavor. Dredging food before frying gives it a nice, crispy coating.

julienne
Cutting food into very thin strips about 1½"–2" long, with a width and thickness of about ⅛". Both meat and vegetables can be julienned. (Also called matchstick cutting)

marinate
Coating a food in a liquid prior to cooking. Stir-fry recipes with meat, seafood, and poultry nearly always include a marinade, both to tenderize the food and lend extra flavor. Cornstarch is frequently added to help seal in the other ingredients—always add the cornstarch last unless the recipe states otherwise.

matchstick head
To prepare matchstick heads, julienne the food and then cut it crosswise into small cubes the approximate size of matchstick heads.

mince
Cutting food into very small pieces. In general, minced food is cut into smaller pieces than chopped food.

mise en place
A French term that translates to "everything in place." In a kitchen, it refers to organizing and arranging your ingredients so that when cooking commences, everything that you need is prepared and helps expedite the process. This is particularly important in stir-frying since the cooking process is typically quick

sauce
A liquid that is added to lend flavor to a dish. In stir-fries, a sauce is frequently added in the final stages of cooking.

sear
Quickly browning meat over high heat before finishing cooking it by another method. Searing meat browns the surface and seals in the juices. In stir-fry dishes, the meat is briefly seared after it is added to the pan, and then finished by stir-frying.

shred
Cutting food into thin strips that are usually thicker than a julienne cut. Meat, poultry, cabbage, lettuce, and cheese can all be shredded.

simmer
Cooking food in liquid at a temperature just below the boiling point.

stir-fry
Cooking food by placing it in a small amount of heated oil and moving it around quickly at high heat. The main difference between sautéing and stir-frying is that food for stir-fries is cut up into uniform pieces to make it cook more quickly.

Online Shopping Resources

AsianFoodGrocer.com
www.asianfoodgrocer.com
Located in San Francisco, AsianFoodGrocer.com offers a wealth of products such as Asian spices, noodles, tofu, and canned goods. Items can be purchased in individual units or in bulk wholesale.

Earthy Delights
www.earthy.com
Based in Michigan, Earthy Delights specializes in supplying specialty foods, from mushrooms and gourmet cheeses to fine oils. They supply a wide range of sauces and seasonings used in Asian stir-fries, from soy sauce to sesame seeds and dried chili peppers.

Mitsuwa Marketplace
www.mitsuwa.com
Mitsuwa Marketplace is the largest Japanese supermarket in the United States. The online stores offer a wide variety of food products, seasonings, and appliances. Mitsuwa offers foods that are used in many Asian cuisines but focuses primarily on products for Japanese cuisine such as bonito flakes and prepared wasabi.

Wing Yip
www.wingyip.com
Based in the United Kingdom, Wing Yip has recently launched an online shopping site to accompany its stores located throughout Britain. They carry a wide variety of ingredients used in stir-frying, including their own line of products. Although they carry a few specialty items such as shiitake mushrooms and sushi ginger, the focus is primarily on Chinese cuisine.

Williams-Sonoma
www.williams-sonoma.com
Williams-Sonoma is a renown specialty store offering quality cookware, electrics, cutlery, and food products. The store first began selling French cookware but now has expanded to offer a wealth of international cookware and spices.

The Wok Shop
www.wokshop.com
Located in the heart of San Francisco's Chinatown district, this family-run business has been in operation for over thirty-five years. The store is an invaluable resource for anyone who doesn't have easy access to an Asian market. In addition to their line of carbon steel woks, cleavers, and other basic equipment, they carry a number of harder-to-find utensils such as tempura racks, Chinese spatulas, and wire-mesh skimmers.

Standard U.S./Metric Measurement Conversions

VOLUME CONVERSIONS

U.S. Volume Measure	Metric Equivalent
⅛ teaspoon	0.5 milliliter
¼ teaspoon	1 milliliter
½ teaspoon	2 milliliters
1 teaspoon	5 milliliters
½ tablespoon	7 milliliters
1 tablespoon (3 teaspoons)	15 milliliters
2 tablespoons (1 fluid ounce)	30 milliliters
¼ cup (4 tablespoons)	60 milliliters
⅓ cup	90 milliliters
½ cup (4 fluid ounces)	125 milliliters
⅔ cup	160 milliliters
¾ cup (6 fluid ounces)	180 milliliters
1 cup (16 tablespoons)	250 milliliters
1 pint (2 cups)	500 milliliters
1 quart (4 cups)	1 liter (about)

WEIGHT CONVERSIONS

U.S. Weight Measure	Metric Equivalent
½ ounce	15 grams
1 ounce	30 grams
2 ounces	60 grams
3 ounces	85 grams
¼ pound (4 ounces)	115 grams
½ pound (8 ounces)	225 grams
¾ pound (12 ounces)	340 grams
1 pound (16 ounces)	454 grams

OVEN TEMPERATURE CONVERSIONS

Degrees Fahrenheit	Degrees Celsius
200 degrees F	95 degrees C
250 degrees F	120 degrees C
275 degrees F	135 degrees C
300 degrees F	150 degrees C
325 degrees F	160 degrees C
350 degrees F	180 degrees C
375 degrees F	190 degrees C
400 degrees F	205 degrees C
425 degrees F	220 degrees C
450 degrees F	230 degrees C

BAKING PAN SIZES

U.S.	Metric
8 x 1½ inch round baking pan	20 x 4 cm cake tin
9 x 1½ inch round baking pan	23 x 3.5 cm cake tin
11 x 7 x 1½ inch baking pan	28 x 18 x 4 cm baking tin
13 x 9 x 2 inch baking pan	30 x 20 x 5 cm baking tin
2 quart rectangular baking dish	30 x 20 x 3 cm baking tin
15 x 10 x 2 inch baking pan	30 x 25 x 2 cm baking tin (Swiss roll tin)
9 inch pie plate	22 x 4 or 23 x 4 cm pie plate
7 or 8 inch springform pan	18 or 20 cm springform or loose bottom cake tin
9 x 5 x 3 inch loaf pan	23 x 13 x 7 cm or 2 lb narrow loaf or pâté tin
1½ quart casserole	1.5 liter casserole
2 quart casserole	2 liter casserole

Index

Note: Page numbers in **bold** indicate recipe category lists.